306
.740941

D1149389

For many years a freelance journalist, Allegra Taylor is author of *I Fly Out with Bright Feathers (The Quest of a Novice Healer)* and *Acquainted with the Night*, a book on death and dying. She is married with six children, has three grandchildren and lives with her documentary film-maker husband in Twickenham.

HAVERING SIXTH FORM COLLEGE LIBRARY

WITHDRAWN FROM HAVERING COLLEGES SIXTH FORM LIBRARY

PROSTITUTION
WHAT'S LOVE GOT TO DO WITH IT?

ALLEGRA TAYLOR

HAVERING SIXTH FORM
COLLEGE LIBRARY

48073

An OPTIMA book

© Allegra Taylor, 1991

First published in 1991 by
Macdonald Optima, a division of
Macdonald & Co. (Publishers) Ltd

A member of Maxwell Macmillan Pergamon Publishing Corporation

All rights reserved

No part of this publication may be reproduced,
stored in a retrieval system, or transmitted,
in any form or by any means without the prior
permission in writing of the publisher, nor be
otherwise circulated in any form of binding or
cover other than that in which it is published
and without a similar condition including this
condition being imposed on the subsequent
purchaser.

British Library Cataloguing in Publication Data

Taylor, Allegra *1940–*
    Prostitution : what's love got to do with it?
    1. Great Britain.   Prostitution
    I. Title
    306.740941

    ISBN 0-356-15444-0

Macdonald & Co. (Publishers) Ltd
Orbit House
1 New Fetter Lane
London EC4A 1AR

Typeset in Ehrhard by Leaper & Gard Ltd, Bristol

Printed and bound in Great Britain by
The Guernsey Press Co. Ltd., Guernsey, Channel Islands.

For Louise

With love and admiration

CONTENTS

PREFACE

This preface is an attempt to disarm anyone who might quite justifiably say, 'Who does she think she is?', 'What does she know about it?'

To know nothing is a curiously pregnant state to be in. An expectant patient state in which things grow and change and take shape by themselves in the warm, nourishing darkness. It's really the opposite of being a scholar, an expert, an authority.

I began with an open mind, an open heart and open ears. Every day I learned something new and was continually astonished by the variety of the human experience. I had manifold opportunities for my favourite occupation of loitering with intent. I had some wonderful laughs and made some lifelong friends.

I used to feel embarrassed when I was totally ignorant about something. I'd bluff and hope I wouldn't be found out. But I no longer feel apologetic. Ignorance is neither blissful nor woeful, it is neutral. It just means you have limitless possibilities for learning. It is a very good place to start.

So this is not an academic work, an encyclopaedic survey, or a definitive thesis. I draw no conclusions except that the variety of ways the resilient human spirit finds to survive is a constant inspiration.

ACKNOWLEDGEMENTS

Many people have helped and encouraged me during the writing of this book. In particular I would like to thank Harriet Griffey of Macdonald Optima for her great faith in the project, my editor Melissa Brooks, Nina Lopez-Jones and the English Collective of Prostitutes, Helen Buckingham, for permission to quote from her unpublished writings, Caduta Massi, Tuppy Owen, Jackie, Martin, Raoul, Carol, Fiona, Katrina Donegan, Pam, Peter Wright, Lindi St Claire, Dolores French, Eva, Miles, Angel, Dr Susan Edwards, Nadia, Heather, Rickie, Mark, Mike, Carol, Diane, Val, Lisa, Roz Caveney, Caro, Ayten, Jean, Frances, Colin, Jill, Nieman, Judy, Louise, Claire, Chief Inspector Neil Doak and The Metropolitan Police at Paddington Green. And finally, a particularly loving thank you to my husband and best friend, Richard, for his trust and support.

Everybody's names have been changed (except for those who preferred not to) and some locations have been altered to protect identities.

ONE

Love for sale seems to be a puzzling contradiction and yet the pull of it is so strong that public figures risk careers and reputations by pursuing the promise of some ultimate sexual experience or erotic scenario or maybe just some fantasy so vague it can never be realized. Do they find what they are looking for, or is the gulf between expectation and reality too great? Is it a longing for some kind of intimacy, or a flight from intimacy? Is prostitution a simple pragmatic transaction, or is it symptomatic of a deep melancholy in our society born of alienation, loneliness and unmet needs?

This is a book about prostitution. All around us, on the street, in brothels and bed-sits, in expensive hotels, discreet clubs and suburban semis, the oldest profession continues to flourish. Why? What makes someone become a prostitute? Who are their clients? There are so many questions I want to ask, not least the uncomfortable one – why does it fascinate me so much? I want to know if people become prostitutes from choice or from absence of choice. Do they pay a high emotional price? Is prostitution fundamentally damaging to the human psyche? Do prostitutes provide a vital safety valve in a sick society? Is it possible to sell your body and keep your self-esteem? Who is exploiting whom?

It is a subject about which most people are endlessly intrigued and almost completely ignorant. 'Vice Girl' scandals sell more newspapers than any other type of story. We lap it up. The perfect opportunity for a bit of vicarious titillation combined with some satisfying righteous moralizing.

The eighteenth-century essayist, Oliver Goldsmith, once wrote that love was 'an abject intercourse between tyrants and slaves'. A more romantic view is the Suzie Wong or Sweet Charity myth – the tart with the heart of gold. Reality is probably on a sliding scale between those two extremes – a subtle, complex mixture of needs and desires, fact and fantasy, yearnings and sorrows.

When I was a child my family moved to Brazil. My father, the eternal fugitive from impatient creditors, was headed for greener pastures yet again. He managed to get himself a job on a Yiddish newspaper that served the little community of European Jews building a new life in South America and he rented a small apartment for us in the less salubrious area of downtown Sao Paulo.

In this new world where we hadn't yet learned to speak the language or find our way around, my sister and I used to kneel up at the window on chairs, resting our chins on our folded arms, and amuse ourselves – looking down on the street life five floors below. It didn't take long for us to realize that the same women stood waiting in the same places every day. Men would come up and talk to them and they'd go off for a while. Sometimes they'd stand there for hours and nobody would approach them.

'They're whores', my mother said, 'and that's not a term of abuse. It's a good, honest biblical word for an honourable profession of ancient lineage. They make love with men for a living and don't you ever think badly of them for doing it. Any woman worthy of the name would do the same if her children were hungry. Remember, never judge someone until you've walked a mile in their mocassins.' Or their high-heeled gold mules, in their case.

From then on we were rather in awe of them. At that age, sex was a pretty disagreeable prospect and the thought of such heroism for the sake of their hungry children was motherhood at its most selfless. We each 'adopted' a favourite and kept score watching anxiously from the window, sometimes for hours until she'd had at least one customer.

'Mine's got one! Hooray!' I'd cry.

'I think mine has too, a man's talking to her. Oh no! He's gone off again!'

My mother had a great friend who'd been a prostitute in wartime London and had married one of her clients, a Dutch businessman who was besotted with her. Bette was loud, generous, vulgar and humorous. I thought she was wonderful and she showed me how to put my hair in pincurls so I could look like Debbie Reynolds. She wore amazing red snakeskin shoes with bows on and carried a red snakeskin clutch bag to match. My mother said she most likely hadn't given 'it' up entirely and occasionally kept her hand in, so to speak.

My mother was full of good advice on being a woman, rather out of fashion in today's climate but daring in its day. 'A good woman would be able to be a lady in the drawing room, a char in the kitchen and a whore in the bedroom,' she'd say dramatically, giving us the concept quite early in life that womanliness was a subtle, complex thing. 'A good woman plays the hand she's been dealt with dignity and to the best of her ability.' She certainly lived her own life by these precepts and enjoyed a very unconventional creative marriage for forty-five years, as well as being a working wife and bringing up three children.

One day, as we watched from the window, my father came and stood behind us. He put a hand on each of our shoulders and told a poignant story from his time as a journalist in the Spanish Civil War. As an innocent, idealistic young man he had been appalled at the numbers of women reduced to working as prostitutes in Barcelona. The fact that so many were young and beautiful seemed to make it worse. He wanted to find out what circumstances had caused them to seek their living on the streets so he approached one, agreed to her price and followed her up a flight of rickety stairs to a curtained cubicle.

Upon hearing he only wanted to talk she looked at him quizzically, rebuttoned her blouse and sat down for twenty minutes. She couldn't afford to waste too much time, she hinted delicately, as she could cater for several more clients before the night was over. He said he would like to take her out for tea on Sunday and she readily agreed.

When he arrived for the assignation in the botanical gardens at the appointed hour, he hardly recognized her. There she was, demurely dressed in a high-necked blouse and shawl, not a scrap of make-up, her river of thrilling, black, waist-length hair neatly confined in a single plait down her back. She was accompanied by her mother, her grandmother and two aunts. An invitation from a young suitor of serious intent required chaperones and they followed along behind at a discreet distance the whole afternoon, fanning themselves.

My father had been very moved, he said, by the way the family still maintained their deep traditional protective regard for their daughter while accepting the reality of her life. My mother disagreed and said it was sad that they were such hypocrites. Why did she have to maintain the fiction of being a virgin by day while she was a whore by night? A man would not have to keep up such a pretence.

My mother's great heroine, about whom she once wrote an unpublished play, was Aspasia, the most famous of the Greek hetaerae, and lifelong partner of Pericles, the leading statesman of his time. The hetaerae held very honoured positions in society as the mistresses of the country's most powerful men. Aspasia successfully combined intelligence, political astuteness, sexual expertise and motherhood. She taught and spoke in public. She was universally loved, respected and acknowledged. She didn't have to choose between being a good wife or a fallen woman. She was who she was. I understood that my mother admired her because she appeared to integrate so many of the female archetypes - The Mother, The Whore, The Priestess, The Goddess - into one total woman.

Now, all these years on, having become interested in the role that disharmony and disintegration play in illness and disease, I want to explore the fragmentation that is still so much a part of the experience of being a woman. I've spent years being the wife, the earth mother, the healer, but what happened to the whore? I want to reclaim all my component parts and see what sort of a woman I am.

Who better to go to, to ask, to learn from than prostitutes themselves?

But who is the whore? How do I recognize her and where do I find her? We have become very divided from one another and yet I don't feel she is very far away. I have never been a prostitute in the accepted sense of the word, but I have slept with men as a trade-off when it's suited me. There is also a prevalent viewpoint amongst certain feminist separatists that people like me are the most hypocritical whores of all, having accepted financial security and married respectability in exchange for sexual, domestic and child-rearing duties. Perhaps most women barter sex for something. The uncomfortable fact that a sexual relationship in modern Western society frequently involves a substantial economic element is rarely admitted openly.

A prostitute is defined in the *Encyclopaedia Britannica* as 'a person who for immediate payment in money or valuables will engage in sexual activity with any other person known or unknown'. The edges of the subject are actually a little more blurred than that. The exchange of sexual favours for money, security or protection can range in style from a king's mistress showered with jewels to a brief encounter in a back alley for the price of a couple of drinks.

I don't know why we find such an exchange strange or shocking. After all, prostitution is not called the oldest profession for nothing. This is very ancient primate behaviour, genetically programmed into us. Female chimpanzees, for instance, will often present themselves sexually to a male to appease or to solicit attention or to get food. Most women have a whore component somewhere in their total personality, even if it's just the fantasy of being the seductress. I know I do and I am simultaneously fascinated, excited and appalled by it, by the confident, matter-of-fact expression of the power of female sexuality. I want to own that part of me and integrate it with the rest. Even if I have chosen a monogamous relationship it can include all of my sexuality not just the respectable part.

The difficulty was I didn't know any hookers and I didn't know where to start. I was rather shy and inhibited about approaching any. Should I go and lurk in a red-light district, approach one in the street and introduce myself? Supposing she isn't one and was just waiting for a friend? Supposing she tells me to mind my own business? What if I call one of those numbers stuck up in a phone box? Would she be hostile? Insulted? Misunderstand my intentions? Hate my guts for everything I represent?

4

Prostitution may be legal, but it is still surrounded with punitive legislation and generally treated as unacceptable. Prostitutes have been denied so many aspects of life that non-prostitutes take for granted. They are the scapegoats, discriminated against and regarded as outcasts while the rest of us have been denied access to the mysteries and secrets they hold. Why can't we reclaim the whole woman in all of us?

I feel strongly that the oppression of women flourishes in this divisiveness. It's not prostitution itself that is oppressive, but the hypocrisy that surrounds the whole subject. When prostitutes can hold their heads high, all women will have more power and yet I was facing the fact that there is no common meeting ground for whores and non-whores.

Then one day a friend of mine was buying a tracksuit at a street market from a woman with a clothes stall. While she was trying various garments on they got talking about how hard it was to earn an honest penny these days and the woman disclosed that she used to work as a call-girl. My friend, knowing of my quest, asked her if I could contact her sometime. And that's how I met Helen Buckingham.

I couldn't have had better luck than to meet this witty, courageous and articulate woman, one of the first to 'come out' and speak openly about her profession, challenging centuries of sexual repression, self-deprecation and feelings of worthlessness. On talking to her, I was struck by just how strong the parallels are between society's attitudes to prostitutes and its attitudes to people with AIDS – the moral censure, the stigma, the scapegoating, the oppression and judgement leading to isolation, loneliness and shame are all similar.

The longer other women insist upon ostracizing or patronizing the prostitute, Helen believes, the longer it will be before prostitutes trust other women and come to join them in the search for a true female identity. We live in a society so long dominated by men that we have lost touch with what womanhood is. We have only our deepest instincts to rely on. The way we treat the 'common prostitute' in our society is born of a primitive urge to punish our own shortcomings via the weak and vulnerable.

Helen lives in a little flat with her six-year-old son who was home from school with a slight temperature the first day I came to visit. He sat on the floor playing with his train set and eating frozen prawns and loganberry icecream. A mouse was making himself at home, running boldly round from room to room. Helen had given up being on the game seven years ago when she became pregnant with this second, late child. Apart, that is, from the occasional telephone job passed her way by her friend, Connie, who organizes a telephone credit-card set-up.

'I earned a fiver yesterday by agreeing to have a gentleman put through on my line. "Hello," I said pleasantly. Nothing. "Hello, are you there?" "I'd like to suck your bottom," he lisped. And then he hung up! That was it. Pathetic, isn't it?'

She told me this story doubled up with mirth, sitting at her sewing machine looking like that Posy Simmonds cartoon character with straight black hair and outsize specs. Described once by a journalist as 'a librarian type who hasn't discovered Smirnoff', Helen embodies, in her own words, 'The unerotic nature of the appeal of prostitution to women who find themselves threatened by economic disaster, hand in hand usually with a sense of social isolation and emotional insecurity.'

Over the course of the next year, Helen and I met together many times. She shared her journals and writings with me and introduced me to other working women. We cooked meals for each other and sat around talking for hours. She has been a most generous and loving friend.

Helen grew up in a middle-class puritanical family where 'God was a terrible presence, an all-pervasive power who watched me so that I could do nothing without this oppressive intrusion into my privacy.' She was a disturbed child in a world of double messages, with a powerful, controlling mother whom she could never please and a father 'constantly haunted by the demons which rode him in and out of demented states of mind'.

'I was never far from believing myself insane because I had been surrounded by highly neurotic people all my life and it seemed obvious that eventually I should become like them and take my turn at the mental hospital too.'

At 16 she shocked a roomful of her mother's friends by announcing that it was, in her opinion, the courtesan who was the only free woman. As soon as she was able to Helen came up to London, 'set almost vengefully upon a course which was to lead to a life style for which, in many ways, I was ideally suited.' In the midst of the bright new moral climate of the sixties, she threw herself into the spirit of the times. Yet there was a great naivety and innocence about her and she was still conditioned to see marriage somewhere at the end of it.

Her first great (unconsummated) love was for a Roman Catholic priest.

'We never spoke of our great yearning for each other. By admitting it there might have been consequences which would have changed the destinies of us both. We might have married and lived happily ever after, but then neither of us would lead the lives we both lead now, not exactly imprisoned in the archetypes we represent but contained so that our lives are structured by them, and in some ways all the richer for that.'

6

That relationship and its aftertaste, she says, was what kept her heart open to men through all that followed so that neither prostitution nor feminism could poison or harden it. The fury that still fuels her recollection of that time came not from disappointment over this relationship but from disillusionment with the new promiscuous society which seemed to promise women more than it delivered. 'Somehow there was an underlying assumption that women owed sex to men and to themselves, but that society in general and men in particular owed nothing to motherhood.'

Then she fell in love with an irresponsible rotter and found herself poor, pregnant and abandoned at a time when abortion was illegal, counselling non-existent and illegitimacy still a stigma. In shock and despair she accepted the propositions of the various men who wanted to bed her because she dreaded a night on the streets and because she was hungry. She began to find men repugnant. Each one another face of the betrayer.

'There is no pain like the pain of a woman insulted in her womanhood. The pain and the attendant wrath doesn't always show but, in one form or another, I believe it is there in a high percentage of women. It is *always* there in prostitutes. Sometimes it festers and emerges later in life in the form of cancers, nervous breakdowns, drug addiction, alcoholism and hopelessly masochistic relationships with men. It motivates political lesbianism and feminist separatism. At the back of it all is not sexual frustration but love frustration.

'I couldn't believe what had happened to me. Surely motherhood was sacrosanct and that was what bound a man to a woman. In this I was as much a slave to romantic fiction as my mother had been.' She found herself slipping into an attitude of mind that wanted to close doors between herself and men.

After the birth of the child she was confronted by the total lack of childcare provision for the pre-school age children of working mothers. The social services, she said, and the politicians seemed completely ignorant of the needs of women. She couldn't live under the same roof as her controlling mother, 'not just unpleasant or undesirable, but actually impossible', so her situation was one of stalemate: no private means, no provider, no equal job opportunities, no childcare, no supportive family, no state help – 'You didn't qualify for council housing, a mortgage or even legal contraception unless you were married!' More crippling than any of these was the feeling, at a much deeper emotional level, that she had nothing to offer except sex. The final crossover point came when she was engaged as a very poorly paid researcher on a series of articles on single mothers and their plight. The editor offered her money in exchange for sexual services. He was courteous, kind, gentlemanly and generous so she reckoned, why not?

From there it was a short step to the escort agency and the world of the high-class call girl. Most of the women she met at the agency were also casualties of the sixties sexual revolution, left to bear the brunt of liberation as the sole breadwinners of one-parent families.

'Middle and upper-class women who would have died of starvation rather than go on the streets or into some Soho brothel found this way of earning money out of the sex they had been giving away for free, a perfectly acceptable way of life. Free sex had not got anyone anywhere except into single motherhood. Unfortunately, their neediness led to them seeking warmth and protection from clients and not being business-like enough.'

The women who dealt with the job most successfully were the married housewives with families who wanted to get home as soon as possible. 'They were brisk and to the point, like well-trained nurses, and usually took no more than ten minutes flat between taking a contraceptive out of their beaded handbags and flushing it down the Dorchester loo. Then bustling into the lift and changing into their flat shoes they drove off home leaving the client, somewhat dazed by the speed of events, tottering into his pyjamas.'

In her heart Helen knew that, for her, becoming a prostitute was a statement of dissatisfaction, disillusionment and disenchantment with the state of affairs between herself and men.

It was also a statement of revenge. 'Prostitution seemed the only way to make my family notice my wounded feelings. I could launch myself against those who hurt me with the devastation of an atomic blast simply by claiming a relationship with them. Every time I did so I was bound to make people who knew me thoroughly uncomfortable. Unfortunately, the neurotic disposition of my family made it quite impossible for most of them to appreciate the gesture as having any relevance to their relationship with me.'

Not everyone, says Helen, is cut out to take their basic assets into their own hands and exploit them against all the mores of society. It takes extreme circumstances and exceptional courage. Women are particularly sensitive about being sex objects; after all it is the very antithesis of the role of the beloved or soul-mate which is the highest compliment that men and women can pay one another. It is very alien to get paid for sex in cold blood and the plunge does take a psychological somersault.

She talked about how important it is to set boundaries. Most women who don't become sickened and repulsed by the job specialize in something they can live with. Once you start being tempted by big money to do things you really don't want to do, you're in danger. And it does seem like easy money. To begin with, she says, you can't believe how much you can earn. But £50 once in a while becomes £50 a day, so why not £50 an hour? And then you get burnt out. The offer of £500 to do something distasteful to you adds to the cost: burn out *and* self-loathing.

This is quite different from the women who might try prostitution once or twice just for the hell of it, rather like doing one parachute jump or white-water rafting down the Colorado River. One friend of Helen's, a doctor, accepted an engagement with an Arab sheik just the once to prove that she could do it and that her high-flying career had not 'defeminized' her. She was furiously competitive and had to be best at everything.

Helen's new high income as a prostitute made a remarkable difference. 'You've become a person of consequence,' remarked a friend. 'People actually credit you with an opinion. Before you went on the game, you were so demoralized.'

'As a matter of fact,' said Helen, 'I was salvaging my self-esteem by proving I could muster some dignity and self-respect. What I had discovered was that, in fact, no one loved me. Men did not attach themselves to me because they loved me but because I was the best they could get their hands on.' Only much later did she come to realize that she had 'set too much store by marriage and not enough by woman-hood'. A woman's primary relationship should be not with a man, but rather with herself and her identification with other women. She found no solace, she said, until the birth of her second child late in life 'put such a distance between myself and men that I rarely see one these days, and it has been the happiest period of my life'.

Going on the game not only took care of practical considerations, but gave her some measure of control. She could hand over the sex without handing over herself to those who would pay for it and refuse sex to those who would not. She was also surprised by the men she came in contact with: 'I did not expect them to be half as civilized as I found most of them to be.

'The more I familiarized myself with the world of prostitution, the more "natural" I was to find the clients compared to the egomaniacs I encountered in my private life. The most poignant difference between lovers and clients is that the thought of the client fills one with moral repugnance while the encounter, in fact, leaves one feeling untouched (unless something has gone wrong), whereas the thought of a lover selected from free choice fills one with a sense of optimism, sexual desire and moral acceptability, but so very often leaves one with a sense of having been touched by betrayal.'

Underneath Helen's veneer of professionalism, the pain and vulnerability have always lain very close to the surface. A Frenchman once challenged her with a double fee to achieve an orgasm. She did and they promptly fell in love 'for two whole days'. But it was doomed from the start. She had to turn up at the club and he had to go home to his wife and she never saw him again.

'Withholding orgasms has always been part of a woman's integrity and her protection against falling in love,' she says. 'Giving way to it can have catastrophic consequences, broken hearts, decline in health, suicide, because a woman steps beyond the threshold of caution and into an area of her feelings.'

Interestingly, she says the older a woman is when she goes on the game the better she will cope with it. Women who have children and have come into prostitution to support them, seem to survive psychologically much better than childless women who lack the emotional anchor and love outlet that motherhood provides.

'All the prostitutes I have known who have gone to pieces and eventually died have been childless and child-like, dependent upon masochistic relationships with men, drugs or incessant "good fun". They have been quarrelsome, petty, hysterical, paranoid and vain. They have related to their customers in only the most superficial way, offering themselves as nothing but sex objects and providing nothing but a petulant consent to be "used" in order to get money. They therefore attract only the most unscrupulous and boorish of men, amongst whom are bound to feature every kind of pimp and ponce.'

She, herself, never became involved with pimps although she did work for a while for a frightful madam, the infamous 'Countess Viviana' – 'the most evil person I ever met. She clearly demonstrated that it isn't always gender which determines whether you are oppressor or oppressed. She did a roaring trade in Third World women who hand-embroidered her linen napkins and silk underwear by day and saw to her clients by night. Totally exploited, they always remained in debt to her and never had enough money to go home. One particularly pathetic young girl took so long saving up to retrieve her child from an orphanage that it had died by the time she returned to South America. This incident sickened all of us, but Countess Viviana only said that if it was so sickly it was perhaps a blessing in disguise.'

Helen left in disgust and thereafter only ever worked for herself operating, with a few other women, a discreet brothel cooperative which was never shopped by neighbours and never raided by the police. They serviced a wide variety of clients from the man who wore women's clothes under his business suit but could never tell his wife for fear she would lose respect for him, to the man who enjoyed giving a woman things – flowers, underwear, wine – but was married to a woman who did not enjoy receiving them.

Sometimes Helen and a few friends would be engaged for an 'orgy'. These occasions were more like prep school pillow fights than anything Caligula might have attended. The whores, obtained often at great cost, would sit there in the nude getting on with a bit of knitting. They were completely ignored while the men cavorted amongst themselves, stark naked, spraying each other with champagne and generally acting like men do in rugger changing rooms.

'We were there to lend an air of heterosexual respectability should anyone feel uncomfortable about the homosexual overtones,' she said. 'I never got the impression that any of the men *were* homosexual. On the contrary they seemed to be a little afraid of each other and this regression to childish behaviour was an attempt to be at ease. The evening would have to be rounded off with sex in the last few minutes as part of the rite, but my impression was that none of the men would have missed it had we refused to oblige. The sex was always perfunctory and the men too interested in each other's larks to give it their full attention.'

Helen very rarely got involved in bizarre sex and dealt mainly with straight, rather pathetic sex. 'Englishmen *always* keep their socks on!' she said, laughing. 'That's how you can tell their nationality if in doubt. Often some of the older ones still wear those sock suspenders too. There is no sense of body awareness, physical pride or sensuality. Sex is like a dose of syrup of figs. Not exactly unpleasant but good for you. "Keeps you going," said one old boy, exactly as if he were referring to a laxative. Many don't even have orgasms, they merely ejaculate.'

Being left alone by the police was by no means to be assumed – witness what happened to Cynthia Payne. As long as the nonsensical prostitution laws exist, any attempt to organize on the part of prostitutes results in arrest, closure, heavy fines. They are not free like other people to operate from premises which are suitable for their purpose. Even two women sharing a flat for safety, economy and companionship can be prosecuted for running a brothel.

Since prostitution of itself is no offence, it seems crazy that criminal sanctions are applied to women trying to find ways of pursuing this activity. As Dr Susan Edwards in her lucid investigation *Women on Trial* says: 'It becomes increasingly difficult to understand the motivation for criminalization of a "prelude" to an activity which involves consent and no concept of a victim, with the possible exception of the woman herself. The National Association of Probation Officers support this view. They see no reason why the penal system should be involved in the control and suppression of an activity which is not in itself illegal and in which there is no victim.

'Also it seems illogical that whilst a woman may be committing a crime by loitering or soliciting, a man in "accepting" and being party to her unlawful solicitation does not. The punter is beyond the law.'

Helen laments the demise of the big madams (with the notable exception of Countess Viviana). Most were hounded out of business by the law, leaving the prostitutes who worked for them terribly vulnerable to criminal pimps. 'Since prostitutes tend to be young and their lives in disarray, which is why they are on the game in the first place, they need to be kept in line.' She mentions the famous Madam Liza and others like her who kept girls off drugs. They knew the warning signs and moved in to nip it in the bud. They had all been pros themselves so they knew what the pitfalls were, what the emotional problems were and they cared. They cared about their businesses, their own reputations and the reputations of their clients.

'If only for reasons of self-interest, it was enough to make caring for the girls an essential part of the service,' Helen explained. 'They understood the boyfriend troubles, the moral repugnance that can seize a woman up, the financial worries that force her to swallow the moral repugnance and get on with paying the bank manager, the depression that can follow a humiliating experience with a client, and the desire of the young to have fun with money, drugs, kicks and instant gratification.'

These women also understood the problems of those with children to care for and school fees overdue. They would make little alterations in rostas to help a woman in financial trouble. They would arrange new girls to go on double bookings so that an experienced girl could help them get the hang of things. Cleanliness and good health were important.

It is a completely different story where pimps are concerned. 'Wherever men are in charge of prostitution as a way of making a fast buck,' says Helen, 'the standards drop at once and it is instantly recognizable in the appearance and morale of the girls who work under them.'

Eventually, the vengeance motivation which had led Helen into prostitution in the first place, took her into campaigning for a better deal for women like herself who found themselves 'knocking at the door of social ostracization'. She founded a pressure group called PUSSI

(Prostitutes United for Social and Sexual Integration), later renamed PLAN (Prostitution Laws Are Nonsense). Her intelligent, honest, articulate observations on prostitution made her into a public figure, a pundit invited onto chat shows and discussion panels, courted by sociologists and psychologists, but less popular with some hard-line feminists.

One of the great tragedies has been the polarization of the women's movement on this issue. Many prostitutes feel bitter that the feminists have contributed to their oppression by forcing moral judgements on them. Feminists accuse prostitutes of pandering to destructive male stereotypes and thereby prolonging inequality and abuses. Prostitutes accuse feminists of contributing to their marginalization and isolation by being as bad as the rest of society if not worse in ostracizing and criticizing them.

Perhaps the most positive and helpful thing any one woman can do is to support and validate those who for whatever reason have chosen to be prostitutes. In any job there will be people who do it because they've drifted into it, because it's all they think they can do. And there will be those who do it with vitality. Prostitutes are no different. Some feel they are victims. Some *are* victims. Some are most definitely not and celebrate their choice. All of them, like anyone else, need love and acceptance.

The morality question is a complex one not solved by moral indignation and self-righteousness. Insight into the reasons for prostitution do not emerge in atmospheres charged with hostility and injustice.

'Prostitutes are quite as aware as anyone else of the moral dilemmas which confront us as individuals and as nations,' said Helen and went on to tell me about the waterfront prostitutes in Haifa who refused to do business with the sailors who had come off a nuclear submarine. They had agreed unanimously to boycott any man with any connections to nuclear warfare because of their belief that it threatened the safety of the world and was therefore immoral.

Getting to know Helen confounded many of the standard stereotypes and was the beginning of a time of great learning for me. Through her, doors opened and a network of contacts began to form. Because of the enforced isolation they are subjected to, many prostitutes only feel relaxed in each other's company where they don't have to live a double life. I feel privileged to have been included so often, both in their working lives and their off-duty confidences. And I have been greatly moved by the courage, humour and sadness I have seen. Everything which follows is the result of conversations, experiences and friendships that happened over that year. One prostitute I met through Helen was Connie.

'Sometimes you get a dead horse at the other end!' said Connie. She was talking about the perils of phone sex. 'If you get no feedback, it's difficult to know how they're coming along. If that happens I might say: "Would you like to know what I look like? Well, I have long red hair down to my bum and a lovely body which I'm very proud of. I work hard to keep it in perfect shape. I'm quite slim with big firm breasts."'

Silence.

'"Would you like to know what I'm doing right now? I'm lying on my velvet couch totally naked looking at myself in a full length mirror. Now I'm gently caressing my left nipple ..."'

Silence.

'"If you were to walk into the room right now, what would you like to do?" Bingo!'

The whole process costs just £29.50 by carefully checked credit card. It doesn't usually take more than three minutes.

Connie is, in fact, 58 with a care-worn face, a pretty good figure, dyed black hair with white roots showing and a sensational voice. She has been a whore since she was 17 and now feels too old and too tired to lie on her back any longer, so she uses her considerable experience and understanding of male sexual fantasies to home in on what they want to hear.

She has a discreet ad in a sex magazine: 'Discover the art of good conversation. Ring Salome.' Sometimes a whole day goes by and no one calls, other days the phone rings midday, tea-time, late at night, once even at 5 am. If she's not in the mood she switches the phone off or puts on the answering machine with a very seductive sounding message asking callers to try again later. She keeps very erratic hours herself and often stays up all night writing poetry, mostly rhyming doggerel, but heartbreakingly poignant expressions of her innermost feelings:

Don't wake yet, sleep a bit longer.
I don't want you to see my hot tears,
My dark fears.
Wait a while and soon
I will be ready to greet you.

Connie lives alone above a florist's shop in Kentish Town. The place is a mess. Cats' litter trays, dog hair on all the furniture, kittens nesting in the remains of what was once a very expensive lynx and leopard skin coat, unmade bed and full ashtrays. She shares the place with two enormous German Shepherd dogs, two senile, blind, matted old dogs that look like sheepskins left out in the rain, a tortoiseshell cat, a black and white mother cat and four kittens.

Her life seems to have been a succession of wrong decisions, mistimings, and disastrous love affairs. She has two daughters (one of 40) and an adopted uncontrollable delinquent son of 19 who is the child of a West Indian lover. Connie took the lad in after he had found his mother dead from an overdose and the father had declined to look after him. It cramped her style somewhat as she was running a kind of salon from her home in Swiss Cottage at the time.

This, by all accounts, was an elegant establishment where she held private parties for groups of businessmen, say, or football supporters. Connie would have pre-arranged the right number of classy, beautifully dressed women at £200 each and they would all meet up for a glass of champagne at her place, then go off for the evening to do whatever. Each girl would be given a discreet envelope by her with £150 in it. So for ten men she'd make £500 for herself.

Having young Clifford around the place wasn't ideal, so, against everyone's advice, she sold the flat and moved into this flat. Her life seems to have been a relentless downward spiral, despite the huge amounts of money that have been through her hands.

The first time we met she told me about a sure-fire way to get rich quickly. This involved some telephone chat-line scheme which she was just about to embark on, but it transpired that her erstwhile business advisor tried to ease her out and everything hinged on the son of a friend who used to work as a telephone engineer and would know how to set the whole thing up. Then if she could just borrow a lot of money from the bank or sell her house and move to the country, everything would work out at last ...

There was a wistful optimism and touching impracticality about her plan. She rolled a joint, picked the dog hairs off her tracksuit and peered at herself in the mirror muttering, 'Must make an appointment to get my roots done.'

Connie was the only child of a dreamy father and a tyrannical mother who used to lock her up and not allow her to play with the gypsy children who lived near by and to whom she was very attracted. One day when she was 13 she escaped and went on a thieving expedition with her chums for a dare. She got caught and put on probation. Her mother sent her to a punitive boarding school from where she escaped again a year later and ran away to London never to return home again.

She arrived at Victoria Station to find herself sitting in a pool of blood as her periods had started. In the Ladies' lavatory, a kindly woman asked her what was the matter and why she was crying. Learning she had nowhere to go, the woman took her in. She turned out to be a prostitute. She took Connie under her wing, took her along on jobs to sit outside and wait, never coerced her into anything but offered a tempting example. Suddenly fun, wickedness, wildness, danger and excitement were the accepted way to live. Connie remained a virgin.

'I believe a girl should wait until she's in love, than she's ready for sex. You need to be wet and willing and practically swooning, then you are anaesthetized. A man on the other hand should be taught, *shown* by an older, more experienced woman how to be a good lover. A girl only needs to be told verbally,' Connie explained.

Connie had fallen in love and lost her virginity, but the guy turned out to be a rotter and married to boot. She got picked up by the police because she was still underage and on probation, sent to a remand home, met lots of girls who were on the game and decided, quite definitely, that she would become a prostitute. These were the people with whom she belonged. The polarization was complete – them and us. Her loyalties now lay firmly with the outcasts and criminals.

She fell in with a gang of burglars, married one, got pregnant and was arrested for receiving stolen goods. The baby was born in Borstal, taken away from her and, the final irony, brought up by Connie's mother. This daughter is now respectably married, never wants children and has nothing to do with Connie.

The pain of these recollections brought tears to her eyes and she rolled another little joint. She talked about her dream of setting up a place of sanctuary where girls who want to be prostitutes could go. There they could tell their story to someone kind who would not judge them or pressurize them. If they had made up their minds, they could be shown the ropes, warned off the sharks, pitfalls and minefields and helped to get started. If they were just desperate or scared or hard up and didn't really want to go on the game, they could get advice, help, shelter or whatever to keep them off the streets. It seemed such a worthwhile dream, that maybe, one day someone would make it reality.

Connie has perfected her husky, sensual voice, a cross between Edith Piaf and Fenella Fielding made raspier by smoking. When she talks she has a whole repertoire of quaint, old-fashioned seductive little wiggles and facial expressions, a parody of girlish coyness. She does a little bit of business with a lace handkerchief rather in the manner that women used to do a little number with a fan.

She never ceases to be amazed at how quickly a man can be processed once you know the trigger factor. In her old days of contact as opposed to telephone sex, she could often suggest a candle-lit bath with a client. 'Two minutes of soaping each other and more often than not they come in the bath and it's all over – nice and clean. They can very rarely manage it a second time. The important thing is not to rush them or hustle them. If you make it seem as if you've got all the time in the world, they'll be happy and relaxed and no trouble. I do feel you should give value for money.'

Connie has always enjoyed the acting and performance aspect of the job and is proud of her skills and expertise, but that's only one side of the story. She has clearly found the social isolation of having an unacceptable profession hard to bear. She is disillusioned with men, with so-called friends who let her down and rip her off, and her optimism is looking as threadbare as her old fur coat. When she says she's going to get out of this place, make a fresh start, pay off her debts, get out of the sex business, re-decorate the house, she only half believes it herself. So she has a little smoke and everything looks a bit better for a while. She skates a fine line between coping and despair.

'Whoring is boring, but lucrative,' said Connie when I went to see her a second time. Our arrangement had been that I would pick her up and bring her out to Twickenham for a change of scene, a day at my house, a walk by the river. But when I phoned to confirm she said, 'Oh darling ... I didn't write it in my diary. You're not angry with me, are you? I'm in a bit of a spot. You see, Access is going to withdraw so I've go to make as much money as I can. I've only got a couple of weeks. I daren't leave the house. I've banked quite a lot on this weekend and ... you do understand, don't you darling?' I said, no problem. I would pick up some food and bring her round a picnic lunch. Then she could man the phone and teach me how to handle the clients at the same time.

When I got there she was in an even greater muddle than last time, wearing a stained pink tracksuit and ancient dog-chewed fluffy pink slippers. Archie, her 87-year-old platonic gentleman friend, had gone to the bank with the credit slips. Archie likes to keep active and run little errands for her. She's known him since the days when she ran her soirées in Rosetti Garden Mansions. He'd always made himself useful and would fetch drinks for the gentlemen clients when they arrived. 'Afternoon tea or evening wine with congenial company' was how the soirées were advertised and Connie liked to make the introductions personally to ensure that the transactions went smoothly and discreetly. It never felt like a brothel.

On this day Connie had half her bottom teeth missing. 'I've got to have a bridge made, darling, and it's going to cost a fortune. I hate wearing the temporary crown, it's so uncomfortable.' She looked in the mirror above the mantelpiece, licked her finger, smoothed her eyebrows and patted her hair which was trying desperately to escape from a bun. 'Must get my roots done,' she muttered absently. 'You've caught me on an off day. I'm going to get a housekeeper as soon as I can find one. I hate living in all this squalor.'

The off day seemed like the latest in a long succession. The little kittens played among the huge paws of the Alsatian dogs and Connie looked on affectionately. All her love and a lot of her income are lavished on the animals who are happy and contented. 'Isn't it interesting how some women are always trying to make families?' Helen Buckingham had said to me the last time I saw her. 'They are disappointed with men and frustrated by never being allowed to pour all their loving onto anyone so they collect waifs, stray cats, sick donkeys, lame ducks, and any other creatures who need mothering. They set themselves up to be exploited.'

'If I had my time over, I would never have adopted Clifford,' said Connie. Although she has now thrown him out, the crazy, disturbed boy has been the cause of her downfall she now thinks. He was the reason she moved from Rosetti Gardens, he is the one who has bust the place up, torn down her beloved lampshade, broken her best vases, stolen her money, kicked a hole in the door. 'I loved the little boy he was, but I don't love the monster he's become,' she said, encapsulating a lot of what happens between unrealistic, generous-hearted women with mothering needs, and the inadequate, immature men they often choose to lavish this affection on.

We ate our picnic and in between lamenting her misfortune, Connie instructed me on how to conduct an erotic phone call. Apart from describing to the man how she looks, long red hair, secret places, big breasts ('say "breasts" lingeringly, sometimes that's enough'), hard nipples which she's fingering, playing with herself and so on, sometimes they want to get into a bit of domination. Then she scolds them and tells them to get down on their knees and kiss her boots. Within seconds they're breathing heavily and it's all over.

The phone rang. 'I make them wait a bit,' she said, sipping her tea and picking up the receiver on the tenth ring. 'Hello,' she said with a perfect mixture of huskiness, girlishness and promise. 'Ooh yes, darling, I love talking about sex but this is a service and there is a fee. Did you realize that?' She asks the caller for credit card details and promises to ring back. She rings Directory Enquiries to check out that the address and the phone number match. They don't. Another time waster.

'We talk about intimate things, darling, anything your heart desires, whatever gives you pleasure.' The phone had rung yet again and she was describing her service for the umpteenth time to a potential client enquiring as to the nature of the 'pleasurable conversation'. He balked at the £29.50 and didn't ring back. A lot of them are incensed to discover she wants to be paid. 'They think it's free and that they're going to be talking to a woman who has the same needs as them. A sort of mutual fantasy. Can you imagine! Men are so stupid.'

All the time I was there she received about ten dud calls and no genuine ones. A 12-year-old kid rang with his father's credit card. 'It's not worth the money,' she told him. 'Why don't you go outside and get some fresh air.' 'His voice hadn't even broken yet!' she said to me.

Then something shocking happened. She received a really vicious hate call from a woman. 'You fucking shit cunt,' said a rough voice. 'You suck men's cocks, don't you?' She could hear other women cackling in the background.

'How rude and coarse you are!' Connie replied in her best upper-class accent. There was more foul-mouthed abuse and she rung off. They phoned back several times. 'Either they are a bunch of lunatics in an asylum or a bunch of charladies using the boss's phone in the lunch hour,' she said. In the end she suggested in her most aristocratic voice that they put their collective head down the toilet and flush the chain.

She was laughing but the incident left her very unsettled and upset. It was the first time she had ever encountered such hostility from other women. The realization that she was the repository for so much irrational hatred left her feeling depressed and paranoid. Reality had intruded in a very violent way upon her elegant erotic fantasy world. She took a couple of aspirins and rolled a little joint.

TWO

One day, Helen called me to say that the American prostitute Dolores French was in London to publicize her recently published auto-biography, *Working: My Life as a Prostitute*, and would I like to come over to meet her. Luckily I was at a loose end and jumped straight in the car. Helen cooked us a risotto and opened a bottle of Beaujolais.

Dolores is a sweet-faced, friendly woman in her late thirties with a ready sense of humour who carries her abundant body with ease and assurance. One of the myths she is keen to dispel is that prostitutes are damaged people who come from damaging backgrounds. She herself had a reasonable and loving childhood, the identical background, as she points out, that produced her sister who is a nurse. Her family have made the difficult leap of adjustment to knowing what she does for a living.

She told them just before she went on national television in the United States as she didn't want them to find out from anyone but herself. They, and her husband, a defence attorney, are very supportive and accept that she has made a rational choice and that the work suits her. Many people in many different jobs are damaged she says – typists, school teachers, business executives, 'and what about *gynaecologists!*' – but the connections and motivations aren't scrutinized quite so assiduously.

Dolores' father ran a gas station and was the local sheriff. Her mother was a tireless, exemplary homemaker but also encouraged Dolores to make herself strong and independent and not to take any nonsense from men. 'So, amateur psychologists,' she challenges, 'what in my history "made" me become a prostitute?'

Dolores has no children, by choice, and concedes that it would have been difficult to have been so open about her life if she had. Not because she would want to hide it - children, she believes, are very adaptable; what they can't abide is dishonesty, secrets and hypocrisy – but because the courts can take your children away, as they can in England, if you get into trouble with the law.

As a profession, prostitution is, she feels, one of the best ways that a woman can come to understand and explore her own sexual pre-ferences. People keep asking her how long she's going to stay on the game. Her answer is at least until she grows up and decides what she wants to do!

Dolores told me about her mentor, Elaine, the beautiful elegant woman who introduced her to the profession. One day after years of unhappy marriage and five children, Elaine simply packed a small bag and left a note telling her husband where to find the car. Then she left the car at a layby on the motorway and, figuring it was as good a place as any, hitched a lift with a trucker who was going to Atlanta. She was 35. After the truck driver found out she didn't have any money, he offered her cash in exchange for sex. 'I was pretty naive at the time', she told Dolores. 'I never for a moment thought it was prostitution but that was my first job – or my millionth depending on how you look at my marriage.'

Dolores learned from Elaine that it doesn't matter how you go about selling sex. Men expect sex almost everywhere. Once you understand this fact you're in business. She also learned that no matter how much money she made she still had to deal with how society treats prostitutes. 'You have to maintain your own integrity,' she said, 'and no matter how well-adjusted you think you are, you will constantly have to deflect criticism. Even if you know in your heart that what you're doing is OK, you might start to feel devalued or degraded so it's important never to think of yourself as a bad person or to act like a bad person.'

Dolores read Dale Carnegie's book, *How to Win Friends and Influence People*, and she began to see prostitution as a noble profession right up there with nursing and teaching. 'All the things he talks about such as the need to appear to be truly, deeply interested in a stranger, make a good courtesan, a good healer, a good counsellor. People think that prostitutes hate men because you usually end up talking about the weird clients who make the best stories. But even weird clients are usually nice people. You're providing a valuable service to these men – all of them. You're helping someone with a crippled sense of self-esteem. Part of the art of prostitution is using sex to create a feeling of trust and intimacy, to bring people in touch with their sense of self-worth.'

As Dolores started working she became aware of how many of her clients were isolated and lonely. They came because they didn't have anyone else. She realized that if she could make a man walk out of there feeling good about himself, feeling he might actually be interesting and fun to be with, she had performed a great service. 'To do that a person has to love men and enjoy being with them, which I do. Even if a man wanted to engage in quite bizarre sexual behaviour, it seemed to me that my job was to respond with understanding and compassion. I was willing to consider anything short of having pain inflicted on me.'

Dolores is obviously gifted at putting people at ease, calming men down, making things all right. Many are terribly shy and have screwed up all their courage to come to her. Englishmen, she confirms, do leave their socks on, turn their heads away, shut their eyes, tell her to 'do it' while practically gritting their teeth. 'For some of them it's like taking a nasty-tasting medicine,' she laughs. 'They know it's something they ought to have, but prefer to get it over as soon as possible!

'Men think they keep coming back for sex, but they're coming back because we touch them emotionally, because we're real people.'

Dolores loves what she perceives as the honesty and independence of the prostitute/client relationship. She feels that when a woman has an 'affair' she nearly always starts to want to make demands on the man. She wants more time, more love, more devotion. She wants to have his baby, spend her birthday together, or have him leave his wife. What changes the equation is money – 'the great equalizer' as she calls it.

'By living off the money men gave me for sex, I was able to achieve the sort of independence from men my mother always wanted me to have. Having always been overweight, I began taking good care of my body. Being told I was beautiful made me begin to see myself in a new light. Women choose to go into prostitution because they need money and they need flexible hours so they can deal with all of life's problems. Prostitution is not the problem.'

In her quest to get to know all aspects of the profession Dolores has tried out many different styles of prostitution from the windows in Amsterdam to a waterfront brothel in Puerto Rico. 'I love the intimacy, the serenity, the fluidity and the safety of the whorehouse. In a whorehouse there's an acceptance of everyone's place in the universe.'

I felt, talking to her, that she really does like men and has a natural daredevil, adventurous streak in her. She has always found the danger, the risks very exhilarating, that frisson of fear, the adrenalin rush, getting herself out of tricky situations. Within three years, she says, you're either completely addicted to it or you give it up and get out.

I remember once doing a series of articles for a magazine on women who do dangerous sports – gliding, downhill racing, hot-air ballooning, mountaineering. The parallels are quite striking. Dolores likes living on the edge and compares herself to a commando or an undercover agent, 'Rambo in Rhinestones,' she says, laughing. A great deal of energy, wiliness and ingenuity, not to mention experience, goes into spotting vice squad cops posing as genuine clients and avoiding arrest.

Both Dolores and her husband have been very active in campaigning for prostitutes' rights – for medical care without moral judgements, for legal reforms, for people to understand that a prostitute can and should press charges against anyone who commits a crime against her, for fairer media representation.

A good example of how the media misrepresents prostitution is the following quote from the *New York Times* (25.11.87) which Dolores used in her book: '"The disease [AIDS] appears to have entered the Philippines, in many cases through prostitutes who have had contact with servicemen near two large American bases," the doctors said.' The statement doesn't read, 'American servicemen have brought AIDS to the Philippines.' The fact is, says Dolores, that military personnel, if found to be HIV positive, will often prefer to say that they caught it off a hooker rather than from a homosexual encounter or through intravenous drug use. There is no stigma associated with the former and the latter two are offences against the military code of justice and carry severe penalties. Naturally the authorities collude in dumping all the blame on the prostitutes as they aren't all that keen to publicize homosexuality or drugs in the army.

Research carried out in both Britain and the United States has shown that HIV infection in prostitutes is no more common than in any other group of sexually active single women. Its prevalence amongst street prostitutes is nearly always associated with a history of intravenous drug use and shared needles. It's also related to poverty. 'Safe sex requires the money to buy condoms,' says Dolores, 'and most importantly, a sense of self-worth, a sense of a future worth living for. If a woman is in a spiral of poverty, despair, and negative self-image, her suicidal impulses will be strong.'

This was confirmed by Katrina Donegan, a trained nurse, who works with the Praed Street Project on AIDS and prostitution. About 200 prostitutes from the Paddington area in London form a cohort which the team are studying. The women come for health checks, medical advice, drug dependency help, counselling and support. There is a drop-in centre for informal social get togethers and cups of tea. The findings indicate, so far, that HIV infection is not significantly higher than in any other section of society (less, it would seem, than amongst Roman Catholic priests!). In fact only three women in their sample are HIV positive and of those, two are intravenous drug users and one has a bi-sexual lover. So, in other words, it's not the prostitution which is the high-risk factor. The team are hoping to show that allegations about prostitutes spreading AIDS are largely unfounded. They, more than most people, have a vested interest in protecting themselves.

As an expert in safe sex Dolores is often asked to speak at hospitals, universities and so on. Her party trick is to demonstrate how to blow a condom onto a banana. She claims if you hide one in your cheek, you can get it onto a man without him knowing. I have tried the banana routine in private with singular lack of success.

Dolores' dearest wish while she was in England was to visit Sissinghurst Castle as she is a keen gardener. I'd always wanted to go as well so I offered to take her. We met up a couple of days later and hit the road. Even though she was off-duty wearing an old tracksuit with her natural blondish straight hair hanging loose, she still had her false eyelashes and astonishing long black fingernails fixed on with super-glue. She had threatened to come in camouflage army combat fatigues and heavy disguise after appearing on the Wogan show the previous night but, in fact, I don't think anyone would have recognized her. She looks quite different without her cascade of auburn wig.

I had watched the TV show and been enormously impressed by her quiet dignity in the face of hostile questions and moralizing asides. The other guests on the show were Shere Hite and Jackie Collins. Dolores was by far the most relaxed woman present. The studio audience, who seemed to have been hand-picked for crassness, guffawed every time she tried to make a point and didn't really listen. In a typically British response to any discussion about sex, they seized on anything that could have a double meaning and made it into a smutty innuendo.

The worst ordeals in Dolores' working life (apart from one maniac who pulled a gun on her, and that, as she says, could happen to anyone in a bank or a shop) are always when she makes public appearances in her efforts to advance prostitutes' rights, break down stereotypes and inform people what the job is really like. Her most unfriendly, disrespectful, antagonistic encounters have always been with media people who set her up for either ridicule or pity or revulsion.

She has perfected a technique of patiently riding it out, not getting defensive, angry or upset. She goes into a sort of state of meditation, she says, to keep herself sane and centred. She is asked again and again, 'Doesn't prostitution make you feel dirty and degraded?' 'On the contrary, I'm proud of it and I love it,' she replies. 'It is the most honest and rewarding work I've ever done. The overwhelming majority of clients are pleasant and on their best behaviour.'

She is asked how she can bear to use her body as a commodity, but she has no problems with this either, 'I sell my services in the same way as anyone else who has to be *present* to do their job.' A dancer, a gymnast, a model, a psychiatrist, an actress, all use their bodies, or their relationship skills or their ability to make-believe convincingly in order to earn a living. A whore does all three.

When asked how she could do what she does and be happily married she reflected on how interesting it was that so many people seem to think the fact that she has a husband is the most extraordinary thing about her. She says she has never had any difficulty dissociating her working body from her private life, certainly no more than, say, a gynaecologist! ('Ah, but that's different,' she was told. 'Their patients aren't there for pleasure.' What a bizarre answer!) She said that both she and her husband do not regard sex as the ultimate intimacy in their relationship. For them, making choices and decisions together, sharing ideas and a home are the real closenesses. Our society gets sex out of proportion, she thinks.

It was good to have the long journey (made longer by a terrible traffic jam on the motorway) to talk more and get to know each other. I think she was glad to be just a person, not an interview subject, or a prostitute, but a tourist, a gardener, a new friend. We bought rolls and cheese and fruit and ate as we went along enjoying the beautiful Kent countryside in the afternoon sunshine.

She was interested in my experiences of living with the Aborigines while researching my book about healing. I was telling her how demoralized and invisible they were, their customs and wisdoms devalued and destabilized by the dominant colonial culture until their only choice was to become 'integrated', that is to say submerged and swallowed up, or to die out.

She made the interesting connection that there is an obvious parallel in the way prostitutes have been treated – an automatic assumption that they, too, are benighted victims of ignorance and circumstance, an assumption that they have nothing of value to say or teach, that the best thing you can do for them is to rescue them.

'That attitude instantly devalues any choices they have ever made,' said Dolores. 'They don't need to be saved, they need to be recognized, respected, celebrated. Prostitute lore is very ancient. Women have passed it on by word of mouth. Prostitutes learn about the trade only from other prostitutes.

'What most reformers mean by "integration" is really a form of colonization, of absorption. It means the rejection of a unique cultural identity, in exchange for adopting that of the conqueror and accepting the missionary viewpoint that your "backwardness" is something to be pitied and deplored.

'The first thing a person is entitled to,' said Dolores, 'is the dignity of feeling she's made the best choices she knew how at the time with the resources she had, based on survival, ego-integrity, and the need for love. Those are the only reasons anyone does anything.'

We talked a lot about looking for ways to bring all the parts of being a woman together. I am body and spirit, sex and guts, intuition and intellect. I am healer, goddess, whore, mother, wife, witch, crone. I am looking for the whole woman, but we have been set against each other as watchdogs and judges, kept submissive by a divide and rule policy each bit relegated to her own compartment.

Ivory towers for madonnas, pedestals for divas, gutters for whores, kitchens for wives, stocks and stakes for witches and crones. All these categories keep us from each other and keep us from becoming whole. Each part denying the other. I am all these women and every woman. Our strength lies in recognizing and accepting one another's unique beauty and worth. Prostitutes have carried their art of womanhood alone and unsung for long enough.

After a decade of courageous campaigning, the situation, Dolores feels, is changing fast. There have been a couple of international conventions on prostitutes' rights, for instance. Paradoxically, one of the fears is that the decriminalization of prostitution will come so rapidly that, like a newly, independent country, it will run away with itself and the things of value that are worth preserving might get swept out before anyone acknowledges that there were any in the first place.

'What none of us wants,' she says, 'is a situation like Las Vegas, with licensing and state control. The trouble is we've been fighting so long for women's rights and the decriminalization of prostitution that now that it's nearly upon us we haven't agreed on what sort of structure or lack of structure we want.'

I asked Dolores, in view of her great enthusiasm for the job, if she had any boundaries in her working life, things she would not do for a client no matter how much money might be offered. About this she was quite categorical: she wouldn't do anything which involved another person who was not willing or was a child; anything which would be harmful to her or cause any permanent damage to the client; any kind of genital contact without a condom; unethical sex to obtain information for a third party (a paid set-up).

After our day out, we came back to my house and showed each other family snapshots. She admired my garden and phoned home to speak to her husband in Atlanta. I cooked her some supper while my youngest daughter admired her black fingernails and her diamond watch. Dolores taught her how to say the only words she knows in Spanish, 'Es necessito dinero primo' – you have to pay first.

THREE

One astonishing piece of good fortune I had while researching this book was meeting the wonderful Sophia, an ex-prostitute who now works with a research project in Birmingham looking into the risks of HIV infection related to sexual behaviour. The job involves going out and contacting street prostitutes where they work, offering health education, free condoms, opportunities for counselling and HIV testing. They maintain strict confidentiality while at the same time compiling a great deal of useful data.

A friend from London Lighthouse introduced us and there was an instant rapport. Sophia is 28 years old with long, bleached blonde hair, pale skin, very blue eyes and a smile of great sweetness. Having chosen to give up full-time prostitution, she now feels that an essential part of her own healing process is to reclaim the pejorative labels such as dyke and whore which have defined her, so that she can acknowledge them, own them, and love those parts of herself that they represent.

When I met her she had been in analysis for six months and had already made tremendous progress in both understanding and forgiving herself. She spoke with profound insight into her motivations and emotions beginning with her bleak childhood.

Sophia is the eldest of four children and, on the face of it, comes from rather an exotic family – one of her grandfathers was a lion-tamer in a circus – but the reality of her life was nothing to be envied. From the age of seven she was sexually abused regularly by her father. As she sees it now, she tried to take the 'badness' onto herself – 'Look what I've made daddy do' – in order to protect her mother from the reality. Her mother did nothing to stop what was happening. She was a wretched and silent conspirator who wouldn't see what was going on in front of her nose. Sophia's role became one of sacrifice overlaid with power and control. Taking upon herself all the sexuality that her hugely overweight and unattractive mother was unable to handle, she offered herself almost as a decoy in an attempt to shield both her and the younger children for whom she felt responsible.

In analysis Sophia has been able to see how it is that children who have been sexually abused often display seductive or sexually provocative behaviour; in a sense their survival depends on it. It is the only way they know of getting affection. They also have the immense power of being the guardians of the most intimate secrets in the family, the mistresses of the household, the mother's replacements.

Her childhood was characterized by this confusion – on the one hand exploited and abused, on the other precocious and omnipotent. Sophia was very clever and did well at school, coming top of the class in almost everything. As she says, she desperately wanted to please her teachers, seeking their approval and hoping that they as good, responsible adults would take care of her.

Her home life was a complete lie. Her mother was a sadistic woman – showing Sophia up, holding inquisitions and humiliating her. Her father, 'flabby and hairy, with a repulsive pink body and a pink penis', exploited his total control over her life and will, forcing his daughter to pay with her body for the affection and care which should have been hers by right, dishonouring the protective bond between parent and child.

When her parents began basking in the reflected glory of her scholastic achievements, taking the credit away from her, claiming the merit for themselves as exemplary parents, she deliberately failed all her exams to spite them.

She started taking drugs, quickly moving on to injecting heroin. 'In a sense it was an act of purification, deliberation, perhaps, in retrospect, also punishment,' she says, 'but it was my choice. I was doing what *I* wanted with my body for the first time.'

She left home and fell in with Carlos, an attractive, clever, manipulative man who exploited her neediness. At first he was loving and fatherly and persuaded her to come off heroin. The fact that he was black and as different as possible from the hated hairy pink body of her father made him seem safe, 'almost like a third sex'. There were no connotations or echoes of the dirty, guilty sex of her childhood. She wanted his approval, wanted to belong somewhere.

He then suggested that if she loved him, she could help pay off some of his gambling debts by working as a prostitute. In mute despair she agreed. It was, after all, consistent with her innermost view of herself and, apart from the first time with a client when she cried because she felt so bad, it began to seem logical. It confirmed all her most negative feelings about herself as somehow contaminated, only good for delivering sex.

Wanting to please Carlos, wanting to fill up the emptiness inside, she played out the fantasy. She even enjoyed the masochism and the serving, doing the cooking and the housework and then going out and earning the money. And it was good money – £200 to £500 a day. Apart from buying a few clothes, she gave Carlos all the money. He beat her but to begin with she mistook his possessiveness and domination for affection.

Sometimes she'd meet other women on jobs, and in bathrooms and toilets they'd have a chance to get to know each other a bit. They'd exchange jokes, experiences, information, embraces. She became aware that the only time she ever experienced any comfort or warmth or understanding was during these encounters.

When Carlos realized that she was attracted to other women, he brought another, younger girl to come and live with them – more money for him, companionship for her. The girl he found was only 15 and Sophia felt protective immediately towards her. They'd do jobs together, lesbian displays, but Sophia would tell the clients that if they wanted intercourse it could only be with her as the girl was a virgin.

Together they hatched a plot to run away, but Carlos got suspicious and watched them like a hawk. He often threatened that if she ever tried to leave him he would slash her face and cut off her clitoris. One day the two women planned an all-night job with a high fee to tempt him to let them out, but while Sophia was trying to smuggle out a suitcase, Carlos caught her and knocked her out with a punch in the face. When she came to, he had tied her wrists and was dragging her across the floor. He tied her to the bed and held a knife to her throat.

She had appeased him and defused him before by crying and by submissive cowering which always worked. This time, though, he tortured her. He dripped hot wax on her from a candle; he ran the knife over her body; he said he was going to pour a kettle of boiling water over her face and went to get the kettle from the kitchen. He did throw it in her face, although the water was cold and he laughed when she screamed.

Luckily the other girl came back and he eventually let them go. They went to stay with a few women friends, but it wasn't long before the young girl went back to Carlos. Sophia felt betrayed and confused, but it was the turning point.

After being sadistically tortured by the man you have regarded as your lover, where do you go? How do you heal? It has been a long and painful journey finding, in analysis, the tools and the self-regard for rebuilding her life. In retrospect now, in spite of her anger towards Carlos, she feels a certain amount of compassion. Knowing that, in reality, he was seen and, more importantly, saw himself not as a man but as a 'big buck nigger' in our deeply oppressive WASP society, when what he had longed for was position, influence and respect. He had seen Sophia as a symbol and used her neediness to feed his own hunger for power. 'Being a prostitute taught me to see men in another light,' she says, 'as weak, as sometimes pathetic, as victims too.'

Sophia told me a dream she had had recently about meeting a lot of prostitutes who were disabled and who were with disabled clients. 'I awoke from the dream very relieved that I wanted to be a prostitute again. I felt quite happy about it. In analysis it became clear that the dream was about feeling crippled and disfigured and that when I'd initially become a prostitute I'd done it to *name* and make clear my role as a sexually available person. I felt that whoredom had been imposed upon me by my father and that I'd had to give of myself sexually in order to be loved and parented. In acknowledging this in the dream I then felt that I had a choice whether to be a prostitute or not. It would be a positive decision for me.'

Sophia, when I first met her, was living with a woman partner in a rather turbulent relationship. Although she had given up being on the game full time, she still occasionally saw one regular client, partly because the money was handy but more importantly because of wanting to own and face all the parts of herself. Her woman friend was not happy about this but, as Sophia said, 'If she loves me, it must include that part of me too.'

A few months later, I went to Sophia's house for supper. She lives in a neglected old house in the suburbs, alone now that the other women who were sharing it had moved out and she had split up with her partner. In the basement flat where the curtains were never opened, a solitary, violent drunkard crashed about shouting abuse at the whole world, filling the air with the disturbing and frightening sounds of irrational anger. The place was a bit of a mess for which Sophia apologized frequently. She hadn't had time to clean up since the others left; she hadn't the heart to bother since she was shortly to be rehoused. The council wouldn't let her stay in such a big three-bedroomed place alone and anyway she would be glad to get out.

Sophia cooked me a beautiful dish of stir-fried vegetables with tahini and garlic sauce. I'd brought a bottle of wine and we had a lovely supper together. We had both changed a lot since we had first talked. My own experience of coping with breast cancer and having to confront some of the pain of my life and the myths of my childhood made me feel closer to her than ever. Although her experiences had been infinitely more horrific than mine, I could identify more closely with her pain and our dialogue was more a sharing of equals.

With the remains of the wine we went and sat cross-legged on her bed, a large four-poster, the only personalized part of the house. It was a riveting sight, all hung about with spurs, hand-cuffs, feather boas, chains and other accoutrements. On the wall behind was a huge collection of lesbian sado-masochistic photographs and on the other side of her room, a rack of her clothes consisting almost entirely of several different black leather outfits and boots.

Sophia had been quite involved in sado-masochistic sexual practices, both in her private life and in the prostitute/client relationship. She explained that she tried to explore these issues in a place of safety – lovingly, enquiringly, openly – rather than pretending they don't exist. In sado-masochistic sex between consenting adults, issues of surrender and power can be experimented with in an atmosphere of mutual trust, but it's dangerous ground. It's a fine line between acting out fantasies and fears and actually getting hurt emotionally and physically. 'People need to be pretty sure what they're doing,' she says. 'I don't want to make it sound like an élitist pastime, but you are dealing with such deep and potent forces that there is a risk of getting out of your depth. This happened with my previous lover. The sex we had brought up loads of stuff for her about having been abused as a child which would have been a lot better coming through slowly and gently in therapy. I don't begin to have adequate resources to deal with that with a lover. I think S/M sex is good and it can be great, but I'd only want to do it with someone who has extensive self-knowledge.'

Sophia went on to say that she is trying to learn how to have real, loving relationships with people and to exorcise the template, the prototype of sickness and destructiveness out of her life. Her questions are clear and her honesty is stunning.

Sophia read me a piece of her own writing, an autobiographical incident from her time with Carlos, the pimp who beat and tortured her. She writes well with a mixture of dreadful immediacy and black humour. I was both moved and impressed. There were many points that she'd raised the first time we spoke, particularly about why prostitutes are scapegoated, which I was hoping she'd enlarge upon.

As she sees it, part of the unconscious imagery of a prostitute in our society is that she absorbs excess sexuality. All that semen, all that lust and carnality, all that kinkiness is poured into her. The very image of the whore with her high heels, split skirt and fishnet stockings is one of exaggerated, excessive femininity. Wherever there is excess, there has to be surplus. And where there's surplus and waste, there's pollution and the attendant fear of contamination. The prostitute absorbs contamination merely by the presence of her physical imagery. 'We all have our prejudices,' says Sophia. Even people who have done a lot of work to try and resolve issues of racism and sexism still feel comfortable with regarding prostitutes as bad people. It's almost the last bastion of prejudice.

In this context there is also a problem for anyone working with prostitutes in sexually transmitted diseases clinics or outreach projects. Because prostitutes are seen as 'other', beyond the pale, different from the rest of us, the health workers, merely by associating with them in an intimate way, pick up some of the same stigma. Consequently they are marginalized and kept apart too. They work in buildings that are not part of the main hospital, in basements and portacabins.

All of this came to light during a support group for health workers that Sophia helped facilitate. A lot of the workers felt that they, too, by actually touching the genitals of prostitutes in STD clinics and by listening to their life stories, were absorbing the excess. By becoming privy to this forbidden knowledge – knowledge of sex and 'naughtiness' and people's guilty secrets – everything was being finally off-loaded onto them. They had become the last repository for all the contamination. They felt they were becoming full to bursting with all these emotions and problems.

Part of the threat of prostitutes is that they *know* – they know about sex, they know about men. The unspoken fear is they might know things about my husband, my boyfriend, my father, that I don't. They might even know things about me. And maybe one of the reasons for the eternal fascination and 'research' into prostitution is that people want to *know* what prostitutes know.

One of the issues to which Sophia has given a lot of thought is her role as the 'token' prostitute in the research project. Although it is generally felt to be good and valid that prostitutes should participate in projects of this kind, there is still an unease around the subject, a fear of the area of life that prostitutes inhabit, a fear of the unknown fringes of the twilight world they haunt. So in order to protect themselves against contamination, health workers and research workers need to have a 'vaccine' to make their project immune. The need to have a real live prostitute, one who is identified with them. They can then embrace her and make her part of the project, thereby immunizing themselves against the threat of contagion.

Sophia feels that perhaps the directors and management of such projects want access to the knowledge without somehow getting their own hands dirty. To achieve this they have created a new sub-species akin to the Hindu caste of 'untouchables', the garbage workers, the abbatoir workers, the night soil workers, those who do the shitty jobs but are never acknowledged. This leaves the workers and, in particular, the token prostitute, feeling unsupported. It is rather like the token blacks that were annexed to social projects in the early days of racial integration. Like them, Sophia carries a mass of projected fears and a lot of responsibility.

The other important point Sophia had touched on was that of other women's attitudes towards prostitutes. Why is it that other women can be so judgemental, I wanted to know? Sophia's explanation is that most women live with a complicated confusion of feelings about their own sexuality and a repressed urge to uncover that part of themselves which the whore represents.

'A lot of non-prostitute women I have talked to have fantasies about being a prostitute,' she says. 'there is a love/hate, love/fear relationship with that particular part of their entire personality which has never been allowed to be seen as respectable enough to explore.' The inner command is, 'Don't look at it!' It is seen as the really dark side and the only safe thing to do with it is to project it lock, stock and barrel onto prostitutes for them to carry alone. Because of the low status imposed upon her, the prostitute is unlikely to have a forum to speak about the things that she knows, and is even less likely to be taken seriously if she does speak out and so the divisions between women are perpetuated.

In ancient Greece, a woman before she married was required to go to the temple and have sex with a stranger. With the stranger she was awakened to her innate feminine nature of giving, receiving and containing love. It symbolized having sex with a god and thereby becoming the goddess incarnate, the embodiment of the goddess's love and fertility, bringing the mystical and the mysterious into the human sphere.

Nancy Qualls-Corbett writes about this in her fine book *The Sacred Prostitute*:

> She did not make love in order to obtain admiration or devotion from the man who came to her, for often she remained veiled and anonymous. She did not require a man to give her a sense of her own identity; rather this was rooted in her own womanliness. The laws of her feminine nature were harmonious with those of the goddess.... In this union – the union of masculine and feminine, spiritual and physical – the personal was transcended and the divine entered in.... Her human emotions and her creative, bodily energies were united with the suprapersonal. She touched the basic regenerative powers, and thereby, as the goddess incarnate, assured the continuity of life and love.

The goddess had then paid her due and money was given to the temple. To be 'taken' in that way, to be wanted for a purely sexual reason, re-established a woman's eternal link with the goddess. It confirmed her initiation as a sexual being, comfortable in the knowledge that sex can be a good thing and of itself.

Alas, in the centuries that followed, all of this became eroded by the triumph of a dominant monotheistic patriarchy. The belief in masculine supremacy was to exclude women from any role apart from that of Mater Dolorosa, the sexless image of a weeping, impotent *virgin* mother. No longer was there an image of the divine feminine. The very qualities for which woman had once been considered sacred now became the reasons for which she was reviled.

It is a great tragedy that women should have endured this split in their being. As Qualls-Corbett writes: 'On the one hand the feminine was untouchable because it was elevated to extreme, heavenly heights; on the other it was debased as wicked and vile. The image of the sacred prostitute, simultaneously deeply spiritual and joyfully sexual, was completely unviable.'

So women have to choose between these two images; they are not allowed, as a man is, to be whole. A man can be a sexual being, a husband, a father – he can be all those things which are part of being a man. A woman cannot. She must label herself: pure or dirty, nice or bad, wife or whore, worthy or unworthy of respect, a woman who can take any amount of abuse or a woman who isn't free to explore.

Maybe that's why, once a woman has made a choice to be a whore, other women are secretly envious because it is a part of themselves they have had to deny and renounce. The only way to deal with that envy is to despise and condemn the whore. Sophia's point about contamination is important here: because prostitutes are perceived to be foul vessels, full up with excess whether that be semen or forbidden knowledge or perverted sex, there is the anxiety that they may be cancerous in some way, that the excess may seep through, become malignant and be impossible to get rid of. Therefore it's reassuring for the rest of us if prostitutes are ritually and frequently chastised, even annihilated.

Enormous amounts of police resources are expended in catching and punishing prostitutes. As Sophia says, 'So many cop films and killer hunts involve prostitutes being killed that one must assume there is something fundamentally cleansing about this. When people get anxious they need a sacrifice. Somehow the offering has been made, the debt is paid, and a shaky equilibrium restored. A woman who has lots of sex must not be permitted to survive. If she does it seems an outrage.'

Sophia told me of another dream she had had about a woman who had a hole in her chest between her breasts. 'She was floating among the stars in the sky and I could see the sky through her breasts. She was like the reed that could be bent but would not break. The hurricane would not affect her, it would blow through her. People were angry with her because she had the qualities of absorption, endurance and indestructibility.

'I believe there is a whore in all women, an instinct to unite with the goddess, to become very skilled in the sexual arts, to be desirable and to take their own pleasure as well. This gets very truncated and curtailed in the average married situation. There's a sadness and a wistfulness, a feeling of loss which turns into anger and revulsion. A punitive attitude develops of "what I can't have, you're not going to have either, not without paying a high price, not without forfeiting the right to respectability and inclusion in the human race."'

It was after the disabled dream that Sophia had the profound revelation that all the time she had been a prostitute and for quite a long time afterwards she had never fully honoured the prostitute part of herself. 'I hadn't even recognized that I was a product of my abused childhood. I feel very liberated now. Before I felt a lot of confusion about whether I wanted to be on the game or not. I felt a compulsion to live out the thing that had been projected onto me, almost as an act of defiance but at the same time I longed to protect myself. I don't feel a victim any more. I feel I can work or not as I choose.'

My impression is that Sophia is rare in having confronted so much head on. She agreed that probably most prostitutes have little space or motivation to explore these issues. We tend to think of 'a nation of prostitutes', but of course they are a collection of individuals separated by isolation, buying into the stereotype themselves. As Sophia says, 'There are very few points of reference for an isolated prostitute to come in from the cold. I'm "out" to all my friends, but at the same time people do react, even at an unconscious level, to that information. If we lived in an ideal world there would be adequate support, adequate resources available to help people feel good about themselves and about sex. But I feel quite anxious that the scapegoating and hypocrisy can only get worse with the fear of AIDS and the return to so-called Victorian values.'

FOUR

Lindi St Claire, whom I had been trying to contact for ages unsuccessfully, was there one night at Helen Buckingham's house at a little party to introduce Dolores to some English working women. She looked like a Via Flaminia whore from a Fellini movie – fat but pretty – all 15 stone, 5′2″ of her poured into a smart, black tailored suit. Lindi St Claire hit the headlines after a celebrated tax demand for £150,000. She told the Inland Revenue she was perfectly happy to pay tax the same as any other citizen, but if they were going to tax her on her earnings from prostitution she wanted it recognized for what it was.

She went to her accountant and he recommended forming a limited company. She wanted to call it Prostitution Services Ltd, but she was not allowed to put 'prostitute' in the name and had to make do with Personal Services. It wasn't long, however, before the Attorney General insisted that her company be struck off the register. It was against public policy, he said, to form a company specifically for immoral purposes.

So Lindi refused to pay any tax. 'They're such hypocrites,' she says scornfully. 'They want to take my money, but they won't acknowledge what I do. If I'm paying tax as a prostitute, I want "prostitute" included in my company description.' The battle is still unresolved, with the Inland Revenue now threatening to take her to court and make her bankrupt.

Despite being called 'Miss Whiplash' by the tabloid newspapers, who relish the more bizarre aspects of her speciality, Lindi is very serious about her role as a public voice for prostitutes. Recently, she has been running for election to the Euro-parliament as leader of the Corrective Party. Their election manifesto includes the legalizing of brothels, allowing advertising in the Yellow Pages, licensing prostitutes and abolishing censorship laws.

She only got thirty-nine votes in the last election and was ridiculed by the media who simply refused to take her seriously. 'They asked me questions but didn't use any of my responses,' she complained. 'They just used the out-takes and asides when I was messing about. They made me look stupid. So this time when I have a press conference I'm only going to repeat the statements that I've practised and not say anything else.' She asked me how I thought she came across and I suggested that if she concentrated on the important issues and acted confident and dignified she would do just fine. She invited me to come along to her press conference to be held on the following Sunday morning at her working premises in Earl's Court. 'It's a dump really,' she said apologetically, 'just a dungeon.'

I turned up at 11 am the next Sunday to find only Sophia and her brother loyally wearing big pink rosettes sitting outside Lindi's front door in the basement courtyard. Poor Lindi looked rather embarrassed at this overwhelming display of apathy on the part of the press. She'd rung each newspaper personally to inform them. However neither her leaflets nor her manifesto were quite ready in time. What coverage she had had, had been of the 'Whipping Up Support' variety, treating her as an easy target for cheap laughs. This had been very hurtful for her. 'I've brought it on myself, though,' she admitted. 'I've made a lot of mistakes. At first I encouraged the titillating tart approach – I thought it was fun – but they've made me look like a wally.'

After a while a couple of other people showed up. Linzi Drew, the porno star and editor of *Penthouse*, arrived in a traffic-stopping outfit of acid-drop yellow stretch jersey, a sleeveless, plunge-neck, figure-hugging micro dress with white stilettos and a cloud of teasel candy-floss platinum hair. She was a living work of art, female sexuality personified, and was accompanied by her man, a porn photographer who looked like a rock star. The atmosphere was very supportive and, largely due to Sophia's subtle guidance and advice, Lindi looked confident and serious, having prepared a recorded statement for the press so that there could be no ambiguity or misrepresentation.

An elderly gentleman, a character actor, veteran of 700 films, so he said, and founding member of the National Association for the Reform of the Obscene Publications Act also turned up to lend support. Lindi hoped he might add class to her campaign because he spoke nicely and looked distinguished.

At last someone from the press showed up – a reporter from the *Daily Star* (who also sometimes wears a different hat and writes for the *Sunday Times*). Lindi ('The Lady of Laxton Manor, leader of The Corrective Party') played her three-minute statement and then Sophia, as campaign manager, said a few words. She was brilliant, emphasizing Lindi's courage in being prepared to stand up and raise important issues of human and civil rights, health education, safety and sexual freedom.

She spoke about the under-utilized, undervalued rich resource of prostitutes' knowledge and experience and how in this age of HIV infection, prostitute women know how to eroticize safer sex. There's an urgency, she said, to put the health and safety of the general population before out-moded laws. There is more censorship in Britain than most of the free world and nobody ever caught AIDS from looking at pictures. Ours is a country of sexual hypocrisy and sexual intolerance and as long as prostitution is suppressed, forcing prostitutes into isolation, the big porn barons and criminal pimps are able to get in on the act.

Lindi can be prosecuted for running a disorderly house, Sophia explained. If she has anyone else working with her for companionship and safety, she can be prosecuted for running a brothel. She is subject to VAT and income tax demands, but she is not entitled to the protection of the law and can't claim expenses. She is proud of being a prostitute and has immense courage. She wants to abolish all those farcical laws that waste police time and court resources.

When Sophia had finished speaking, the reporter made his few salacious, snigger-type comments, but I think he had actually heard what was being said and perceived the importance of doing justice to the arguments. I don't know what he wrote in the end, but I'll give him the benefit of the doubt.

After everyone else had left, Lindi, Sophia, her brother and I repaired to the pub to discuss her campaign strategy, particularly the need to produce a manifesto putting Lindi forward as a caring, thoughtful person with other issues at heart as well as the ones relating to the decriminalization of prostitution.

I asked Lindi if I could have a look at her work premises and although I thought I knew what to expect, I was still amazed by the sheer volume of props and costumes. It was like a theatre warehouse or a film set. Hanging on pegs on all the walls and corridors were hundreds of outfits – nurses' and policewomen's uniforms, gymslips, black rubber knickers, dozens of pairs of boots from green wellies to storm troopers riding boots, whips, canes, chains, hoods, anything you could imagine having a fetish about.

There were three rooms divided from one another by wooden partitions – again like theatre flats. One was a torture chamber stocked with cages, hooks, whipping posts, stocks; one was a bedroom with black satin sheets and one was an operating theatre where she has to act out all the medical scenarios. Clients send Lindi written scripts and she learns them just like a part in a play. One man, for instance, likes to have his teeth pulled out, or rather Lindi has to pretend she's going to do it! Things I've never even conceived of as having any possible erotic connotations. There seems to be a terrible poignancy about becoming trapped in re-enacting forever a compulsive behaviour that at some stage in your childhood became associated inextricably with sexual excitement.

Amongst all the bizarre equipment were hanging a couple of little woolly knitted baby outfits. Thinking maybe she'd bought them for a niece's christening or something, I made a remark about them looking so out of place there. Lindi told me there's a whole area of deviant behaviour called Babyism where the client likes to dress up in a nappy, suck a giant dummy or one of her breasts and just be rocked.

I found myself gasping with the sadness of it. Lindi and other women like her are dealing with this kind of thing everyday. Where does it come from and what would happen if they weren't there to provide an outlet, a safety valve? What help or support do they get?

After meeting Lindi, I realized how much I didn't know about this particular aspect of the life. Sophia had been promising to introduce me to her friend Amber, a 'dominatrix' or dominance mistress. Dominance work is a highly specialized branch of prostitution. Most prostitutes dabble in it as an optional extra since so many clients request it, but Amber is the acknowledged High Priestess. As she is always on the lookout for assistants my idea was to ask her for a temporary job in order to get some first-hand experience of what actually goes on.

Amber is naturally wary of any outsiders, but she accepted Sophia's assurance that I could be trusted. So we met up at Sophia's flat in London first for a plate of pasta and a bottle of Australian Chardonnay before going over to visit Amber. Sophia had just taken part in a debate organized by Women Against Pornography where she had been very much in the minority speaking on behalf of Feminists Against Censorship. She had received quite a lot of flak from the opposing camp, but felt quite sure of her ground.

The principal issue, as she sees it, is that of integration and wholeness. Censoring pornography means separating off the 'image of the whore' and only displaying it in seedy pornshops while her counterpart, the decent, chaste woman as portrayed in *Family Circle* and *Good Parenting*, is marketed as the ideal image. This further divides us from one another and reinforces the stereotypes. Whereas a mother is never associated with sex – she is cocooned in her domestic bliss and happy in her castrated role – a whore is never associated with children and family life. She is deemed unfit for motherhood. So who is the woman in the photo? She is the slut, the slag, the tart, the bimbo.

What are women saying when they find pornography offensive and harming? Is it 'I'm afraid that men will think it represents me when it doesn't'? Is it 'If I banish and deny the image of the whore, my halo will shine more brightly'? 'If I can't be sexual she can't either without giving up her right to be a human being.'

Sophia is also angered by the attitude that supposes that whores are so oppressed they don't even understand their own oppression, therefore chaste women must take up their cause. The anti-porn brigade, says Sophia, have a lot invested in their own chastity and, like modern-day missionaries, they are carried along on a tide of self-righteous and religious fervour. But what about the whore who doesn't want to be saved?

We went over to Hackney where Amber lives and met her in the corner pub with her husband Dennis, a mild-looking businessman. Amber is a motherly woman, in her late forties with five grown-up kids. She was dressed in a black velvet jump suit, high heels and a diamond choker. Her jet black hair and dramatic eye make-up give her a rather awesome look, but she was very friendly and easy to get along with. Sophia has always admired her because she represents her ideal of a mother – a sexy, fun, unshockable, live and let live mother.

We had a drink and talked awhile about the current pornography debate and public fears that the satellite television channels will flood the nation with 'unstemmed filth'. The general consensus was that a lot of confused thinking exists in this area. Erotic material of sexual activity between consenting adults, no matter how unusual, should not be muddled up with criminal activity which is already covered by adequate legislation; for example, anything involving minors, animals, unwilling participants, rape, drugs, etc.

The question of where 'healthy', legitimate sado-masochism as a perfectly acceptable practice between individuals who both want to play ends and unacceptable violation and brutality takes over is a hard one to define precisely. It is also a dangerous area. The very existence of the unspeakable and repulsive so-called 'snuff' films where an unsuspecting woman, often a Third World prostitute, is actually tortured to death, her agony recorded in detail, is proof enough that there is no limit to the sickness and evil of which human beings are capable. These videos are in circulation all over the world, including Britain.

After our drink, we all walked round to Amber's flat nearby – the ground floor of a small terraced house – and she showed us into her sitting room, a cosy, chintzy little parlour with a log-effect electric fire, holiday souvenirs and Amber's knitting lying on the sofa.

'Is this where you work?' I asked, somewhat incredulously. Amber and Sophia exchanged looks. 'Do you want to vet it before we show her?' asked Amber. 'No, I'm sure she can take it,' replied Sophia laughing. 'Well, let me do the lighting first then,' said Amber with the air of someone about to illuminate the Christmas tree, and disappeared into a small back room. There were sounds of switches being flicked on, then she stood proudly in the doorway like a fairground barker and said with a flourish, 'Da Dummm!'

There, bathed in a Stygian red glow was the most fearful dungeon you could imagine, recently redecorated with brick-effect wallpaper, a mirrored ceiling and a vast collection of neatly arranged sado-masochistic apparatus. There was a very expensive steel cage (picked up cheaply secondhand), a whole shelf of different sized dildos, the largest of which looked like it had been modelled on an elephant, another of tissues, vaseline and KY jelly laid out in an orderly fashion. There were weights, pulleys, harnesses, racks, shackles and chains.

'Oh, haven't you done it up nicely!' I said ridiculously, trying to appear nonchalant, while Sophia enthused at the comprehensive range of equipment, admiringly fingering the quality of all the bits of rubber and leather. The walls were hung with photographic portraits of Amber looking mean and masterful in her full dominatrix regalia. Some included the mild mannered, balding Dennis dressed in a pair of leather shorts and a little leather toga.

Dennis busied himself getting refreshments and we all settled ourselves incongruously in the torture chamber, perched precariously on the various custom-built black vinyl couches and whipping stools, their restraining straps dangling harmlessly.

I found the room very disturbing. Who on earth comes to this fearsome place? 'I only like top class clients', says Amber, 'Proper gentlemen who know how to behave. I can't be bothered with riff-raff.' Her regulars include solicitors, Harley Street doctors, senior police officers, business executives and churchmen. They come to be punished, humiliated, frightened and tormented to the limits of their endurance. Amber doesn't do straight sex at all, never has done. What she administers is pain.

This is not something that should be attempted by amateurs, she points out. It is a very skilled job, knowing how to eroticize it, how to administer it safely, avoiding parts of the body prone to injury such as the kidneys, how to give a person what they ask for, to enter into their mind and to know when they've had enough.

Nothing surprises her and nothing shocks her, although some things disgust her and she has definite boundaries. She will not comply with certain requests, for example, anything to do with excrement. (This is another whole branch of erotic taste, if that's the right word, known in the trade as scatology or 'scat', where clients have become stuck sexually around the age of two years old, the era of botties and potties, poo poo and toilet training, and now find themselves unhappily inhabiting the bodies of respectable grown-up men.)

Amber can call on the services of a couple of 'submissive' girls who themselves enjoy being beaten, to service the needs of the few 'dominant' men who want to dish it out rather than take it, but the majority of her clients come and pay a lot of money in order to submit, to relinquish themselves, to suffer. There seems to be a hypothesis to be made for finding some significance in the fact of extremely powerful men in society needing to do penance, even the score, expiate the guilt which the mantle of power imposes on them and purge themselves. Judges, for example, who wield immense power are notorious in prostitution circles for their leanings in this direction. (One prostitute I met some months later told me that a client of hers who is a magistrate confessed to her that sentencing a prostitute in court always gives him an erection.)

Dennis talked openly and frankly about the pleasure he derives from being a submissive male. His relationship with Amber has been a mutually satisfactory one for twelve years. He serves her and she bosses him about, but there's a great deal of tangible affection between them. He said he wasn't beaten as a child nor can he pinpoint any particular incident that might have fixated him on the erotic possibilities of corporal punishment. He was born with it, he says, and just remembers always having found the thought of it sexually arousing.

When he met Amber she was an unhappy housewife with a job in a maritime insurance office. The masochist in him soon brought out the sadist in her. She discovered how much natural flair she had for the work and, encouraged by Dennis, went into the business. She loves her work. During the week they camp out in the little flat and every weekend they take off for their country house where they garden, walk in the beautiful countryside and exercise their handsome Dobermann dog.

So what about a temporary job in Amber's bondage parlour? I'd have to answer the phone, greet clients, maybe dress up in a bit of kinky gear and occasionally add to their frissons by witnessing their ordeals. 'Yes,' I said, acknowledging that I was completely green and didn't know what to expect. I admit to being both appalled and excited by the idea of dabbling in these dark waters of the psyche. 'You can always go out and make yourself a cup of tea if it all gets too much for you,' suggested Sophia.

I reminded myself that only those who want to be hurt and come specifically for that purpose are hurt but how will I feel knowing about it at close range? Amber and Sophia are both very articulate on the useful, safety-valve, psycho/sexual drama therapy aspect of the work and how if you could get a degree in it and put letters after your name everybody would respect you and you would be asked to chair learned discussions instead of being reviled as the lowest of the low, a sewer in which to flush all the effluent and toxic waste of society.

At one point Dennis left the room to fetch drinks and Amber said in a conspiratorial whisper, 'Can we fix something up for him, he's getting awfully itchy.' She suggested setting up a scenario to give him a 'good going over' as she put it and asked Sophia if she'd oblige and me if I'd like to watch! I think her idea was to test me out and see if I was going to feel comfortable around the work she does. They decided to meet the following week to discuss strategy between them. I would be told when to come.

The whole evening disturbed me. When I got home I couldn't sleep the whole night. I was aware of a lot of turbulent, painful energy in Amber's dungeon. Those walls must have witnessed many scenes where very deep childhood grief and trauma, fear and anger were re-enacted for sexual release. It was a room in which secret compulsions and violent interactions were re-created by people who prefer the familiarity of punishment to the hardship of change and new choices.

I was also awed by the overwhelming strength of the emotions and behaviours that are acted out in the sexual arena. The men who come to Amber are among the most powerful and influential in the country and the only people who really know them are prostitutes, women like Amber. Their wives don't know them, their families don't, their colleagues don't. All this ferocity and vulnerability is zipped, buttoned, tailored away behind good Savile Row suits. At the same time women remain fragmented into their component parts – the whore divided from the mother, the lady, the healer, the goddess. What a mess we've made of our sexuality.

Unable to integrate our sexuality we bury it, take it out on children, create hypocrises and scapegoats to make us feel better about our repressed desires. As Sophia said, 'Acknowledging the whore in ourselves doesn't necessarily mean going on the game. It can mean having the kind of sexual relationship you want with your husband.' With that in mind I decided to take up the invitation to be a voyeur.

FIVE

In my fantasy world women are always the superior sex. It is my place to serve and amuse those women who know and understand that they are dominant. When dominant ladies require interludes of amusement and entertainment, it falls to me occasionally to provide this to the limit of my miserable ability. I will try to offer Madame a good time by suffering for her and her friends.

There then followed an itemized list of punishments. This letter was sent to both Amber and Sophia by Dennis in anticipation of the evening. I met up with Sophia first at her place while she got dressed up for the part. She looked amazing, like an Alan Jones sculpture, in a shiny basque, G-string, black stockings, thigh-high pointy boots, lots of make-up and rhinestone jewellery. She just put a coat over her undies and we drove over to Amber's. The clothes are a very important part of the fantasy. When we arrived Amber was wearing a rather hilarious Barbarella-type outfit in black vinyl with little detachable, pop-on nipple covers, net stockings and red and black lace-up boots. Another woman friend, Jane, had come along too, to add to Dennis's delicious discomfiture. Our role as disinterested observers was to maintain a haughty aloofness and, if we could bring ourselves to do it, toss the occasional insult in his direction.

We four women sat in the living room and when Dennis appeared he was dressed in little white underpants and vest, looking terribly harmless and pathetic with his glasses on and his bald patch. He began by serving drinks. Amber and Sophia found fault with everything he did, gradually humiliating him more and more, making him crawl on his hands and knees, using him as a foot rest, reading his letter out loud and laughing at his 'insolence'. They ridiculed and sneered at him, calling him a miserable slug, a worm, a snivelling creature and so on, culminating in tearing up his letter and throwing it all over the floor from where he had to pick up the pieces in his mouth and drop them in the litter bin.

He took his clothes off and they tied up his balls with leather laces and clamped weights on his nipples. In the dungeon they hoisted him aloft in some fearsome harness. They pinched and tormented him, with simulated evil glee and shoved a dildo up his arse. There was a great deal of grimacing and groaning, but I couldn't help being reminded of all-in wrestling which has something of the same sense of theatre about it. Next Dennis begged to be allowed to drink his mistress's 'vintage wine', her 'sacred golden drops', so they took him to the bathroom. He lay in the bath while Amber clambered above him, her high-heeled boots teetering precariously on the ledges of the bath, undid her G-string and peed all over him. He adored it and tried to drink as much as he could.

Jane and I were invited to watch as little or as much as we wanted, either looking through the one-way mirror or wandering into the room making any disparaging remarks that might add to his humiliation. Apparently it heightens his pleasure a hundredfold to have other women witness his ordeal. There are a few rules, however. Earlier Amber had said, 'Say whatever you like while the scene is going on, but don't laugh and don't do what someone once did – they asked me if I *loved* him and when I said "yes" they said, "then how can you beat him and hurt him?" It was a terrible turn off. The answer is, yes, I do love him and that is why I do this for him.'

This was all preliminary to the main event which was his beating. He chose the weapons – whips, crops, canes of varying sizes – then lay over the stool with his bare bottom in the air. Amber and Sophia took turns to beat the hell out of him. He could certainly take a lot of punishment and kept begging for more. They hit him over 150 times until he bled and took photos of it all with a polaroid for his later perusal and further mileage.

Finally it was all over. Off came Amber's boots in relief and she put on her slippers. Dennis got up and gingerly put his pants on. He was instantly transformed into a normal, confident, assertive man. He kissed everyone and thanked us. He gave Sophia an envelope with her fee (she normally charges £200 but this was a special rate for friends) and a surprise present he'd bought for Amber in gratitude – a beautiful diamond watch.

We all stood around chatting and having a cup of tea. 'You've got to get inside their heads,' said Amber. 'Powerful men come here to have their power taken away, to be made helpless. It's a blessed, wonderful release for them to be totally at the mercy of someone else.' Dennis seemed to be almost in a state of altered consciousness while he was undergoing his ordeal. Afterwards he looked very happy and proud to have endured so much. Nobody at his work place, of course, knows anything about his secret life.

The whole drama took about four hours and required a lot of concentration and hard work from Amber and Sophia. Both Jane and I were rather bemused and astonished by the whole performance. I hadn't, contrary to my fears, found it a distressing experience because it was, in reality, quite safe. There were very clear boundaries. It didn't feel evil, just bizarre. I was reassured by the knowledge that Dennis and Amber really love each other and have devised a mutually satisfying sex life.

Amber says she can get into a detached frame of mind which enables her to give Dennis, or a paying client, what he wants without confusing it with her everyday feelings. When she and Dennis are not acting out a scene, they relate quite differently. More than once a client has phoned the next day and thanked her for a most rewarding and cathartic encounter. 'Now that's the part I really like!' she said. 'That's real job satisfaction, knowing you are using your skills to help people.'

After this introductory personal session, I felt I would be able to come back again to help with some other clients. A couple of weeks later I had my chance.

When I arrived at lunchtime Amber was in the bath getting ready for a busy day with three bookings, one after the other. She'd chosen this day for me to come because it would be 'good for my education'. When she was all perfumed and creamed she squeezed herself into a black leather mini-skirt, black stretch-lycra bustier and silver stilettos, no stockings – 'He likes bare thunder thighs!' she said. She was knocking back pints of tonic water in readiness for the 'water sports' enjoyed by her first client of the day, an advertising executive named Boris. 'He's not into any serious bondage or pain, but likes grovelling at his mistress's feet and being humiliated,' said Amber.

She had asked me if I would care to participate in this one and I had worn my lace-up Victorian boots just in case. When Boris arrived he got himself undressed in the fantasy room. Amber made him stew a bit because he'd been late. Then she went in and I followed a few minutes later to find him naked on his knees in front of her and her silver shoes resting on his head. He heard my footsteps, but she wouldn't let him look up. Finally she told him he could kiss my boots which he did fervently.

She sat astride him as if he were a horse and he had to carry her around the room. Then she asked me if I'd like a ride. Er, um, I'd only wanted to be a fly on the wall, not ride a naked man around the room, but he was obviously loving it and to have refused might have spoiled the whole charade. I had no right to be faint-hearted at this stage. He had a big erection by this time so Amber rode him into the bathroom, made him put his head down the toilet, sat on it and peed. 'Can I play with myself, Madame?' he asked. And that was it. He came in a few seconds.

Thereafter his whole demeanour changed. He stood tall, reasserted himself and had a shower. He got dressed in his baggy home-knitted woolly jumper with a badge of a little sheep pinned on, a present from his youngest daughter. A nice looking artistic man, he was laughing and joking with us, marvelling at how strange it was that all desire to grovel and debase himself disappeared the moment he had his orgasm. He was quite happy to talk and recollected the first erotic childhood occasion when a frolic with an older girl cousin had led to a sexually exciting humiliation. Alas there wasn't much time to linger as the next client had arrived and was being entertained in the front room by Molly.

Molly who works one day a week with Amber is a 'submissive'. The rest of the week she lives deep in the Shropshire countryside, devotes her energies to environmental issues, has a respectable job and is trying to develop her skills as a writer. She first met Amber at one of the contact clubs on the sado-masochistic scene and Amber 'trained' her.

Since the next client required a school scene, Molly had dressed up in a PE kit several sizes too small. Amber asked me to wear something appropriate for a 'member of staff', so I'd come along in with a longish black skirt and blouse and a tweed jacket. She introduced me as 'Mistress Alex'. Fred, the punter, was very approving. Amber changed into an astonishing black wet-look, skin-tight vamp dress and stockings, quite unlike any headmistress I've ever seen but Fred was thrilled.

He was a jolly RAF type in blazer and slacks. He helped himself to a large whisky and radiated confidence standing at ease in front of the fire and rocking back and forth on his heels. He and his wife, he told me, have been into this sort of thing ever since they got married, with her dominating him, but about once a year he likes the excitement of coming here which he's been doing for years. 'I know I'm kinky,' he said with a self-deprecating grin, 'but the only thing you can take with you when you die is experience. I'm here to have an experience.' On one occasion he had even brought his wife along to participate, but she was too shy and didn't enjoy it so now instead she sends a letter which Fred brings and hands to Amber.

It is addressed 'To Mistress from Madam' and lists all his recent misdemeanours (persistent untidiness, leaving doors open, cheekiness) with the hope that he will learn a lesson and show an improvement in his behaviour. Amber read it gleefully and Fred put on the schoolboy clothes he had brought in a duffle bag.

From then on it became an elaborate theatrical improvisation lasting about two hours with Amber and I playing the stern, disappointed, punishing schoolmistresses, Molly playing the tell tale and Fred the naughty boy having his bottom caned. At one point Fred switched roles, went out of the room and came back in as the gym master. He reprimanded Molly for her sloppy work, made her do a few exercises, then told her to bend over the vaulting horse for 'six of the best'.

This was the part that worried me. I identified with her. I was both horrified and fascinated. Most difficult of all was to face my own feelings because here on this thin front line I was meeting both the victim and the oppressor within myself. It is a country of extremes. The uneasy eroticism of 'The Story of O' side by side with all the revulsion evoked in me by brutality, sadism and injustice.

I was concerned for Molly and I asked her, when there was a suitable opportunity, if she was all right. She smiled sweetly, 'Oh, I like the pain,' she answered. 'I can take a lot of pain, but only on my bottom. I can't bear to be hit anywhere else and I go mad if anyone actually harms me or cuts me.' I realized that I was in a surreal Alice In Wonderland world where the usual assumptions about human behaviour no longer applied.

Fred, with bloody stripes on his backside, examined himself in the mirror with satisfaction and wincingly put his shorts back on. He had a happy look on his face and went off home bearing his battle scars to show his wife. I suddenly perceived Amber as the Hindu goddess Kali, the terrible mother, the omnipotent mother of early childhood; the one who gives and withholds at a whim; the fierce giantess, the punishment giver, the one who makes you cry. Fred had faced her fury and survived. The canes went in the bath with some disinfectant.

The final session of the day was even more disturbing and confusing. By the time I got out into the fresh air again I really felt the need to talk to someone about all this. Any psychoanalyst working with a patient on such material would have supervision and support for all the issues it brings up. I confess to being right out of my depth in these dark waters and can only offer my layperson's reactions.

The drama unfolded in a misleadingly nonchalant way. First, Geoffrey, a beautifully spoken elderly gentleman, arrived at the door. A tall, elegant, silver-haired man, with impeccable manners, he was immaculately dressed and carried a suitcase from which he extracted a bottle of chilled white burgundy, a home-made birch, a table tennis bat and an enormous black strap-on dildo.

Amber changed once more into a totally see-through silver lurex body stocking. Molly and another girl who had come especially for this job (Ursula, an East German lesbian with a sad face and a perfect body) changed into suspenders, stockings and nothing else. Dennis had arrived home early from work and changed into a little Spartacus slave number complete with dog-collar and lead. Amber led him around the house for a while, then instructed him to sit at my feet holding his lead in his teeth. He was allowed to lick my boots from time to time.

I felt distinctly over-dressed and thought the least conspicuous thing I could do was to strip down to my underwear and sort of melt into the background. I'd come prepared in a black silk basque and stockings just in case and felt proud to associate myself with the working girls. Anyhow, I enjoyed playing the part.

Amber introduced me as her friend Alex. The old boy whose face I vaguely recognized, but couldn't quite place, was the epitome of charm. In a trice he had stripped down to his shrivelled, septuagenarian birthday suit and stood sipping a glass of wine. 'You like CP (corporal punishment), do you?' he said in the same cocktail party tones he might have used if he had been asking if I liked ballet. I muttered something non-committal adding that I preferred being dominant just in case he got the wrong idea.

'Oh, me too!' he said enthusiastically, adding, 'public school, you know,' by way of explanation. 'I like beating girls and then sucking them off.' And for the next two hours that's what he did. I thought my heart would stop. He beat Molly with the bat, he put Ursula over his knee and spanked her really hard. Then he kissed them both and rubbed their bottoms. 'Good brave girls,' he cried and, hardly pausing for breath, began again.

He birched Molly with his twigs and fucked her up the arse with the dildo. I had to walk into the kitchen at this point and get a drink of water. He ordered them to play with each other's nipples while he sucked Ursula off. He then put on a video of 'correction therapy' which was just an endless succession of girls confessing their misdeeds to a faceless man in a suit followed by strappings, canings, riding crops, hairbrushes, slippers, spankings, etc., until they cried and begged for mercy promising to be good. Amber seemed to know most of the 'actresses' and one of them was Molly.

While the video was on Geoffrey had both women with Dennis in the middle all bend over in a row while he fingered their arseholes and paddled them on their bare bottoms with the bat. Then he took Molly off to bugger her again and she pretended to come. He was in a frenzy.

All this time his own little penis hung limply. Finally he slumped exhausted on the sofa and while both women sucked his nipples Amber knelt in front of him and masturbated him with a rubber-gloved finger up his bum. He was delirious with joy, kissed everyone and had a cup of coffee. He couldn't stop praising Molly to me. 'So sweet natured ... can take a fantastic amount of punishment.' His eyes lit up when Amber mentioned she had a new girl for him if he'd like to come back next week. Then he transformed himself back into a Savile Row suited Lord, for that is what he is in the outside world.

After he left the girls stayed behind for a while. I asked Ursula how as a lesbian she could stand having sex with a man. 'I never have sex with men,' she answered indignantly. 'This wasn't sex as far as I'm concerned.' 'Then how could you allow him to beat you?' She shrugged, 'I like it. My father used to beat me.' She hates men, she said and only has sex with women. She beats her own girlfriend. Then she stood up, a slim child the age of my daughter. Her beautiful, perfect body with a life-size tattoo of a rat on her left shoulder blade had been abused all her life. She put on her exterior self – DM's, shapeless dungarees, a big leather biker's jacket, crew-cut hair sticking up like hedgehog's prickles. Amber gave her £75 and she went off back to the commune she shares with six other lesbian women in south London.

Molly also got paid £75. With her poor bottom covered in welts and bruises, it was hard-earned money. She put on her thick-lensed myopic specs, a pair of jeans, boots and a woolly jumper. She tied her hair up in a messy pony-tail, knelt on the floor and then, as if nothing had happened, produced from her shopping basket her Avon cosmetics catalogue for which she is a representative. She managed to interest Amber in a few items and we all sat around flicking through the pages as if we were at a coffee morning. Meanwhile Dennis, still in his Spartacus outfit, swept up all the broken bits of twig from the disintegrated birch. It was totally surreal.

When Molly and Ursula had gone Amber and Dennis were still dressed in their fantasy clothes and feeling playful on the sitting room rug, rolling around like tiger cubs. They decided to go out for a curry so I thanked them for their hospitality and said goodbye. The outside world was just as I'd left it. I could hardly believe it was still early evening and not some midnight hour.

My head was crowded with disturbing contradictions and I felt faint with hunger. I realized I hadn't eaten all day so I stopped at the Sea Shell Restaurant in Lisson Grove and bought myself an enormous portion of take away haddock and chips which I stuffed in my face as I drove along burning my tongue in my haste to fill myself with comfort and normality.

What does it *mean*, all this sexual arousal from pain and punishment and humiliation? Since it's so widespread, why doesn't anyone talk about it honestly? Helen Buckingham once told me about a prostitute she knew who did a lot of heavy dominance work. Every once in a while the need would well up in her to go and get roughed up by a man, so she'd pick up some likely looking thug in a pub or a wine bar and provoke him into beating her. She was always shattered and depressed afterwards in a way that her clients never seemed to be. For her, being driven to satisfy the urge brought no fulfilment, only a terrible sense of despair.

Maybe the difference is that the male clients have made a conscious choice to pay for it in a clearly defined situation where they can still feel they're in control. The payment is the significant part. What if Geoffrey had no whorehouse to visit where the women knew exactly what they were letting themselves in for? He might have picked up a street prostitute who, with no witnesses and no protection, would have been in great danger. At least, thank God, today's activities were contained within set boundaries and there were non-participants around to make sure things didn't get out of hand.

Given that there will always be buyers and sellers of bizarre sexual practices, surely it's better to have brothels where it can go on legally with experienced professional people like Amber in charge. The alternative is driving it underground where it falls into the hands of organized crime or amateurs and where somebody could easily get badly hurt or killed. Lindi St Claire told me once that there are prostitutes who specialize in rape scenarios, even gang rapes. Does this defuse or fuel the beast?

I tossed and turned all night with images haunting my mind. Where had this touched me? Where do my own fear, hate and deprivation lie? What would it take to make me into the fiend? What turns a cultured, educated, sensitive man into that cold-eyed monster barking orders ('bend over, get across my knee, turn round, stick your bottom in the air, do this, do that, whack, whack, whack') to lovely young women who could be his daughters or even his granddaughters in age? The image of Molly's helplessly compliant body being buggered by an impotent old man with a big black dildo strapped to his groin is a manifestation of the utmost alienation. He was like a man possessed by demons. She was like a voodoo doll.

What extraordinary schizophrenic splitting allows the woman to dissociate herself from the job? How does she preserve a sense of self-worth while allowing an old pervert to hurt and abuse her tender womanly body? This is the reality of the darkest side of prostitution. The arena where hatred, violence, pain and shame are all mixed up with pleasure and gratification.

My instinct is to defend myself and block it out. What we fear, we try to keep contained, and yet I want to understand it, to allow my fantasies, however distressing, and to acknowledge my own involvement. Emotional responses are complex and full of so many contradictions.

A psychotherapist friend says that when she's dealing with very disturbing material brought by a client she often asks her unconscious for a dream, for any clues to help her understand the nature of the discomfort in herself. The work actually becomes interesting at this threshold of the terrifying. The questions she asks herself are, 'What part of me could murder or rape?' 'Where does the monster live?' 'Where does the beast reside?' 'What does she feed on?' 'How do I integrate these characters into my psyche?'

That night I dreamed I was at the bottom of the sea trying to reach a pearl in a clamshell. I could see it gleaming, but each time I put my hand in, the jaws of the clam snapped shut. Two or three times I got out, but then it caught my arm. I struggled trying to wrench myself free. My lungs were bursting. I was drowning. Then I woke up.

Joseph Campbell, the great authority on mythology, says that the place where you find yourself shipwrecked is where you have to go down, down into your own abyss, into the underworld, the 'night sea' to find there the forgotten, the omitted energy which should have been informing your life but which was being excluded by your conscious posture. In mythological journeys, he says, there are two ways of going into the underworld. One is by being swallowed, like Jonah, where the unconscious seizes you and takes you down; the other is by killing the monsters that guard the gate. I had felt shipwrecked and it seemed important to face my monsters. The events I had witnessed were shocking, but I also knew they were mutually agreed upon and entered into by all the consenting adults involved, including me. What did I feel about the participants? Pity? Revulsion? Actually neither. The recurring image I had was of damaged children doomed to re-enact forever the place where they became trapped, where sexuality became equated with something else – pain, humiliation, bullying, fear. Love as 'an abject intercourse between tyrants and slaves' as Oliver Goldsmith called it.

I had been an accomplice in the event and I still cannot decide whether what I saw was an acceptable, inevitable slice of life, a safety valve, a tragicomedy, or the saddest thing in the world. I am also confused and disturbed by the fact that I found it both sexually exciting and appalling, my most forbidden fantasies come to life, forcing me to reassess my relationship to my own sexuality, my own primary being.

As Angela Carter writes in *The Sadeian Woman*: 'Into the sexual arena we drag all the cultural impedimenta of our social class, our childhood conditioning, our sexual and emotional expectations, our whole biographies – all the bits and pieces of our unique existences.' She goes on to lament 'the Judeo-Christian heritage of shame, disgust and morality that stand between the initial surge and the first attainment of this most elementary assertion of self,' and she says it is a wonder that anyone in this culture ever learns to fuck at all.

So I feel a strong compassion for the actors in this drama, but it is also important not to make assumptions. At a conference on the politics of prostitution and pornography held in Toronto, a prostitute got up and said: 'Stop looking at us as victims and see us as equals. Address sexuality as it really is. How can you feel loved and respected when you're being invalidated.' She also said, 'Men are people and we're tired of feminists treating them as if they're not.' She was angry at the notion that prostitutes are so oppressed they don't even know they need saving. 'It's offensive, judgemental and patronizing,' she said, 'to save anyone from themselves.'

For one reason or another there will probably always be women who want to work as prostitutes, just as there are men who want to work as soldiers or racing car drivers. In an ideal world it should be a profession of choice rather than necessity. People need support and help to make their own choices.

Safety is not a reason to stop people from doing things either unless, of course, it endangers others. If it were, there would be no trapeze artists, mountain climbers or fighter pilots. No one ever asks them what childhood deprivation caused them to get a buzz from danger or led them into dicing with death for a living. 'What prostitutes need,' she declared, 'are support systems with very clear messages that there are certain things you may not do, such as rape or hurt or beat up or murder anyone.... And if you have a high-risk job like night-watchman, a taxi driver or a hooker, why not have a direct alarm to the police station like a bank cashier does?' Maybe because money is more important.

SIX

Lorraine was being charged when I arrived. She was in a very aggressive mood and didn't want to see me. She never wanted to talk to 'no fucking journalists, never again, no way!' she shouted. She had been betrayed by a magazine that had published her photo when they'd promised not to and lots of people who didn't know she was streetwalking had recognized her. But after she had been released on bail, she simmered down a bit and came to find me in the police station waiting room. She'd changed her mind, she said, so we sat down and had a plastic cup of police dishwater tea together.

Lorraine is a thin, waif-like girl of 22 with beautiful almond-shaped greyish green eyes and long straight brown hair that hangs down in front of her face like a curtain in an attempt to hide the tattoos – a cross on her forehead, a flower on her cheek, a tear in the corner of her eye – relics from her punk days, which she now regrets. She also has HATE tattooed across the knuckles on both hands. No love at all.

She only works, she said, in order to finance her heroin addiction and she was about to go straight back on the street after talking to me to earn the £100 a day she needs. In fact she'd have to work twice as hard because there would be the court fine to pay after this arrest.

Lorraine was introduced to heroin at the age of 15 and has tried half-heartedly to come off several times. Her baby, born last year, was addicted at birth and spent the first weeks of her life going through the agonies of withdrawal. The baby is being cared for by Lorraine's mother and although Lorraine adores her little daughter she also accepts that she is not the best person to look after her. She spoke wistfully about 'one day' how she'd like to come off heroin, come off the game, get a job, have a family.... 'I hate this life,' she said, 'I hate it so much, it makes me feel dirty.'

When I told her I thought she was beautiful, she said, 'Oh no, I'm not. I hate my looks.' Then she smiled behind her hair as she lit another cigarette, 'There I go again, always doing myself down.' Lorraine seemed to be hell-bent on a self-destruct mission. She had a sort of ethereal quality, a resignation, a negligible expectation from life. It was almost as if she was transparent, her sense of self was so non-existent. She smiled a lot, but like a dying person who knows they are not long for this world.

She gave me her address, then reached out and touched me briefly on the arm – like the brush of a butterfly wing – when we said goodbye. I tried to say that just because you hate the job doesn't mean you have to hate yourself. Inside is a good person, a loving person, a person who has not been made hard in spite of the hardship she's endured ...

A real tear slipped over the top of the tattooed one, watered the flower on her cheek, and was brushed fiercely away. HATE glinted across her clenched fists as she drowned her cigarette end in the dregs of her tea. 'Take care of yourself,' I said, and she laughed as she pulled her thin jacket around her and stepped back out into the cold November streets. The police inspector who arrested her this time thinks she'll probably be dead in eighteen months.

I went upstairs to the canteen where the night's team of policemen and women, some in uniform, some in plain clothes, were tucking into enormous mounds of doorstop chips and saveloys and fried fish smothered in tomato sauce in preparation for the chase. Their job is to catch street prostitutes, bring them into the station in the van and charge them. Sometimes they're released on bail, but if the police think they won't turn up in court in the morning, they're kept in the cells overnight.

I was there at the invitation of the Vice Squad to join them on one of their night patrols. I had written asking to speak to some of the senior police officers involved in this aspect of the work because there seems to be a lot of bitterness on the part of prostitutes concerning police attitudes. With the current legislation as it stands, the police are seen as the enemy, the enforcers of unjust laws. This obviously can't be easy for them either and I was curious to hear their point of view. The best way seemed just to hang out with the Vice Squad for a couple of nights and talk to both police officers and the women they picked up off the street.

'What is the point of all the harassment?' I asked the plain-clothes team leader patrolling Soho that night. 'Whose interests are served?'

'If we didn't do our job, the place would be crawling with prostitutes,' he answered. The image of whores as vermin was a recurring theme. But, surely, if they weren't penalized for sharing flats, for instance, wouldn't they just be able to work quietly from their own premises? I wondered. 'Yes, but where?' he replied. 'In your street? In your basement?' It was the old argument that nobody wants their children to see the men coming and going, to begin to ask questions, to find used durex in the back alleys, etc. My argument that our everyday laws already cover any noise, nuisance or litter without needing special prostitution laws was brushed aside. 'Anyhow, if you make it all perfectly legal, that's as good as saying it's a perfectly good profession for anybody's daughter to take up. I certainly don't want my daughter to be a prostitute, do you?'

It wasn't the place to unpack my theories. The police see a lot of terrible things and it's easy to understand how they can develop an extremely warped view of human nature. This led to talk about the strange and furtive sexual behaviour of more than a few powerful figures in public life and the complaint that the existing kerb-crawling laws as they stood at the time made it pretty impossible for the police to actually arrest the punters. 'Our hands are tied behind our back because they know the sort of people we'd be bringing in – the law makers themselves for a start, judges, politicians – and they don't want any embarrassing incidents.'

Of course it is annoying for non-prostitutes to be propositioned by men in the street, but surely if whores and clients were left undisturbed to meet each other, wouldn't the market find its own level and the whole situation be less confusing for everyone? I've heard prostitutes say that although the anti-kerb-crawling Act of 1985 was supposed to have been passed in the interests of women's safety, in fact it made them more at risk with no time to talk to a client and size him up before jumping into his car.

The team leader was unconvinced. One girl had told them of a client, a 'top drawer' gent, who used to pick her up regularly in Park Lane and take her to The Dorchester. He liked her to wear a nappy and sit on his lap. He'd bounce her up and down for a while then, as he became excited, start to finger her inside the nappy and get her to crawl around the floor making 'goo goo' baby noises until finally he'd rip the nappy off and have very violent intercourse with her.

'Where the hell did that come from?' wondered the Sergeant, scratching his head in disbelief. 'What was done to him as a baby or what had he done to a baby himself perhaps? Jesus, what a nutter! Ought to be locked up! Can you imagine even thinking that up? Do you really want people like that running around?'

He did acknowledge, however, that behaviour as weird as that was certainly safer contained in a fantasy scenario with a professional. Thank God the guy wasn't at large with no one to pay to act it out with him. The argument that prostitution encourages this type of behaviour doesn't convince me. It's there anyway. In my opinion the woman prepared to take something like that on deserves the utmost respect. In the circumstances it just seems a shame that the police, frustrated in their inability to curtail the activities of 'pimps and perverts', have to pick on the prostitutes who are such easy targets.

Quite late in the evening, our bold band of vice crusaders finally piled into the unmarked van and ventured forth into the hot breath of Sin City. There was an Inspector doing his last night before being transferred, a new young recruit, two plain-clothes guys, one on attachment from another police station, a uniformed woman PC, and me. We went cruising round the streets of Paddington and before long spotted a woman in a tightly belted silver raincoat talking to a man in a car. Two of the policemen leapt out of the van and closed in on her, but as they hadn't seen her in the neighbourhood before, they cautioned her and let her go.

Although prostitution is not illegal in this country, soliciting is, which makes it impossible for a prostitute to meet her clients without committing an illegal act. She can't advertise, describe her services on the telephone, show herself on the street, display herself in a window, or put a sign on her door unless she pretends to be doing something else such as French lessons or massage where she is constantly at risk of being caught out by undercover Vice Squad cops posing as punters.

The police can stop *any* woman under suspicion of loitering or soliciting in a public place. Merely being in possession of condoms in your handbag is enough evidence for the police to caution you – something of an irony in today's climate of concern about safer sex. Three cautions and you are charged. Once convicted you are branded a 'common prostitute' for life. You could lose custody of your children, be deported if you are an immigrant, find it impossible to get another job.

If a 'common prostitute' appears in court as a defendant, her past history will be brought up. This makes a mockery of the possibility of an unbiased hearing. It doesn't happen to any other citizen. Not even a convicted murderer or rapist has his record read out in court *before* he has been tried. If a prostitute is attacked or raped and appears in court as a witness for the prosecution, her past history can be used against her to discredit her evidence even if she is the victim!

It was to expose these chilling facts and many other bizarre and unjust effects of the Kafkaesque legislation surrounding prostitution that the English Collective of Prostitutes came together as a self-help organization. Some years ago, following a series of brutal murders in Lyon, a group of French prostitutes occupied a church in order to draw attention to their plight. Their action was an inspiration to hookers all over the world who began to come out for the first time and demand some basic civil rights.

Amongst those who gained courage was the English Collective of Prostitutes which has never been funded and operates entirely on voluntary labour. They feel that prostitute women are both the safety valve and the scapegoat of a very sick society. From their headquarters at the King's Cross Women's Centre they handle dozens of requests for help and campaign for, among other things, the abolition of all the laws against prostitutes and for more state help for any woman who wants to get off the game.

Nina Lopez-Jones, one of the Collective's spokeswomen, is a passionate campaigner for change. 'Prostitution laws keep you so isolated that you can't speak out for yourself,' she said. 'In our experience, at least 70 per cent of women on the game are mothers and most would do something else if they could. If you've got children, you have to feed them. It's a question of priorities. We don't think prostitution is a wonderful job, but it may be the best of two evils.'

I also talked to Fiona, one of the volunteers at the King's Cross Women's Centre. She is a single parent with a one-year-old daughter. 'I was on Social Security and we just couldn't survive on it,' she told me. 'I was borrowing from friends every week and getting into debt just to live. After a while I just couldn't bear how humiliating it was, nor could I make that kind of money anywhere else so that's why I went on the game. Now we have a much better standard of living. We can afford to eat, I can afford to pay a responsible child-minder. I can buy clothes for myself and my little girl, transport, heating – simple things like that. Once you get used to a decent standard you realize what a basic right it should be for everybody to be able to have those things.

'I'd love to get off the game, but I need at least £200 a week. I don't live in council property and you know how expensive private rents are. Decent quality housing has always been my main problem. I save most of my money. What I want is to buy my own place. I want things that'll last. I couldn't stand to be old and humiliated by doing a cleaning job, or having to choose, like so many old people, between having enough to eat and being warm. The only other way I could earn the same amount of money would be to marry a rich man, and that's only a respectable form of prostitution and a lot more work. At least I've kept my integrity and don't have to depend on anyone. I can choose who I have a relationship with. I can say "no" to people because I can afford to be without them.'

The English Collective believe that the real issue is an economic one. No 'women's work' is sufficiently recognized or financially rewarded, therefore women are forced to choose between low-status, low-paid jobs and prostitution. 'Most jobs that women have to do are degrading,' said Fiona. 'I used to work in Woolworths on the tills. It was like a prison sentence. Such pitiful wages for such shit work. I'd rather work voluntarily for women's rights here at the Centre because it's the only job I can see that's worthwhile. Being on the game is just for the money. I know so many families being supported by prostitution, it's become just like a normal job.'

Prostitutes feel their isolation and their vulnerability very acutely. 'One of the cruel consequences of the prostitution laws is that your boyfriend, particularly if he's black, is likely to be accused of pimping off you,' said Fiona. 'Anybody that you know can be guilty by association.' Prostitutes are the only section who, by law, can't dispose of their income in any way they want without incriminating others. Husbands, lovers, children over 16 can be prosecuted for 'living off immoral earnings', which makes it very difficult for a working woman to have any relationship with a man outside of her job.

Adding to the irony is the fact that since loitering and soliciting ceased to be imprisonable offences, the courts impose high fines instead, thereby becoming the biggest pimps of all. Either the women end up in jail anyway for non-payment of fines or they have to go straight out on the streets and work even harder to earn the money to pay the courts – all for a totally victimless crime. 'We don't see why it should be an offence to facilitate an activity which is in itself not an offence,' says the Collective.

'Even the co-habitation law is, frankly, telling women to be prostitutes,' says Nina Lopez-Jones. 'It implies that if a man is living with you, he is obviously paying for sexual services and therefore you are not entitled to Supplementary Benefits.'

I was talking about all this to the guys in the van when just then, a small, thin woman broke cover like a little mouse and started running, trying to get away from the police. It was like a game safari in East Africa – small, shy creatures flushed out of their habitat and pursued by a minibus, and I was left with the uncomfortable feeling that some of the police saw it as a sport. Dawn, the WPC, jumped out of the van and chased after her on foot finally cornering her by a fence. She was arrested and put into the back of the van where she immediately started wailing, 'But I'm not working tonight! Honest, sir! I'm starting a job tomorrow. I was just on my way back from celebrating. Look, my uncle's come to pick me up. That's him in that car over there.'

'Come on, Christine, I'm not stupid,' said the Inspector who knew her by sight. 'If that was your uncle, why did he drive off in such a hurry? And who was that black man sitting next to him? Was that your ponce?'

'No, sir!' she cried in anguish. 'I'm not with him no more. I wasn't working ...' and so on. The police didn't take any notice and drove her back to the station. This was the girl, they told me, who had been grievously beaten up by her pimp not so long ago but, to their frustration, never showed up to give evidence against him when he was arrested. I tried to talk to her a bit, but she was too upset to speak and just sat there crying and chain smoking. At the police station she was charged with loitering and let out on bail. No offer was made to give her a lift. She was just left to find her own way back in the middle of the night with no taxis about.

The rest of us piled back in the van again fortified with polystyrene cups of tea for the next big assault on the vice of the metropolis. One of the policemen had quite a lot to say that was critical. In his opinion the police didn't manage to recruit from a wide enough social spectrum with the result that they concentrated too much on 'working-class' crime and were insufficiently equipped to deal with middle-class crime such as fraud, for example. Picking up street prostitutes, he acknowledged, didn't do much good; it really didn't solve anything or help anyone. They weren't encouraged to be interested in the women's social situations or personal problems. They were merely serving the local residents' interests by sweeping it off their patch and moving it somewhere else. Cleaning up King's Cross, or Mayfair, meant a sudden increase in street prostitution in Notting Hill Gate or Peckham.

We cruised around Mayfair and it wasn't long before they spotted a woman hurrying along carrying a shopping bag. She hardly looked as though she were loitering. 'Good evening, Donna, I assume you're on your way home,' said the Inspector and, turning to me, added, 'Donna's a very friendly person, I'm sure she'll talk to you.' He suggested that they leave me standing on the street corner with her for 15 minutes or so while they went off cruising around a bit more. Donna agreed and we huddled in our coats on the windy November street, me feeling glad I didn't have to do this for a living.

Donna is a very attractive woman in her late twenties with a rosy country-girl complexion, naturally curly black hair and a pronounced Belfast accent. She reckoned to earn £300 a night, she said. She was, indeed, on her way home having just been given £200 by a regular client, a wealthy South African businessman who, apart from his family home, keeps a small, one-bedroomed flat in Mayfair purely for the purposes of entertaining prostitutes. He had taken her out to dinner at a lovely restaurant, then she'd gone back to his flat and they'd just talked. He is a very sweet, lonely man, said Donna. He never wants sex, just company.

Donna has three children, a little boy of six and three-year-old twins, all fathered by a man whom she'd fallen for in flight from her own harsh, loveless childhood. She told what had now become a familiar story: her lover had deceived her, used her and persuaded her to go on the game.

And she had done it to please him. She's rid of him now and employs a full-time child-minder to look after the children. There is no other way that she can earn the kind of money she needs to give her children what she never had – education, security, material comforts. Prostitution is enabling her to save for a house and open a business of her own. She seemed optimistic, practical and fairly undamaged with no hard feelings towards the police. 'They're only doing their job. If we treat them right, they treat us right.' As the van came round the corner to pick me up she blew a kiss to the chaps inside and went on her way.

The last arrests of the night were two girls in a mews trying to hide behind a car. The police flushed them out like a pair of grouse and stuck them in the back of the van. One of them, with touching bravado, went into a brassy burlesque routine, being very saucy and suggestive to the youngest, red-faced, uniformed police constable, putting her arms around his neck and detailing all the things she could teach him that he'd never forget.

When told what I was doing there she screeched, 'No way! I'm not talking to no journalist!' and stuck her nose in the air, indicating to the other one to do the same. They were very chatty to the cops, cracking vulgar jokes, offering off-duty delights, but completely ignored me. I can't say I blamed them. I would probably have felt the same way.

On a more sombre note they began talking about Cheryl, a prostitute who had been viciously raped in Hyde Park by a punter who refused to pay. I had heard this story earlier from Lorraine who had gone with her to the police station to report it. Alas, many women feel no confidence in reporting acts of violence against them, fearing that the police will only give them a hard time and not take any action. The police, on that occasion, had behaved well, she said, and taken it very seriously.

WPC Dawn was pretty representative of the unsympathetic point of view: 'I don't have much time for those sort of complaints,' she said. 'How can it be rape? Five minutes earlier she was prepared to have sex with him for money. How can the same act be rape just because he didn't pay?' That reasoning seemed pretty flawed to me. I protested that it was no different from being prepared to sell someone a television set or give them a haircut for an agreed price. If they refuse to pay and take the goods or services anyway, isn't that theft just the same? The woman is making a living selling sex which it is not illegal to do. If someone forces her against her will or reneges on the contract, that is a violation of her civil rights and she deserves the same police protection as any other citizen.

Helen Buckingham once said to me, 'As every woman knows, the straight sexual act has nothing to do with rape at all. It is the psychological circumstances surrounding a confrontation with a man which makes the act rape or not. Rape does not even have to involve penetration of the vagina to be experienced as a deeply shocking and terrifying experience because, if it takes place against a person's will it is a psychotic breech, a violation of the terms of being a human being, experienced at the deepest possible level.'

Dawn was unmoved, implying that rape and violence were occupational hazards – Cheryl didn't have to be a prostitute, did she? Meanwhile, Cheryl had not been seen for some time and there were fears for her safety.

By the time the two women were charged it was 2 am. Finally I went home and fell into bed. Anyone arrested has to appear in the magistrates court the following morning. Proceedings begin at 10.30 and I wanted to be there to follow up what happened to them.

There were several cases to be heard before the loitering offences, so I sat in the court room and listened to the chronicles of sadness and pain. There was a battered woman with ugly bruises on her face who sat shaking in the dock. She had been charged with arson for trying to set fire to her sleeping, drunken tormenter. There were two men – one a deaf and dumb labourer who had to have a sign-language translator, the other a pin-striped banker of 'good character' – charged with gross indecency at Baker Street gents' toilets. There was a homeless, destitute kid from Liverpool arrested for begging in the Underground with a sign around his neck saying 'broke and hungry, any job offers gratefully accepted'. There was an old man charged with shoplifting a pound of onions and a piece of steak from a supermarket....

The 'learned magistrate' appeared to be reasonably conscientious and fair, but the whole edifice of our legal system seemed so remote and out of touch. The glimpse into another reality with its oceans of tears was an eye-opener. People barely coping or not coping at all in our alienated, materialistic, consumer society.

Eventually first Lorraine, then Christine were stood in the dock and their offences read out: 'Lorraine Martin being a common prostitute, you were arrested for loitering with intent to commit prostitution. Guilty or not guilty?' 'Guilty', a small voice and blank eyes that were somewhere else. 'Fined £50 with £10 costs, payable within seven days.' It all took less than a minute. 'Revolving door policy', as one woman contemptuously described it. 'You're arrested, charged, fined, and let go. Then two days later they arrest you again. It's a bloody stupid waste of time.'

Lorraine waited until Christine had been through the same routine. They'd both seen me sitting there and gave a wave and a smile. I decided to follow them out rather than wait for any other cases to be heard. I caught up with them round the corner where they were joined by a young man, the archetypal pimp with flashing gold teeth, gold jewellery, full-length leather coat and built-in peacock strut. I was introduced to him with great pride by Christine as 'Lloyd, my man'. She clung to his arm and looked up at him adoringly. We went off to have some breakfast together at a workman's cafe and they were all in a talkative mood.

At close range I could see more clearly the terrible damage that had been inflicted on Christine by the man she wouldn't testify against. She had two deep purplish scars in the middle of her face just above the eyebrows where she had been punched repeatedly by a fist wearing a large signet ring. The skin around her eyes was still puffy and the vision in her right eye is blurred three months after the incident. Not so visible were the scars from knife stab wounds on her arms and legs and the cigarette burns on her breasts.

The story was that the pimp who beat her up, a violent schizo-phrenic, is Lloyd's brother. He used to insist she earned £300 a night and would punish her if she came home with less. If she was arrested he would beat her worse than ever so in the end the police would deliberately look the other way when they saw her on the streets so as not to put her at further risk. The reason they picked her up this time was because she had failed to show up on three occasions when she'd promised to help nail the guy once and for all. Finally he'd disappeared, having stolen a video belonging to Lloyd, so Lloyd felt no compunction about stepping into his brother's shoes.

'Some pimps like to put their girls "under the manners",' he told me, 'to get the proper respect. But I'm not like that.' Christine agreed that he had not harmed her in the few months they'd been together. She obviously loved him and would do anything to keep the relationship going. It seems inevitable that anyone raised in an atmosphere of violence and betrayal will come to associate it with love because, of course, as little children they passionately needed to love the parents who ill-treated them. This becomes the behaviour pattern that triggers their bonding habits. It seems as if so many prostitutes have this sado-masochistic relationship with their pimp. The worse he treats them, the more they love him. It's like a Billie Holiday song.

Christine's life story makes grim telling. Both her parents used to hit her about the head a lot when she was a kid, as a result of which she is deaf in one ear and finds it hard to remember things or articulate her thoughts. 'I know I'm a bit funny in the head,' she said. 'I swear at myself sometimes, "You bitch! You slag! What are you so stupid for?" I hate myself when my brain doesn't work.'

She got into glue-sniffing when she was about 11 and was put into 'care' where she was sexually abused regularly by one of the members of staff and frightened into keeping silent. At 15 she finally ran away and went back home to find her mother had married again. Her new stepfather regarded her unwelcome return as a provocation and one night he raped her brutally. Christine had a nervous breakdown, tried to kill herself and was prescribed strong tranquillizers by her GP. Shortly after that she ran away again and, feeling she had no other options, went on the game. She married at 16 to an extremely violent man who is the father of her two children, aged five and two. She showed me a small crumpled photo of two blond angels she carries in her handbag.

Finally Christine left him in fear and loathing and ran away to a battered wives' hostel. Because she had walked out the husband got custody of the children. She suspects that he is sexually interfering with her little girl, but nobody will take her worries seriously, thinking that she is motivated merely by revenge.

I asked Lloyd how he felt about pimping off her. It didn't bother him, he said. She was on the game before he met her. She can do what she wants. If she wanted to come off, he wouldn't try to stop her. He goes out and hangs around in the shadows when she's working 'to make sure she's all right'. It was him in the car the night before, driving off with the 'uncle'. He keeps an eye on her, takes the number plates of whichever car she gets into.

Christine 'don't do sex, only blow jobs' for which she tries to insist on a condom. She is physically very shy and, ever since her rape, hates anyone to see her body. She is very small and both her babies were born by caesarean section. She has tried other jobs, but can't stick them. If anyone gets up her nose she becomes extremely pugnacious and belligerent. It's as if she only has two ways of relating to people – hopelessly dependent and childlike or hard-nut toughie.

Having finished our breakfasts, we walked to the Tube station. On the way we passed a shop selling ridiculous furry slippers shaped like tigers' feet or reindeer faces. They adored them and each bought a pair. We fell to talking about teddy bears. Both girls love cuddly toys and their ideal house would have a bedroom full of them. 'Did you ever have a teddy bear?' I asked Lloyd. 'I still have him, an' all!' he answered sheepishly. So much for the pimp image. Lloyd spent quite a lot of time in a children's home himself. His mother had eight children and when she became pregnant again she had all the five boys taken into care – the three girls were allowed to stay at home. Lloyd was only four years old. No wonder he has ambivalent feelings towards women. There is a kind of poignant desperation in his swaggering macho outward projection of confidence and independence. He *dare* not drop the façade. Inside his true self is fearful and ravenous for comfort and validation. In order to survive, the abandoned baby has nurtured a grandiose ego which forbids even a semblance of need or weakness while he masquerades as a hard man, an indefatigable mean black sex-machine.

Lorraine got out at Bayswater and went back on the streets in mid-afternoon to earn her fine. Christine, Lloyd and I went on to where I'd left my car and I gave them a lift home. They live in a big old house in West London divided into flats, one of which Christine got through a housing association after two years on the council waiting list. The place looks pretty bleak with a dirty old bed cover pinned across the window instead of curtains. Nothing has been done to make it feel like home.

They grumbled about the trouble they've had with the neighbours who object to the volume of the music they play. 'I 'ave to 'ave it loud, doan I?' reasoned Christine, 'because I'm deaf.' The neighbours also complained to the police that she was bringing punters back to the flat. A CID man came round to investigate and agreed not to arrest her if she obliged him with a free sample. 'Bloody pervert!' she snorted. 'I'd rather go to prison!' Lorraine had already told me that there's one policeman at the station who, whenever she has been kept overnight in the cells, will only let her have a cigarette if she pulls her top up and shows him her breasts.

When I'd raised the question, back at the station, of policemen taking advantage of prostitutes by this type of bartering, I was assured it was very rare. No sane policeman would want to have sex with a prostitute in this age of AIDS, I was told. However the fact is that a lot of men, when they can get away with it, *do* exercise sexual power and take advantage of women. A prostitute is terribly vulnerable to this type of harassment. She commands even less respect than other women. By the nature of her job, she's there for the taking.

I got the feeling that neither Lloyd nor Christine had the faintest idea of how to go about making a home. They were two children playing house. Christine made me another cup of tea and the two of them sat next to each other on the tatty, sagging sofa. Take-out pizza boxes were piled in the corner, dirty clothes were strewn all over and a gigantic television dominated the room. The years fell away and I saw not a prostitute in black fishnets and a pimp chewing on a toothpick, but a pale, thin child with scabby knees and a beautiful brown-skinned little boy holding his beloved teddy, surrounded by treachery and duplicity – no match for the hardships of the world they were born into. I hugged them both goodbye and felt like crying.

A couple of weeks later I got a phone call from Christine in a coin box asking me if I'd like to meet and talk on our own. I said I'd be glad to, but when I arrived at our rendezvous she didn't show up. I wrote her a note, but she didn't answer it. I tried to phone, but the number she'd given was unobtainable. I went round to her flat, but the place was empty. I remembered the large blackboard the police sergeant had pointed out to me upstairs in the Street Prostitution Office. On it were written the names of women who had simply disappeared. They had jumped bail, failed to appear in court, gone away to another town. There were warrants out for their arrest, but often they were never seen again.

'I often wonder how many of them are dead,' said the sergeant. 'Some may have moved to a different neighbourhood but most live such dangerous, violent lives.' He pointed to one name. 'Her ponce used to hit her with an iron bar. And this one had burn marks all over her from an electric iron.'

I had returned for a second visit and we were talking in the police interview room. The sergeant is in his late forties, slightly grizzled, fatherly looking with short, grey hair parted on the side and lots of laughter lines creased around his eyes. I have never seen him in uniform. He wears jeans, bomber jacket, woolly scarf and is a very un-stereotypical cop. He particularly wanted me to meet one very young prostitute, Melanie, aged just 18 and he'd rung me to say they had just picked her up.

Melanie, dressed in a long black coat pulled tightly around her body with a demure white collar showing at her throat, looked heart-stoppingly beautiful. She has the face of a young Marilyn Monroe – porcelain complexion, golden curls, lovely features. She lives in Birmingham, comes down to London on Monday evening and stays by herself in a little hotel in Sussex Gardens until Saturday. She reckons to make about £1,000 a week, sometimes only £700, sometimes as much as £1,300 which is rather different from the £30 a week she was getting on the government YTS scheme or the £95 she got from her one straight job as a sales assistant in a jewellers.

It was her boyfriend, again, who persuaded her to go on the game. He has never worked in his life, she says proudly. He's a thief. When he got sent down for burglary she decided to save up and get him a Porsche to cheer him up when he came out of prison. Nobody in her family knows what she does and she couldn't bear for them to find out.

Melanie was an only child. At 16 she ran away from home. 'I used to hate my Mum!' she said. 'She was always ill, always had a stomach ache, always stayed in bed, moaning, seeking attention. She was very self-centred, and never had time for anyone but herself.' Eventually her parents divorced and her father went back to live with *his* mother. 'It's rather strange going over there now,' said Melanie. 'I actually get on very well with my Nan and Grandad. At least they love me and I see them most weekends, but my Dad's always sat there in front of the telly like a big kid. He only grunts at me. He's disowned me completely and shut me out of his life. He's very racially prejudiced; going out with a black man is disgusting as far as he's concerned.'

Melanie says she copes with the job by 'switching off altogether'. It's nothing like making love, she insists; that's for her boyfriend in whom she has invested all her love and care. All her money goes into their joint account. She has bought him a luxury flat, presents galore and the Porsche. She said she'd stop working the streets once she'd bought the car but she's still out there, earning his approval.

Her first week in London brought a terrible experience. She had only been on the street for three days – all alone in London, didn't know a soul, didn't know her way around, didn't even know what the area looked like in daylight – when she caught sight of the police patrol van and darted down an alley to avoid arrest. Suddenly someone grabbed her from behind. It was a Chinese man she had seen watching her earlier. He held a knife to her neck and demanded sex. She says she didn't beg him not to hurt her or anything; all she could think of was pleading with him to wear a durex. She didn't tell a soul what had happened. She went back to her seedy hotel and shook and cried for two days, then she 'blocked it out'. 'I don't know why I'm telling you this,' she said. 'I'm terrified of reliving it. I hope I never happen to find myself in that spot again because it might bring it all back.'

I can't help feeling that if prostitutes were allowed to work freely and could be certain of police protection like any other citizen, they would be encouraged to report incidents of this nature and the police could spend their time more usefully catching the real criminals. In Australia there is a scheme whereby working women, ideally positioned on the front line, contribute to a network of information. Descriptions of dangerous or troublesome clients are circulated, both to warn each other and to alert the police. To a certain extent this happens here, but it's all a bit random and unofficial. The Chief Inspector told me that they had managed to bust a big child pornography operation only with the help of a prostitute who lived in the flat downstairs.

Melanie is very lonely in London and, apart from the hefty fines she has to pay to the Magistrates Court every time she is arrested, she welcomes being picked up by the police. 'The only people I know are the police,' she said. 'I enjoy their company and he's the best.' She gestured towards the sergeant in the next room. 'He's like a father to me. Give us a lift back to my beat in your van!' she said as he walked in. But he said it was against regulations. 'Give us the cab fare then!' But he wouldn't. She smiled and kissed him on the cheek and went off into the night.

'She's the same age as my daughter,' the sergeant told me. 'I'm desperately worried about her. She's so young, so naive. She says she's going to quit in January, but she's said that before.' He shrugged his shoulders and sighed deeply. He told me about a prostitute from Wolverhampton he'd picked up in the van the week before. Another teenager, she was $7\frac{1}{2}$ months' pregnant and still soliciting. She wasn't having much luck getting punters being so obviously in the later stages of pregnancy, 'but supposing she had! What kind of weirdo would want that?' He shook his head in disbelief.

Later on, about 2 am, near the end of the shift, I was sitting in the back of the van talking to one of the plainclothes officers. The guys were smoking and eating chocolate. It was fuggy, airless and hot inside, freezing outside. The windows were all steamed up from bodies. It was boring, tiring and unhealthy. I was telling him how much I admired some of the women I had met.

'Some of them are very nice people – surprisingly,' he answered. 'But we have to keep ourselves in boxes. Stereotypes are very useful. You couldn't do this job without them.' Underneath his world-weary, tough cop exterior, however, was a very thoughtful person. He is married with five children of his own and is currently taking an Open University degree in philosophy to keep his brain alive. His special interests are metaphysics, logic, ethics and poetry. 'I love this job,' he said, 'the adventure, the constantly changing challenges, the element of the unknown, but it has taken my innocence from me and I resent that. Everyone is entitled to a certain innocence. Once you become streetwise you know and see all the wrong things and you can never unlearn it. The cynicism becomes part of you. It's easy to forget there's a world beyond.

'Of course, the stresses of the job get to you. Anybody who says otherwise is lying – or sick. There are plenty of big macho men around, younger policemen who pretend that nothing upsets them. I've cried my eyes out before now and I'm not ashamed of it either. You see some terrible things. There was a crazed father once who murdered his baby by putting a machete through its head, or the case of a very young girl caught up in some satanic cult – she'll spend the rest of her life in a funny farm because of what was done to her ... You have to discharge some of your feelings or you'd go mad. There's one punter in a black Saab I want to get and I can't answer for what I'll do to him. He picked up one of the girls, took her to a hotel and offered her money to submit to a whipping. She refused, saying she wouldn't do it for any amount of money, but he tied her up and whipped her anyway. Nearly killed her, the bastard!'

It's a pity that the police and the hookers are such sworn enemies when they have such a lot in common. They both do a difficult, dangerous job and don't get much thanks for it. I asked the Inspector about the instance of romantic liaisons flowering between his young, virile officers and the pretty women they keep arresting all the time and he said that actually the men most likely to get involved were not the young single guys, but the middle-aged married ones and, yes, it did happen and, yes, it was one of his duties to keep an eye on that aspect.

We went for one last cruise around Mayfair to net a few stragglers before calling it a night. Outside the Hilton Hotel in Park Lane they picked up Amanda looking elegant and expensive in a beautiful coat and classy shoes. She spoke in the well-modulated sardonic tones of someone who has had a private education, come from a 'good' family. Amanda, at the age of 32, is maintaining a £300 a day heroin habit. Her parents have sent her to a de-tox clinic, bailed her out, given her money, sent her away on long holidays, but this time when she went back on 'smack' they washed their hands of her. 'At least they're being honest about their feelings for me for the first time,' she said. 'The fact is they've never cared a damn. It was always money instead of love. But now I know where I stand. I'll have to do it myself this time.' But she didn't look very convinced.

'You'll do it if you think you're worth it,' I said helplessly. She laughed cynically. 'Worth what? I've always had a low self-image. How do I change that?' Her parents never concealed their disappointment that she wasn't a boy. 'When he realized he would never have a son in the Guards, my father ceased to take any interest in me. I had a fucked up childhood, of course. My parents divorced and they sent me to a boarding school. I got in with bad friends, bad lovers, bad drugs.' Her boyfriend went to jail for dealing, she went on the game. She always works the Hilton, either in the lobby or just outside in the street. She had quite a few regulars who drive by and pick her up at a pre-arranged time. Most of the time the hotel security, under the charge of an ex-policeman, throw the hookers out. Amanda, because she looks posh enough to be a bona fide guest, often gets away with it.

On this occasion the police didn't arrest her. I'm not sure what the criteria are; it all seems a bit arbitrary. Sometimes they roar up the street in hot pursuit of someone, other times they just hang out, chatting. They saw Wendy teetering along on high-heeled red strappy sandals and pulled up beside her. 'Oh no!' she said. 'I've only just come out. Don't tell me I've wasted the taxi fare!' 'Do you want to get in the van and have a talk with this lady?' they said, indicating me. She got in. Close up, I could see she was quite a lot older than the other women with a mass of fluffy blonde hair, loads of make up and practically nothing on under her camel coat. She said she was 35.

'I only wish someone would tell the truth about being a prostitute,' she said. 'People think lying on your back is easy money, but it's not. I was made redundant eighteen months ago and took this up for the first time. I'm paranoid about my family finding out. It would kill my husband if he knew. He's a very proud man, but he's been out of work for three years and we've got two teenage kids to support. I don't know what else to do. I'm good at this. I like men and I don't mind the sex – it's only natural after all. What I hate is all the shame and deceit that goes with the job.'

The police treated her with great chivalry and respect and let her go after we'd talked a while. 'One of the nicest women on the game that I've come across,' said the sergeant. 'I wish we didn't have to nick her, but we can't be seen to show favouritism.'

Walking along in the icy December drizzle, her fake leopardskin collar and thin gaberdine coat offering poor protection, Corinne was spotted by the police. When stopped she just gave a resigned little shrug and got in the back. By the light of the street lamp I could see that she was completely cross eyed. Her straight dark hair was clipped back off her face with a bow at the back. She had the brisk, business-like air of a Miss Brodie, a rather eccentric teacher in a girls' school. Corinne spoke in a slow, thoughtful, precise monotone with a broad Glaswegian accent. The cops drove her to the police station to charge her, but let us talk in the interview room while they went off for a final cup of tea.

'What can I help you with?' asked Corinne politely, looking straight at me with one eye while the other looked in the opposite direction. I said I wanted to listen to those who know what it feels like to be a prostitute. 'There's no such thing as "a prostitute",' she said crisply. 'We're just women. Every woman prostitutes herself to a certain extent. If you don't capitalize on your assets, you're crazy. It's just a way of earning a living and it's always been my intention to move on. It makes no difference where you have passed by or what you have passed through in your life, it's only a road you walk down. I'm just the same as I was before I started, so what does the label mean?'

I nodded encouragement and she warmed to her topic. 'Prostitution has made me into a better class of woman. I've looked into the mirror and seen who I really am, and it's given me the incentive to make something of my life, made me the woman I am today. Experience has made me tougher and shrewder. My clients are helping to train me. Please don't portray us as victims. I've had some fantastic clients and I've never been exploited by men.'

It was a brave and dignified speech. I said I respected everything she said and admired her attitude. We talked a bit more in a stilted fashion. She told me she was studying part-time for her 'A' levels at an adult college and that she dreamt of being a writer one day. Then she began to talk about her childhood. Corinne's mother had died when she was only seven, leaving her alone with her father and four older brothers. For the next eight years, until her father died and she became a prostitute, she suffered continuous sexual assault. She wouldn't say more, but it seemed pretty obvious who the perpetrator was. 'I don't feel normal, I've never felt normal,' she said softly. She sat there, straight as an arrow, with her hands folded in her lap. She was the same age as my daughter and I just wanted to hold her in my arms. She stood up to leave and I felt quite overwhelmed with helplessness. I gave her my telephone number and offered to be there for her if she ever needed a friend, but I didn't expect to hear from her again.

Just after Christmas I got a phone call. 'This is Corinne. You probably don't remember me. If you meant it about wanting to see me again I'd like to meet. Maybe I can help you with your book about prostitutes.' I was really delighted to hear from her.

We met in the lobby of the The Green Park Hotel in Half Moon Street and she was already there ahead of me, drinking a cup of tea, when I arrived. Corinne has a very contained outward appearance and looks like a bank cashier or a hotel catering manager in her neat skirt and blouse, no make up, straight dark hair. It would be nearly impossible to guess her profession. We embraced warmly and went off to have lunch together in a friendly crowded Italian restaurant.

'I had no choice,' she answered simply when I asked her why she first decided to be a prostitute. 'I came from a background of violence and sexual abuse. I was deeply ashamed that my body had been violated inside the so-called safety of the family. I felt that somehow if I could cover it up, lose it, dilute it in a multitude of encounters, my father would just become one man among many.'

Once she'd made her mind up to become a prostitute, she set about it in a very single-minded way. She worked in her native Glasgow, in Streatham, in Park Lane. She says her life is a copy of the one portrayed in the film *Mona Lisa* – from the King's Cross meat rack, via the higher vice circles, to a well-organized call-girl set up. But she hated being part of a stable; it made her even more withdrawn than she always was. 'I needed to protect myself,' she says. 'It was soul destroying and very unhealthy living in that plastic, artificial world.' So she quit and went solo. Now she walks the street which has its own terrors but, as she says, you have to meet the fears head on if you want to dispel them. She is who she is and she prefers to do it her own way.

'I found that not all men are beasts and I got a lot of positive feedback about my body, about myself as a woman. Of course, there will be some clients who project a lot of negative fantasies onto you, but I think it's got a lot to do with how you see yourself. If you feel like a victim, you will attract people who treat you like one. If you feel worthless, you will attract people who use and abuse you.' She has a very high regard for herself, she says, and takes her health and welfare very seriously. She has definite boundaries and will not allow any client to mistreat her. 'If you are quite clear in your own mind, they never question your authority. I have a lot of power and control in my job. I'll say to a client, "You have a perfect right to your own tastes, but this one is not for me. You'll have to find someone else."'

She has been asked to dress up and play many parts. One man wanted to see her wrestle with another girl and then let him join in. She enjoys all the characters she has to play. The worst part about being on the game, she says, is not the punters but the police, which is why she didn't want to say much when we met in the police station. In the eight years she's been working on the street she has collected over 300 convictions for loitering. Far from acting as a deterrent the fines force her to work even harder and have made her determined not to be defeated. She feels that the police don't like her because she will not play games with them. She'll neither pander to the fatherly ones nor engage in sexual banter with the lecherous ones. 'I won't give them the satisfaction and they hate me for it. They like to feel superior. They hate my independence and they're envious of my freedom and the amount of money I earn. One policeman is always saying he won't nick me if I do the business with him, but that would *really* be degrading. I'd rather go to prison.'

There are two kinds of danger that go with the job of being a prostitute, she says. The first is the obvious physical danger, the second, much more serious, risk is the emotional and mental stress of other people trying to make you feel bad about yourself all the time. 'Being on the game is a hard life, but you can learn a lot. I've learned that I can survive, I don't need anybody, I'm streetwise, I can take care of myself.'

Corinne has been with the same boyfriend for seven years, an electrician who is thirty years older than her and who doesn't know what she does. 'I wish I could tell him, but I don't know if he could take it. It must be so lovely to have someone you can tell everything to.' But she can't bear to risk it, so she keeps her life rigidly compartmentalized. 'Unfortunately most men still divide women into two camps. They don't like their wife or girlfriend to be too sexual and they can't understand that a prostitute can be a creature of love and tenderness.'

She longs for the day when prostitutes are respected and able to be open about what they do. 'It's such a hard job and we should get credit for it.' We parted with promises to stay in touch, but she wouldn't give me her home address, only the address of the sleazy little hotel where she takes clients. 'Sorry to be so cautious!' she smiled ruefully. 'But that's why I'm still alive.'

I went to meet the Chief Inspector of the Metropolitan Vice Squad in his office on the fifth floor of West End Central Police Station. He is a friendly, good-humoured man ('a PR copper' said one prostitute, scathingly) in his mid-forties, married with young children. His personal view is that many of the prostitution laws should be abolished. As it is, a single working girl in a flat with a maid is within the law. The police only become involved if more than one working woman shares a flat because that is technically a brothel, or if a pimp is living off her 'immoral earnings'. In his area, he knows of a whole block of flats, twenty-seven or so, each with a working girl and a maid and none of them do straight sex. 'They're all into specialities – dressing up, bondage, etc. Don't knock it till you've tried it!' he said laughing.

It is the pimps that they're really after. One in particular attacked 'his' woman with a claw hammer and blinded her in one eye. Her injuries were horrific, but when he was arrested she refused to testify against him out of fear of reprisals. There are also organized gangs who bus girls down from the North to work in London on the streets or out of cheap hotels during the week. The majority are working to support a heroin habit, to which the pimp may well have introduced them in the first place. Although the girls can earn up to £1,000, they only see about half of it. They are often terrorized, brutalized, bullied, coerced.

There are pimps who hang around outside prisons or at main-line stations, homing in on girls who look lonely or lost, frightened or needy. They offer them a place to stay, a bit of counterfeit affection until they're caught in the trap and then feed off them like leeches.

He told me with respect and admiration about the prostitute, a refugee from Germany, now in her seventies, who made a good living for years doing dominatrix work and never once had intercourse with a punter. She is now retired and if you should see her shopping in

Harrod's, she is everybody's idea of the perfect grandmother. It was she who helped them catch a particularly evil child pornographer who was operating out of an upstairs flat in her building. She tipped them off and they were able to catch him red-handed.

I also met the Inspector in charge of Street Prostitution, who has a team of twenty-four officers, nine of them women, under his command. His job, as he defines it, is to 'regulate' prostitution which virtually means moving it along to another neighbourhood. They catch girls soliciting or men cruising and they respond to public complaints about nuisance, car doors slamming at 3 am, used condoms in the bushes and so forth. Their job is not to reform society, but to uphold the law.

SEVEN

'If a man has no arms, he can't even masturbate,' said Tuppy Owen. The tragic imagery of that simple statement made me aware of something I hadn't even thought about before. I was talking to her at Helen Buckingham's flat where I also met Mitzi who specializes in disabled clients. This opened up a whole new vision of prostitution in its healing mode, reconnecting with the sacred, with the best and most beautiful aspect of the feminine. I was reminded of a phrase from *The Sacred Prostitute* by Nancy Qualls-Corbett:

> Our modern attitude makes it difficult for us to grasp what we see as a paradox in the image of the 'sacred prostitute': her sexual nature was an integral part of her spiritual nature. For most of us that conjunction is a contradiction. In ancient times, however, it was a unity.

Tuppy is a tall, thin woman with a bird's nest of fashionably dishevelled hair clamped up in a spring clasp. She is the creator of *The Sex Maniac's Diary*, which she has published for seventeen years. It is a sort of 'Good Sex Guide', which aims to give information about brothels, erotic hotels, contact clubs, publications, and sexual services in various parts of the world. In it she expounds her philosophy of sex etiquette, in particular the etiquette of the encounter between prostitute and client and what each should rightfully expect from the other. There are lots of tips and ideas for ways to make 'safe sex' fun.

I went to visit Tuppy in her amazing underground basement lair, painted entirely matt black, in the bowels of a smart Mayfair block where she's been living for twenty years. She has collected a vast library of erotica and devoted a large part of her life to propagating a healthier attitude to sex. Britain, she believes, comes far down the league table, bedevilled as we are by endemic hypocrisy. It offers a pretty crummy rip-off standard of commercial sex, compared with the stylish, good-value obtainable on much of the Continent, Australia and, in particular, Japan.

Tuppy has learned a lot about the game from talking to men and to prostitutes and, as an offshoot, has formed a club called Outsiders which, among other things, helps put people such as paraplegics in touch with each other and with women who are prepared to service their sexual needs. The Outsiders Club is a register of people who for one reason or another have difficulty making relationships, perhaps from extreme shyness or physical disability. They don't push anything on anyone, but if a person wants advice, counselling or sex information, Tuppy, a trained sex therapist, can help point them in the right direction.

An unusual, tolerant, compassionate and enlightened person, Tuppy is attacked by hard-line feminists for her liberal attitude to porn and prostitution. She is also attacked by organizations for the disabled because she 'encourages them to be disgusting'. But she soldiers on offering her totally non-judgemental service. She reasons that everyone has a right to a sex life and if a person self-selects to join a club of this nature, he (or, less frequently, she) will tend to act responsibly and begin to confront issues that would be worse if left festering.

Club members list their problems and hopes in a confidential directory and are encouraged to get in touch with each other:

John X. Blind. Paralysed from the waist down can give tender considerate massage to friendly, cuddly woman.

Jane Y. Extensive body burns but pretty face hopes to find friendship and romance.

Harry Z. Shy, nervous agoraphobic with speech impediment seeks gentle older woman for love and companionship.

Over a thousand people belong to the club and once a month a lunch is held in London for anyone who can get there. Membership and social events are always cheap so no one is excluded for reasons of poverty. Tuppy is not able to list sympathetic prostitutes because she could be prosecuted for pimping. She is careful to stay inside the law but sails pretty close to the wind; prostitutes and others offering special services are often invited along to meet the members.

I was honoured to be invited to the next lunch which was held, ironically, the day after I got the devastating news of my own breast cancer. I decided to go anyway and it was a surreal experience, having had a morning of tears and terror after a sleepless night, to find myself suddenly in the midst of a roomful of physically and emotionally handicapped people. Maybe it was because of that I felt such a great empathy and ease of communication. My own beautiful breasts were about to be mutilated and I could identify at the deepest level of my being with the horror of disfigurement and the pain of self-consciousness. Tuppy introduced me to several men who had had relationships with prostitutes and I was very moved by the dignity and courage with which they shared their stories.

Terry, who had polio as a baby and can just about walk in that stiff-gaited way with two sticks, is 39 years old and overweight from forced inactivity. He has a sensitive, sweet face and a heart-breakingly jokey manner – a transparent defence against rejection. After ten minutes of quick-fire non-stop gags, I yelled 'Truce!' 'Where are you?' I challenged. 'I think it's safe for you to come out now.' He gave a sheepish grin, his manner softened, his face relaxed and we spontaneously reached a hand out to each other in friendship. It's happened so many times, he told me, that if he is serious and sincere and a girl snubs him it hurts unbearably. Hiding behind the smoke-screen of this larky patter gives him a retreat position. He still feels the rejection just as acutely, but he becomes invisible.

Terry was a virgin until the age of 30 when he finally plucked up the courage to phone an escort agency. He specified his problem and they sent a woman to his house where he had prepared a room with flowers and champagne for the celebration of his own defloration. 'By objective standards she was a plain girl,' said Terry, 'small, plump body, mousey hair, glasses. But to me she was the most desirable woman in the world. I thought she was wonderful. She was tender and kind and put me at my ease. All my fears evaporated and the sex came easily and naturally.

'My problem was that I fell in love with her and had a hard time coming to terms with it being just a job for her. I would have married her on the spot although I can see now how unrealistic that was. I'm not ever going to be anybody's first choice. I see her about once a month – it's actually the high spot of my life – and I try not to be jealous. It's hard, though, and sometimes when I'm feeling down, I wonder if perhaps I would have been better off never knowing how great it is to fuck a woman, but most of the time I just thank God for it.'

Mike was sitting at the same table listening. There is a remarkable degree of frankness among the friends who meet up at these gatherings. The pain and rejection each has had to face has forged a profound sympathy. Mike has a lovely smile-creased face and an obvious intelligence, but the only job he can manage is as a sweeper in a factory. In 1969, at the age of 15, he was in a road accident and spent 117 days in a coma with dreadful head injuries. It is now twenty years on and he has regained an astonishing amount in the way of mobility and speech, so much so that he is about to sit a GCSE exam in economics. But he looks odd, and ordinary, able-bodied women don't want to know.

His brain may have been damaged, but his sex drive remained unimpaired and when he was 20 he bravely decided to lose his virginity, so he came to London, hailed a taxi and told the driver he wanted a woman. The driver took him to Soho and left him there with the instruction to ring any doorbell with 'Model' on it. There then followed a humiliating and disappointing encounter with a hard, impatient whore. He couldn't get an erection, she couldn't be bothered with him, took his money and threw him out. When he eventually managed it with another woman a few months later he thought he was in paradise. 'It was so lovely,' he said and his face lit up with the memory. Mike's sexual experiences since then have all been with prostitutes, most of whom give him little, although there is one older woman who is kind and gives him a cup of tea afterwards. He longs to have a proper relationship and dreams of marriage, 'but no one wants me,' he said. At one point I asked him if he suffered from headaches as a result of the accident. 'No,' he answered, 'but' – placing both hands on his chest – 'lots of heartaches.'

The other young man sitting with us was Tom, a thalidomide victim with no arms. He told how he took the entire £700 he'd been given as a furniture grant by the social services and blew it all on prostitutes in the space of a week! Everyone applauded and clapped him on the back.

Disabled people have normal, healthy sexual desires. Women like Mitzi who do this important work with compassion should be recognized and held in high esteem by any sane and tolerant society.

Mitzi is a beautiful dark-haired, brown-eyed Jewish prostitute who also plays the piano and sings in a jazz band. I went over to her house in Battersea to spend a day with her. She shares a run-down but lovely old place in a quiet square with four women who have a lot of problems accepting what she does for a living. The garden is Mitzi's creation from scratch and her connection with the earth, she says. It is the place where she loses herself and finds total acceptance and peace under the apple tree, amongst the flowers, beans, spinach, grass. Her room is draped with colourful batik, filled with books, warm with sunshine. There are piles of music everywhere. Mitzi has never wanted marriage, a permanent relationship or children. 'I'd be terrified of motherhood,' she confided, 'and at 38, my biological clock is running out anyhow.'

I realized that I would be terrified to do what she does – live alone, confront the wilder shores of sexuality, face the fragmentation and isolation of a prostitute's life in a hypocritical world. I represent one facet of womanhood, she represents another, and it is so rarely that we get to meet. She also does health education work, sex counselling, and sex surrogate work for a psychiatrist with sexually dysfunctional patients. But for all these things she has to wear a different hat. As a health educator and sex counsellor, for example, she cannot let it be known that she is a prostitute and yet who could possibly be more experienced or skilful? She is not allowed to be proud of what she does.

Mitzi sees quite a few disabled clients. It is the most rewarding job you could imagine, she says, and most of the men, particularly the very disabled ones, are tender, considerate, grateful and delightful. One chap she sees is in a wheelchair. ('Nothing wrong with his mind, but his body is completely useless and he's very tiny.') She does a striptease for him, looks at pornographic magazines with him and encourages him to be comfortable and familiar with a woman's naked body. 'I let him feel my titties, stroke my skin, play with my hair. I've helped him learn to masturbate. He's a million years away from intercourse. We just explore what he is able to enjoy.'

Mitzi also has an elderly client whose wife, in forty-five years of marriage, has never let him see her without any clothes on. He travels down from the North of England every so often, bringing her gifts of sexy little outfits. All he wants her to do is to wear them and undress in front of him. Sometimes he caresses her neck or massages her feet. She has never had a bad experience with a client, only with boyfriends who get possessive or jealous although she never tells them what she does.

Some people come just to be held. Some are respecting their wives' wishes not to have sex. 'One old man comes every single week, sometimes twice, either to me or one of my friends. He's 73 and his wife thinks he's too old for it. He'd never, ever had sex outside his marriage until she just didn't want to do it any more and he met us. He's terribly fond of us and very sweet and we have a cup of tea and a chat and we tell him what's going on in our lives. He says he doesn't know what he'd do if he couldn't come to us. Men often feel bad and apologetic for being old,' she says. 'Their anxieties and fears about potency which were bad enough when they were in the full flush of youth and vigour become magnified. Very often an older man on his own, widowed or divorced, may find it very difficult to pluck up the courage to begin a sexual relationship. He is afraid he might not measure up.'

Mitzi first started as a photographic model over twenty years ago doing pretty tame stuff by today's standards – see-through nighties, romps in the hay, bubble baths, etc. There were infinite gradations and girls could make the most money if they were prepared to do 'open-leg' shots. She worked as a stripper as well in a club where you had to walk round the customers with a hat after your number to collect the money. When she finally did a straight fuck for a fee it was a great relief. The honesty and simplicity of the contract appealed to her. It was the same work with no pretence, she felt, and she's never regretted her decision.

Mitzi's mother has known for quite a while about her daughter's double life. She has been very supportive as well, helping her to choose clothes, giving her jewellery, but when Mitzi took part in a television programme about prostitution recently her mother was absolutely horrified that the neighbours would find out her daughter was a whore. 'You can't say publicly and with confidence, "I am a prostitute",' says Mitzi. 'I have tried it. I'm not ashamed of what I do. I'm proud of it. I am a prostitute. But most people fall over backward in horror and that hurts.'

She joined the English Collective of Prostitutes at one time, finding tremendous comfort and release in being able to talk openly about being a whore with other whores. Alas, the apparently immutable aggressive, feminist ethos made her feel increasingly uncomfortable and unwelcome. She has no quarrel with their excellent social and political analysis, but objected to their attempts to re-educate her. Mitzi is saddened by the divisive factions which have split the women's movement. She feels that she has been vilified because her behaviour is not politically correct, because she won't conform. 'Unfortunately they can be very judgemental and unsisterly on the whole. Their angry, man-hating, unforgiving natures make them very hard to get along with and they have alienated many of the women for whom they should be providing a shelter and a forum.'

When I put this criticism to Nina Lopez-Jones she defended their position by saying that as they were primarily a pressure group for change they couldn't compromise. I can see her point and of course it is inevitable that strongly held differing views will emerge in any movement, but at this vulnerable time of healing and emerging, I wish it were possible to heal the rift. Prostitutes, above all else, need acceptance and support, particularly from each other.

Apart from her disabled clients, Mitzi doesn't have an enormously high regard for men. Seeing their weaknesses and their vulnerability day after day doesn't make her like them more because it is so often accompanied by an insufferable arrogance. Men, she thinks, can't do without women's company, maybe because they can never be off their guard with other men. Women, on the other hand, don't need men nearly so much. 'Women are smarter and cleverer than men and much more powerful in bed. They should learn to appreciate this fact and to use it wisely and well. If a man becomes too aware of her power he will try to destroy it, hurt her, free himself from it. It is a constant reminder of his own inadequacy.

'Most men are pathetically inadequate sexually,' she went on. 'Very few have a clue how to please a woman and most women don't tell them what they want for fear of offending them or seeming too wanton.' She, herself, has never had an orgasm on the job and never had a simultaneous orgasm with a lover. It's theoretically possible once in a blue moon, she reckons, but is nearly always faked by women. Men set such store by it but are very rarely able to sustain things to the right degree. A recent client called her over to his hotel to join him and his girlfriend in a threesome. When she arrived she found the man prancing about in women's underwear with his flabby little cock hanging out of a pair of crotchless panties. He, who had set up the whole fantasy of rampant virility, was totally useless and it was the poor girlfriend who needed ministering to.

'I don't feel afraid of men,' said Mitzi, 'especially in bed. That's one thing that prostitution has given me – the confidence to know what to do with men, how to deal with them in a sexual situation, how to read the signals. It's a direct and honest relationship. A prostitute has all the power and control while letting the man think he has. My only rule is that I won't see a punter if he doesn't respect me. People who get their rocks off by despising you – you can sniff them a mile off – I won't have anything to do with.'

We were talking about my experience of working over at Amber's bondage parlour but nothing surprised her and she told me of a German woman she knows who works in a big sado-masochistic salon in Knightsbridge. Her clients are nearly all powerful men – newspaper editors, policemen, industrialists, politicians – who want to be beaten and humiliated and have all manner of peculiar objects shoved up their rectums. What they had in common was a tremendous need to atone for the guilt that is the concomitant of the power and wealth of their lives – to be absolved, confessed, cleansed. One man, a company director, came to her on the day he had just sold a load of dangerous, inadequately tested medicines to a Third World country for a fat profit. 'I've been a bad boy and I need to be punished,' he said and wanted her to defecate on his face.

'It got so she would try to see all the shit jobs on one day,' said Mitzi. 'She would take a laxative in the morning and hold it in wearing a sanitary towel until they arrived, one after the other!'

By comparison, no wonder it's refreshing to be able to bring some gentle, healing pleasure into the life of a disabled person.

Mitzi then told me about another friend, Maxine, who has been able to listen to the wisdom of her heart and move fully into her true instinctive nature – the healer. She had always practised astrology and read the tarot cards as a sideline but now she has done a training in herbalism and switched over completely. I was so excited by this that I rang her immediately to ask if we could meet but she didn't want to talk. She was having a really hard time with her past life coming back to haunt her and just wanted to forget about it. We spoke briefly on the phone: 'Look, I haven't fucked anyone for over a year now. Only a few hand jobs, you know ... and I'm gradually converting the few clients I have left to healing and massage. I no longer want to take anyone inside me, it just isn't my truth anymore. People who are still doing it need so much support, the last thing I want is to create a holier than thou impression. I'm not born again or anything, but it just isn't right for me anymore.'

Maxine was just about to go to ground for a while – maybe to try her hand at writing – until the dust subsided. 'I need the money more than I ever have. I'm in terrible debt and the love of my life has just left me, but I want to use my time and my body more creatively now. Whoring was great when I needed it; it gave me a roof over my head and enabled me to bring up my daughter, but however much I'm tempted by the money now, I know I don't want that anymore.

'I always felt like a healer inside, but I could never break through the barrier of how other people saw me. When you are naked with a stranger your defences are very fragile. I sometimes felt like an animal tamer, knowing I could get clients to trust me. I think prostitutes are more comfortable with their bodies and their sexuality than most people. Taking your clothes off so often makes you aware that there is nothing secret about a body – it's just a body. We don't have "private parts" dismembered from the rest, they are parts of the whole. I wanted to help people and I felt powerful and capable but there is a set of assumptions attached to being a whore – in most people's eyes you are a worthless person.

'Now I don't want anyone to know what I used to do. I've never lied in my private life but the world isn't ready for the truth yet. People can't handle the crossover between healer and whore. One of my radionics and alternative healing patients saw me, heavily disguised, talking in a TV programme with Mitzi and she recognized my voice. It completely freaked her out. She felt betrayed as if I'd contaminated her in some way. "You sick pervert!" she screamed. "And to think I let you touch me!"'

I never did get to meet Maxine. She's set up shop as a healer in a different town under a different name, forced to disown her former self. I remembered a quote from Priscilla Alexander's and Frederique Delacoste's book *Sex Work*: A woman said, 'I wanted to be a priestess, but in this world that job description was a prostitute.'

EIGHT

'So many people just see "the prostitute" – not a woman doing a job, not a person. And when you've been a non-person for so long you become a prisoner of that concept.' I was talking with Angel in the sitting room of her little council flat in Hackney. It's on a grim estate of rain-streaked concrete stairwells reeking of urine and disinfectant, but she's made it into an oasis of cheerfulness and a place of safety and support for other women who want to 'come out'.

'Beginning to feel that you *do* have the power of choice and the control of your own destiny is the most liberating concept and everything follows on from there. A couple of years ago I felt totally helpless. Although I knew all these things in theory it still hadn't hit me that I could actually do something about it. There were so many obstacles around me and it took quite a while to realize that problems are only problems if you look at them like that. If you can just shift your perception and see them as a challenge – as a learning – it all becomes exciting and possible. So much depends on believing you deserve happiness. Subconsciously I always found it very difficult to accept love, to trust it. I never wondered *why* I felt like that, I just assumed I would never find anyone who could really love me or care about me.'

Angel came to England from Portugal when she was six years old and had a violent unsettled early childhood, being brought up by an aunt who beat her and locked her in cupboards. When her parents finally came for her, things did not improve. 'For many years,' she says, 'I was really bitter and angry and mixed up. I had terribly confused feelings towards my mother. On the one hand this great love for her, on the other hand I seemed to be the scapegoat for all her frustrations. It was me that always got whacked, not my brothers. They just pointed at me and I got blamed. I began to believe it was somehow my fault. If you're told you are stupid and bad enough times you begin to believe it. The way I dealt with it was to harden myself. I vowed that no one would ever see me cry. I remember once when my mother was beating me and a cousin was screaming, "Just cry, just cry and she'll stop!" but I wouldn't. My silence goaded her even more but I would have died rather than give her that satisfaction.'

Angel learned early that to trust was foolish and that merely to inhabit a girl's body was fraught with hazards. Just by being in the world she seemed to attract sexual abuse, to invite unwelcome attention. The first time it happened was when a friend of the family read her a bedtime story. She was only seven. 'Even at that age you know something's wrong,' she said, 'but there's an inner voice saying, "This is an adult and adults are always right. It must be my fault, I must have provoked it in some way." It made me feel guilty, dirty and ashamed.'

Nothing was safe. Her ineffectual father didn't protect her. Then a cousin tried to rape her anally. Her world was full of lies, evasions and danger where nobody explained things and people were not as they seemed to be. When Angel was 14, her mother killed herself.

'The worst part about horrible incidents in childhood is that you actually forget them. They are so awful, so painful, that you put the feelings away, beyond reach. You can't recall them even when you want to,' said Angel. 'In the meantime I identified with my mother very much and, influenced by her negative solution, I tried to commit suicide five times. Four of those times I didn't really want to die. I was just saying, "Help! I don't know what to do." But the last attempt was serious. I'd already been on the game and I was in a very confused state. There were lots of things I hadn't dealt with and my head was totally scrambled.

'The good thing that came out of all this was being sent to a psychiatric ward for a while. I didn't give a toss but I went. The funny farm was time out from the pressures. One of the psychiatrists helped me to open up the gates to everything and I began to see how much stemmed from my mother's death and the fact that I had blocked it off.'

I told Angel that one of the things I learned when coming to terms with my own cancer was how important it is to be gentle with yourself at a time when you're trying to make big changes in your life. It is not a time for remorse and regret. The things you have bottled up and battened down in yourself have often been for the best of reasons – survival. If she *had* let those emotions crowd in on her, she would have exploded from the grief of it all. The denial has enabled her to survive.

And then one day you get new information. Your body tries to tell you something and as you begin to see that your old patterns of response are not helpful to you any more, you can start gradually to let them go and move into a new, more honest phase of your life. This is the time when you need support and you need to give yourself a tremendous amount of compassion and understanding for having been as brilliant as you were and coped in the way you did. Whatever you did was the best solution you could think of at the time.

We talked a lot about self-healing and being able to listen to your inner voices. 'What really got me searching, were two terrible dreams,' Angel remembered. 'I was only half asleep when suddenly I found myself paralysed. There was a sound of voices in my ears and a loud buzzing like twenty loudspeakers. I couldn't move and I was very frightened. The hair stood up on the back of my neck. I tried to say the Lord's Prayer, but I couldn't remember it. I strained with all my might to fight back and finally the force seemed to release me. I jerked back to life again and spent the rest of the night huddled in the corner with my back against the wall – really scared.'

Angel said she knew that in some way the dream was a message and then she had the second one. 'I dreamt I was on a spiral staircase going headlong downwards faster and faster. Then I heard that awful buzzing again and felt the pressure of something walking up the back of my legs, pinning me to the bed. I woke up and recognized immediately that it was my own fear that was hurting me, crushing me, holding me prisoner, spiralling me down into a bottomless pit and that if I didn't really begin to fight back it's exactly what would happen to me in real life. I didn't see the experience as something spooky but as another part of my personality talking to me.'

There was also an uncanny encounter with a medium who picked Angel out of a crowd at a mass demonstration saying, 'You had a terrifying nightmare a while back. Well, it wasn't a dream, it was a warning. You know what I'm talking about don't you?' Shaken, Angel began to read all the books on healing and esoteric subjects she could get her hands on. Shirley McClaine's books in particular were a great inspiration. 'I read and talked a lot and began to make myself receptive to new ideas. It was amazing. When you open the door onto that kind of thinking, all the people you need suddenly gravitate into your life. You begin to get a lot of support and to see yourself in a different light.'

She also began to see prostitution in a different light. 'I couldn't stand being treated with a lack of respect. It happened quite a lot without clients even realizing they were doing it. Once they'd paid for your time and your body, they'd think they could do whatever they wanted, whenever they felt like it. They'd grab you or grope you in public, in a taxi and I really hated being mauled. One man got very nasty once when I wouldn't drink with him. He wanted to feel he had the power to force me to do his bidding. But just because he's paid to screw me doesn't mean I'm not a person. I hated it, so I just got up and left! I was beginning to realize I could say "No".

'Some men, perhaps because they're unhappy and hen-pecked at home, feel that paying for a girl puts them in a position of power and they get a big buzz out of insulting and humiliating her. One guy, a very wealthy Arab, would pay for the company of a group of girls and boys. He'd sit there ignoring them then suddenly snap his fingers and say

"You! Up! Dance!" and some of them would. I refused and in the end got on quite well with him because I chose to stand up to him. The more people let him get away with it, the more he did it and the more he despised them for it.

'I've often heard the question, "How come *somebody like you* is doing this?" What do they mean, somebody *like* me? This *is* me. At the end of the day, no matter how nice to you they might be, you're still "a prostitute" and if they had a son and you formed a relationship with him and wanted to marry him they'd be appalled. You've forfeited the respect of a normal human being.

'I don't think it is possible to lead a normal life while working as a prostitute. When you're on the game, you alienate yourself from everyone else. You can never get close to people because there's such a large part of yourself you have to keep quiet about. Your clients never know the real you, your friends and family never know the whore. By your silence you actually buy into the stereotype of what a prostitute is – a split personality, a shameful person who dares not speak her name. I think prostitution is fundamentally damaging for that reason – not because it's a mortal sin.

'I also think that deep in a woman's heart is a feeling that sex should be to do with love and with giving. Many times I would go home from a booking feeling, "Yuk! What have I just done? What have I let happen?" Whereas if I, as a woman, could go into every single booking and enjoy what I have to give and love the person I'm with unconditionally, even if it's just for an hour, then, whether money changes hands or not, I would transform the encounter. But, of course, the majority of cases aren't like that at all. Women do it for the money, but they despise the man and despise themselves for doing it.

'I'm not promiscuous by nature and I don't think many women are. I've never met a so-called nymphomaniac. At the time in my life when I was promiscuous it was only ever comfort screwing. I wanted the cuddle at the end and a bit of affection. It seemed the only way I knew to get it. A man feels great when he's screwed a lot of women. A woman does not feel great when she's been screwed by a lot of men. Maybe this is why very few women pay for sex even if they can afford it. I don't know whether it's a biological difference or simply conditioning; it's certainly very unfair but the fact is a man can spread it about without getting emotionally involved. His participation in the sexual act is very outward, thrusting, focused, one-pointed, conquering, whereas a woman opens herself both symbolically and literally, enfolding, surrendering. It makes her vulnerable and she is more inclined to want commitment, love, security in return. A lot of women who get into promiscuity or prostitution are very self-destructive – spearing themselves on a series of lances, mortally wounding themselves. They don't feel good about themselves afterwards.

'It was around the time I started valuing myself that I started telling people I was a prostitute. I couldn't stand the pretence any more. I thought, "If they like me, they're going to like me for who I am. Why should that change if they know I've been out the night before fucking someone for money? I'm still the same person."'

Angel started telling everyone and speaking openly in front of friends and family about her experiences and feelings. Her flat became a meeting place for other women where they didn't have to hide anything. This grew into a support and self-help group which generated the awareness that whether a person is a prostitute through choice or force of circumstance she is entitled to the same value and respect as any other human being. They talk about the funny side and about the times when you come home and want to scrub yourself till you bleed. They talk about their neediness and their confusions, about their children and the circumstances that led to going on the game.

'Just because we sell ourselves, in our personal lives we're not necessarily *easy*,' said Angel. 'Being a prostitute doesn't mean you'll go off with anyone, doesn't mean you're a bad mother, doesn't mean you can't be trusted, doesn't mean you can't love and be loyal. It's only by sharing confidences, by knowing what kind of people we are in our everyday lives that we've begun to see ourselves more clearly. We're just women – different women who do prostitution for whatever reason. The only common denominator in our lives seems to be some kind of terrible trauma in childhood. All of us have suffered from either sexual abuse, a broken home, the suicide of a parent, rape – something that gave us a negative outlook – and we're learning to talk about those things, learning to look inside, ending the isolation and ostracism.

'Since my daughter was born I've come off the game. I used to get propositioned all the time by kerb crawlers when I was pregnant. And my landlord was always coming on to me. I couldn't bear it at a time when I felt so helpless and in need of protection. The last booking I went on, I had steeled myself as usual and got in a cab but I found myself shaking uncontrollably, so I asked the taxi driver to please just take me home. I don't think I'll go back to it again because I'm a different person to who I was then. I don't need those experiences any more. I've made a lot of change and progress in my life. Going on the game was a liberation too at the time. It was part of my journey. It was the way I chose to take my destiny into my own hands and I'm very thankful I did it. I think we call these experiences to ourselves because of what we've got to learn in this life. The shame is that any woman should have to do it when she's not enjoying it and be drawn to it as a means of punishing herself. If every encounter could be a caring one, freely chosen, it wouldn't damage you.'

Angel feels, as Maxine does, that prostitution is very close to healing. It stems from the same natural impulse to want to give comfort and make love. As many ancient cultures have defined it, it is a way of bringing the goddess's love into contact with mankind, a way of peacekeeping in the world. 'It's only our own stuff that clutters it up,' she said. 'That's when it becomes a vicious or vengeful encounter rather than a kindly one, mercenary rather than merciful. Everyone has the desire to love and be loved but it gets so screwed up. You can express violence, hatred and aggression with the same act that you express love. It's very confusing.'

Two of the young women who come to Angel's flat for support and friendship are Natasha and Holly. They live together with a little kitten for company in an anonymous suburban house in Mill Hill. Holly, with a face like a petulant child, became a prostitute at 16 standing on the street outside the Dorchester Hotel in flight from an unloving family and an alcoholic mother. She later joined an agency where her speciality was being a virgin. Natasha, a sensational beauty with a flawless olive complexion and long, crinkly dark brown hair, worked for the same agency earning up to £500 a night from very wealthy clients. They met and became friends, occasionally doing double bookings together.

'I always felt unwanted,' said Holly. 'My strongest feeling was of disliking myself intensely. I think that's the thing with most prostitutes – absolutely no self-respect or self-esteem at all. I went on the streets partly because of a fascination with it but mostly as a punishment. I didn't think I was worth anything. It's quite shocking to me now when I look back on what we did, what was done to us, the manner in which it was done. I would never do that again. The degrading aspect wasn't even the sex so much, it was the attitude of the punters. The way they'd look you up and down, talk about you as if you weren't there. I played the innocent virgin pretending I was shy and afraid. I'd walk into a roomful of Arabs and they'd continue to talk in their own language. They'd laugh and grab my tits and grope me, deciding amongst themselves which one was going to have me. Unreal! And I allowed it to happen. That's the worst part. I let them do that to me.

'Street work is a lot different. In a sense you have more rights – at least, you kid yourself you're more independent. You set the price. You choose whether or not to go with a particular client. You insist on condoms. I decided I wouldn't get into any other car than a Rolls Royce, a BMW or a Mercedes. *Never* a diplomatic car because I knew diplomats could get away with anything. It didn't occur to me that the very people who can afford Rolls Royces are probably the ones who can buy themselves out of trouble if they have to. I never really thought about the danger, but I had a rough time on the street once. I got into a car and I had funny vibes about it. I should have trusted my instinct because the man pulled a knife on me and fucked me up my arse. I haven't really talked about it. I've sort of blocked it out. What freaks me out about it is that I went straight back out on the street again, which really shows you the state I was in. I really didn't want to live.

'It's very hard coming to terms with liking yourself after you've done prostitution. It's a slow healing process. I don't think prostitution caused me to lose my self-respect; it was lack of self-respect that caused me to become a prostitute. But it's so difficult to think about anything on any kind of deep level because once you start, you're going to have to think about yourself. I didn't want to face anything about what I was doing. I didn't want to go home and think, "Oh yes, I've just opened my legs and let a stranger fuck me."

'Then on a booking once, a guy who was a sort of minder for the punter read my palm. "It's a real shame what you're doing," he said, "because in a couple of years you won't be around to enjoy any of the money. If you die your mother might mourn for you for a little while, but then she'd get on with her own life and forget you."

'That really got through to me. I had wanted to hurt myself so badly in order to get back at my family, but in the end they'd get on with their lives and forget me. I had reached the point where I knew I wanted to change. I decided to go to college to train in massage and aromatherapy. I started meeting "normal" people. My social life veered away from prostitution and I realized how much I was missing.

'It was only after I told a few people here at Angel's that I started asking myself why I did it in the first place because before I used to think, "well, I did it for the money," which is absolute crap. Nobody does it for the money. Money is just a benefit from it that you can use or abuse. Money is just an excuse, a plausible reason covering up a deep hunger. All the while I was playing the virgin I was really longing for the protection and security of a father figure, but I was getting exactly the opposite – child abuse acted out. The reality was 50-60-year-old men having sex with a 16-year-old girl. The younger you were, the better. Girls of 18 got turned away as too old. My faked orgasm was famous in prostitution circles,' she laughed sardonically. 'Men fell for it every time. Honestly, they're so gullible! Picture the scene – there's this fat, ugly, horrible old guy on top of me, no technique at all, puffing and grunting away and I'm in raptures of ecstasy saying, "Oooh! I don't know what's happening. What's going on? I've never felt like this before!" Like, give her an Oscar!

'I realized that my "helplessness", the scatty childish image, the innocent, the victim – which was how I earned my living – carried on into real life. It governed the kind of relationships I used to build with people. It was bad for me. I had begun to get the idea that nobody would want me as an adult woman. Now I've been seeing a counsellor for the past few months because I know how I want to be. I want to grow up.'

Holly has had a hard year facing the reality of her parents' inadequacies. Her mother had just spent a month in hospital drying out, but within three days she was drunk again. 'A little while ago that would have devastated me,' said Holly. 'I used to feel as if somehow it was my fault. If you're a strong child in a family where there's a lot of weakness and unresolved pain, you can allow so much of that to be put onto you. I thought, "If only I could find the key I could make it right." Now I'm beginning to see that my Mum's life is her life. My Dad's life is his life and the only person I can be responsible for is myself.

'My goal had been to retire at 21 with £100,000 cash, a car, and a house. Well, I'm 21 and I've retired but I've got no money, no house and a second-hand Volkswagen Beetle. Even though I've decided that I don't need to do this any more, it's very important that I never forget or deny the prostitute in me. All of us here agree that prostitution is part of us. It's formed our characters and we've learned from it. If you deny it, you're half of a person.'

Natasha came from Iran where her family were quite wealthy. There 'rich equalled happy and people looked down on you if you didn't have money.' When they came to England, her father gambled all the money away and her parents got divorced. 'I had worshipped him when I was little and I was his favourite, but after that I hardly ever saw him,' she said. 'He just wasn't there for us and my Mum told me, "Men are all the same, only after one thing." I was quite rebellious and on the occasions when I did see my father and argue with him he'd call me a lot of names. "You're such a whore Natasha," he'd say.

'My Mum didn't tell me he'd been ill and the last time I saw him he'd been in psychiatric care and had had shock treatment. He was anorexic and his eyes were sunken in. Not long after that he jumped from the top of the hospital and died. The family were ashamed of the suicide and never mentioned it again. There wasn't even a funeral because his brother came and took his body back to Iran. I remembered what my Mum always used to say to me as a child when she was angry with me, "Natasha, you're exactly like your father! So weak!" For years I believed I'd end up the same way.

'I had this image of my Mum that she was totally perfect,' said Natasha. 'I would have done anything not to disappoint her. I got the idea that if I made a lot of money and could be seen to be successful, that would make everything all right.' Natasha joined an escort agency and the first booking they sent her on was to Claridge's. The punter was an old man who wanted her to sit on his knee and talk to him about her studies as if she were his daughter. All her upbringing as a Muslim girl crowded in on her with visions of heaven and hell. She was scared and repulsed, but the sex was easy and he gave her £500.

'I made up a story to my Mum that I'd got a job in an art gallery and was making lots of commission but I was really crying out for her to see what was going on and to care enough to stop me. Both Holly and I felt, "Why can't they see what we're doing?" You're doing it for your family, but they can't even notice you. I used to tell the most amazing lies. I set myself up to get caught but she didn't want to see.

'I went through a period when I really hated the men. All I could see was the negative side and it reinforced everything I'd always been told about men – that sex, young girls and power was all they were into. I mixed with the most powerful men in the world, the richest men, kings – and saw them for what they were, saw them with their trousers down. It certainly took the mystique away. I just despised them.'

All the time she was working Natasha never had a personal relationship that lasted more than three months. She never thought she was good enough or interesting enough. She never thought she could keep a boyfriend or that anyone would ever fall in love with her. She was scared that her emotions were dead and even used to wish she could get hurt just to prove she could feel something.

'After a while, though, I began to feel a lot more compassion for the men. I thought, at least I can be myself but they never can. A lot of Arabs, for instance, are *conditioned* to be big macho men. Right from the day they're born they're not allowed to show their weakness or their feelings. Women have to take the responsibility for this as well. They put a lot of pressure on boys and men about how they should be, how they should measure up. And men feel they're living a total lie. A prostitute is probably the only person with whom they can be themselves.

'What men are showing you at the end of the day is how much they want to be loved and accepted for who they are. I no longer feel the hatred I used to – more pity and sympathy. You can't help feeling sorry for them, trapped in their little fantasies like flies in a jam pot. There's the Englishman who likes to wear high heels and wants you to piss on him. There's a little Greek guy, a billionaire shipping merchant, who liked two of us at once – a little lesbian act. He stood us in the room, naked, and got us to hold each other's nipples. He liked to smoke a cigarette, kiss you and blow the smoke into your mouth! There was a cabinet minister who liked to wear nothing but a boater hat and socks and have cream cakes thrown at him – that would make him come! There was a client who was so rich he had no friends at all, only parasites and hangers on. I tried to make a friendly relationship with him just to prove someone could like him for himself.

'In fact most people have rather bizarre taste when it comes to sex. Who's to say what straight sex is anyway? It's just a pity they can't do it with their wives. I've come to see that a lot of men feel terribly rejected by their wives, even the most powerful men in the world. They feel trapped, frustrated, enraged. You become a kind of a counsellor working out all their shit for them. But then what happens to it? You're left carrying it, that's what! And in the end you feel like a public toilet. I had one very emotionally disturbed client, for instance, who really freaked me out. All he would talk about when having sex was his fantasy of seeing his wife raped and killing his wife and children.'

Natasha had highlighted one of the most difficult problems a prostitute has to face. Any psychotherapist dealing with very disturbing material from a client will always be able to take it to a supervisor for discussion and advice. She is a member of a respected profession and can call on full back up and support. She can discharge the polluted energy and thereby not become contaminated by it. A prostitute is all alone at the end of the line.

'I never saved a penny of the money I made,' said Natasha. 'It burnt a hole in my pocket. Must be something to do with guilt – I'd spend it like there was no tomorrow. I gave the most extravagant gifts to old school friends, I'd take cabs everywhere, take my friends on holiday. But the reality was such a lonely life. Nobody in my family knew and my sister really looked up to me thinking I had a glamorous lifestyle. I could never tell them. I'd sleep until the middle of the afternoon and the day would be gone. I'd read Mills and Boon love stories and lose myself in that fantasy world. It was as if the romantic illusion was the other side of what I was doing.

'The beginning of the change for me came about through a dream. I dreamt a bomb went off and my whole family died. I found myself going up these white stairs, rejoicing that I was going to heaven but when I got there I realized my Dad wasn't there. He'd gone to hell for committing suicide. I wanted to be with him so I found myself running down the stairs which became dirty and black, to be greeted by the devil in a nightclub scene. Some guys grabbed me to rape me and the devil said, "Leave that till later." Then I saw my Dad as I'd seen him last which was when he was dead. He was in a massive double bed, lying there and I went to sleep beside him. Another couple were also in the bed holding hands and the devil told me I had to give the guy a blow job. I was crying and he was crying. His semen was dirty and it smelt and all I could think of was my Dad lying there with no emotions. He was just dead. And the devil said, "This is it. You've made your bed, now lie in it for all eternity!"

'It woke me up to starting to think about my life. I knew I had to let go of the myth of the perfect family and the fantasy that I was somehow going to be able to save them. I came to Angel and with her help I've been able to piece myself together again. My mother still doesn't know, but I've told a couple of friends and almost immediately noticed the difference in the way I was interacting with them.

'I want to contradict people's idea of us – that we're just very shallow, "good time girls". I want to say, "Wait a minute, that isn't me! I've got a brain, I can talk." If you get caught up in a web of lies you never get any self-knowledge. Prostitution takes up your whole life and you can't become a complete person with all your different qualities. It's scary to risk rejection but once you open yourself and let people know you care or you've failed they can be more open about their own failings or secrets. I never used to see it like that, I was so guarded. I feel more childlike now, more trusting and I'm not ashamed of it. I no longer fear that people will take advantage.'

Natasha is now working as a creative special-effects make up artist for television and modelling, trying to make a name for herself in a very competitive field. 'If I was really brave, I'd like to do something environmental, or go to a Third World country and help people. I'd get my priorities straight and realize that nice clothes and a comfortable life style are not that important. I think I have a strong helping, caring instinct so, who knows? Human beings never learn the easy way.'

Another member of the group is Zulema, a small, pretty, Turkish Cypriot woman. She also agreed generously to share her story in the hope that one day all prostitutes will be able to stand tall and the stigma will become a thing of the past.

She was raised in a strict, traditional family where women had no rights outside the home. 'I was brought up to believe that my virginity was the most important thing on earth and if I were to lose it before getting married I was immediately a prostitute anyway. Right back when

I *was* still a virgin, if I came home late from school or anything I would be called a prostitute by my mother. "I know what you're destined to be – slut!" she'd scream. I was the target for everyone's anger, also the embodiment of all their fantasies, hopes and frustrations. They wanted a perfect lump of clay they could mould and shape and be proud of. If they couldn't, I was worth nothing. They wanted me to be a doctor and a virgin. They would choose a man for me. I could see all along what hypocrites they were. Where they went wrong, I wasn't supposed to. Nobody saw *me*. There wasn't a me, only a projection of them.

'Then the man I was in love with got married to someone else. In despair and revenge I lost my precious virginity, my main bargaining tool, to the first guy who happened along. I threw it away on purpose.

'I think I was very brave and very foolish, but I definitely did the right thing. Everything I'd been warned off I had to try. I needed to assert that I wasn't going to live by other people's ideas of who I should be. I would be who I was, whatever that might be, and take my chances. I had to destroy and rebuild and find out for myself.'

Angel and Zulema did their first job together. Scared, excited, egging each other on, flirting with the fantasy of being women of the world, they picked up a couple of guys in a hotel lobby. 'We were playing a part, being daredevils, thinking we were so clever, using men, getting money but we were actually branding ourselves. Inside we felt terrible and bit by bit we bought into the stereotype of what a prostitute is. We took on the whole of society's scorn. Anyone who goes on doing it has to build a wall around themselves. It gets higher and higher, walling off your most sensitive side until you can't see out anymore.'

Zulema worked for a while as a hostess, then spent over three years being, in her own words, 'a sugar daddy's bimbo'. 'I was fond of the old guy, but I felt it was a worthless life. I'd sit in front of the mirror for hours because my life consisted of making sure I always looked perfect. I was just a doll and I'd dress up for him and let him show me off to his friends. The worst part was him expecting love or passion from me. I just wanted his money. He had plenty after all and I resented having to give anything in return. I just wanted a father figure who would spoil me and I added sparkle to my life by double-crossing him.

'I know how horrible this sounds now, but I think it came out of the hypocritical values I was brought up with – seeing sex as a bargaining tool, a woman's only weapon.' After that relationship came to an end Zulema got a job working for an up-market call girl agency. She was in great demand, particularly with Middle Eastern clients, and spent her time being jetted out to exotic locations.

'There was one typical occasion when I went on a fabulous trip to the

Bahamas. The entire top floor of the best hotel had been booked for the Saudi prince, his guests and bodyguards. You had to have a special key to enable the lift to stop at that floor. I was picked up at the airport by a chauffeur-driven white limousine. It felt quite glamorous, but I'm sure people were saying, "Oh look! Here come the whores." I had my own suite and could go shopping in the afternoon, but ultimately the money isn't worth anything if you don't like the company.

'The routine went like this: the prince would rest in the afternoon, so we had to get ourselves ready for about 9.30 to go out for a meal. There were three or four carloads of entourage plus three or four carloads of bodyguards with walkie talkies. We took up about half the restaurant and we'd party all night. Until the prince decided he wanted to sleep, nobody, but nobody, was allowed to go to bed. We'd be there night after night laughing at his stupid jokes. Then we'd sleep till noon, get in a line and trot off down to the beach where there was a tent like a living room with oriental carpets and beds and a buffet with waiters and bodyguards. I'd look enviously at the nice looking hunky ordinary guys on the beach and then look at what I was with and I'd think, Oh God!

'I didn't realize it at the time, but I was really screwed up. I got totally confused by the double life I was leading and I felt dead inside. I wanted to die and I bombed myself out on drugs. I think this happens to a lot of women on the game – the self-destruct mode takes over. I came here to Angel and it was like being in quicksand, all of us were in the same boat, grabbing at each other for support. But we've come through. I came to the conclusion that the lies and self-deception were the most damaging thing of all. I don't think you can start to get better until you can face the truth.

'For instance, some guys like to put the money discreetly in your bag, which suits me fine. I never liked the bit where they hand it over, especially if it's been someone that you've really liked and you've been able to pretend for a while, because it brings it home to you what you are. Once when I was on a first booking from a new madam, the guy did just that. When I got back I realized he'd cheated me. The madam was furious. "Why didn't you count it, you stupid girl?" she said. I replied I didn't like to, I was too embarrassed. "You what?" she screamed. "You take your knickers off for the guy, but you're too embarrassed to count the money!" and she was right. I was pulling the wool over my own eyes.

'The other big moment of truth came for me when Monica, a good friend who was also on the game, got cancer. She was thin and frightened and alone, worried about money and losing her house. Even though she'd lost all her hair from chemotherapy she still went out on a few jobs, wearing a wig over her bald head and a plaster stuck over the tube where she had her chemo. I helped her out as much as I could and collected a bit from some of the girls, but it wasn't enough. So I asked some of my clients – billionaires – quite a few of whom had slept with her, if they could come up with a couple of thousand pounds so she could have some peace of mind and get well. Not one of them came up with a penny. They couldn't give a toss, her family couldn't give a toss and shortly after she died. She was only 25.'

The women in the group are brave and loving. They are discovering ways to help each other explore and clarify their situations, ways of making difficult, life-changing decisions. Each helping the other to view herself from a more constructive viewpoint and, most importantly of all, each giving the other confidence and the chance to be listened to and taken seriously.

I remember when I did the training course at London Lighthouse to become part of their support network for people with AIDS, someone said, 'If a child is made fearful within itself, it holds back its true emotions. If we are not allowed to express our true self, the self we express becomes false. Fear, not hate, is the opposite of love. If we cannot feel or express love, we feel fear. We become afraid of life. Unable to love ourselves or even believe we are worth loving, we begin to doubt the very existence of love or happiness and therefore we become subtly self-destructive.'

NINE

'I've had more pricks than a second-hand dart board!'
'Molly of Tulse Hill' – Retired old male prostitute

My friend Charlie, one of the team workers attached to a health advisory project in the Midlands, did his thesis on prostitution while he was at university. He travelled all around the country and interviewed over 4,000 prostitutes, both male and female. (A sobering 86% of whom had spent time in local authority children's homes and many were abused before and during that time.) 'What surprised me most,' he said, 'was how many men were on the game. Quiet, well-spoken, highly educated men who charge high fees but who can be depended upon not to resort to blackmail, and with whom it would not be an embarrassment to be seen.'

He reckoned that for every hundred girls peddling their wares on street corners, there are a hundred unobtrusive male prostitutes, of all ages, offering their services to both heterosexual and homosexual clients. Students, university graduates, some married, some with other jobs, they are almost invisible and the police hardly know of their existence.

One guy who works for a big male escort agency has a mobile telephone and can be anywhere within an hour. He has full military uniform complete with thunderflashes. Another only has one regular punter who pays him a fortune to dress up in a schoolboy's football kit several sizes too small. He then drives all the way out to Watford where there is a football pitch near the motorway exit. The man only has to kick the football around and pretend to be having a practice session while the punter hides in the bushes and masturbates.

Another man, now retired, was a whore for years, right into his fifties, servicing women clients, mostly rich Jewish widows in the Knightsbridge area. He always visited the women in their own homes and since the hydraulics of his own equipment were as capricious as most men's, he carried with him a briefcase containing a selection of dildos and vibrators. He was very discreet and presentable, drove a Maserati and lived in a beautiful flat. He made his clients feel attractive and cared for.

They were all in love with him, but his own satisfaction was obtained by dating prostitutes and never paying for sex.

I realized how little I understood about prostitution from a male perspective. If male prostitution is so widespread, why is it so difficult to think of it in the same way? I talked about this with Sophia and her theory is that prostitution in women is inseparable from how their honour is perceived; honour equals chastity and any transgression leaves the miscreant beyond the pale. But prostitution in men taps a different well of primitive reactions. Male honour is associated, not with sexual restraint, but with protecting his mother.

As a society we fear 'penetration'. It symbolizes conquest, rape, plunder, infiltration, destruction of the race. A man's role is to prevent penetration of his own community, his territory, his womenfolk. Whores who subject themselves to repeated penetration are therefore symbols of invasion and contamination and any man who takes another man's penis into himself, who passively allows anal sex, who lets himself be pierced, lanced, shafted, is a terrible threat to the established order. He is like a neuter, a non-person, which is why homosexual men become the targets for so much irrational hatred, persecution and oppression.

To leave men out, as most books on prostitution do, would merely widen the rift. So, without trying to come to any conclusions, I wanted to give some space to men. After all, without them the oldest profession would never have existed. These are the voices of punters, both gay and straight, gigolos, rent boys, trans-sexuals and male escorts who have courageously and generously agreed to share their stories.

I met Chris at a cafe in Soho. A mutual friend introduced us, then left us to have a sandwich together and a talk. Chris is a raggedy, stubbly, 24-year-old man with scruffy, fair hair and very narrow, weasel eyes which give him the air of a watchful, practised predator. He was very friendly and open, though, and keen to impart the impression that he's not in the least bit ashamed of his life or damaged by it so far, and is proud of having become so self-reliant.

Chris's mother left home, abandoning him, when he was a baby and he hates her with a deep, abiding bitterness. All he knows is that she is, or was, a prostitute. He has no wish to know her or to find her. He was an only child and his grandparents looked after him until the age of four when he went to live with his father. For a while, there were just the two of them and Chris remembers a brief happy time when his Dad taught him to read. However this all ended abruptly when his father remarried and very soon after had a baby daughter with the new wife. From that moment on Chris was rejected and became the family scapegoat. It was a violent household. His father used to beat his stepmother and when Chris, as a little boy, used to try to stop it, he would get beaten too.

It was an environment from which to escape as soon as he could survive on his own. At the age of 13 he began meeting men at the local gents' toilet and quickly learned how to capitalize on his assets, looking very small and young for his age. As soon as he realized how much money he could earn – £300 a week – he left home and thereafter didn't see his father again until he was 21. He had to prove and is still proving that he doesn't need anyone. He always felt he was much smarter than the rest of the family and wanted to dissociate himself from them. His sister also started prostituting herself from the age of 13 when a neighbour gave her £5 every Saturday to go to his house and have sex with him. 'She knew exactly what she was doing,' said Chris, 'and used to give me a couple of quid to keep quiet about it. Within a couple of years she became a heroin addict and went to London to work as a hooker to support her habit. Then one day she and her boyfriend did over a punter, stole his cheque book and cheque card and got picked up by the police.' Chris's first trip to London was to visit his sister in Holloway prison. She is now off the game, so she says, and just about to get married, but Chris is not very close to her.

Once down in London, he decided to stay, living on his wits, turning tricks. Chris never worked for anyone else or for an agency, but picked up men in bars and parks. He never consented to penetration and only did oral sex if he felt like it. 'I'm not gay,' he said, 'but in my teens I had a very potent sex drive. Going on the game provided an outlet for my exhibitionism, assertiveness and emergent need to gain some sort of control in a world full of treacherous adults.'

He enjoyed the power he felt over his clients, most of whom were very pathetic and got their excitement from being humiliated. 'One man liked to drive to some woods and be ordered to strip naked and run through the stinging nettles!' The only request Chris refused to carry out, because it upset him so much, was when a guy wanted a metal rod to be inserted in his penis and then attached to a battery to give him an electric shock. Because Chris wouldn't do it, the man did it himself and Chris had to watch and to listen while the man screamed. It really freaked him out, he said, shaking his head slowly, his little red, watery eyes reflecting the horror and disbelief of the memory.

The whoring went on for three years. Chris never saved any money, but blew it all on taking his friends out to Pizzaland, 'the ultimate gesture of generosity and high living for us at that time!' he said, laughing. One night he broke one of his cardinal rules and got in a car with two men. One beat him and raped him anally while the other held him down and watched. Then they threw him out of the car by the side of the road. He has no proof, but he's sure they were two plain-clothes policemen because he's seen them since. He was in a terrible state and phoned a gay curate he knew who had been kind to him and never asked for sex. The man let him stay until he'd recovered from his ordeal. He made up his mind after that to get off the game and went to live in Spain for a while.

We ordered some more coffee and he told me something that made me ache with sadness. Sometimes while walking around the streets of Barcelona he would find himself compelled to pick up the oldest, ugliest, most grotesque prostitutes he could find. He was drawn to them with a macabre fascination. Usually these older women preferred not to undress, but to take off as little as possible, do the business and get back on the streets again. Chris's kick was to make them undress completely while he watched sadistically, impassively, never touching them but enjoying their humiliation. Sometimes he would masturbate.

He became increasingly worried about the neurotic relationships he formed with women and with the uncontrollable violence he felt surging within his guts so much of the time, particularly if a woman left him. He started hitting his girlfriend and once nearly killed her. This so frightened him that he decided to get psychiatric help and went into therapy for a year. He has pushed himself to the limit on every type of drug, he has been addicted to fruit machines, losing hundreds of pounds a week, he drinks far too much but his sense of self-preservation is very strong and somehow, in the middle of all this pain, he has managed to care for himself and to survive. He hasn't much sympathy for weaker individuals who fall by the wayside. 'No self-discipline,' he shrugs dismissively.

Chris hasn't completely given up on the human race yet, but the things he has seen are imprinted with dreadful indelibility on his mind and his own wounds run very deep. He was telling me about the heavy S/M scene that exists in some other European countries, Spain and Germany in particular. There, there are some really terrible places, much worse than anything in this country, for those with the stomach for it. If I was disturbed by the beating of Molly and Ursula, at least you could say they were there of their own free will and for their own reasons. These women are drug addicts, abducted children or hapless Third World prostitutes. At one establishment Chris went to, men come to torture women, drive nails through their labia, attach electrodes to their clitorises. Pornographic films are made of these sessions which find their way onto the English black market. A typical smuggling ruse is to record them on top of a normal commercial video, leaving the first ten minutes or so of the original film in case the customs officials see it. There's apparently an enormous international market for these horrors and the more extreme and sick they are, the more people come to accept and expect, constantly seeking ever more depraved fantasies.

Chris has tried to confront and deal with the horrible things he's seen and the bad things that have happened to him in the only way he knows how, by staring them in the face rather than by splitting off from them and pretending they never existed. He says that if you can 'get your head round your existence and meet it face to face', you will survive relatively unscathed. He is surprisingly uncynical about life and kept wanting to make it clear that he does not feel a victim. Nor does he feel prostitution has damaged him. 'It's not so much what happens to you, but how you reconcile it, how you perceive it.'

Chris now lives with his current girlfriend who does not know about his encounters with the gross Spanish prostitutes. He likes to keep a few secrets, he says.

His story reminded me of a pamphlet entitled, 'The Psychopathology of Prostitution', in which Edward Glover writes: 'The choice of prostitution as a profession is determined by the early history of infantile sexual impulse ... an unconscious desire to obtain revenge for neglect.'

* * *

David I have known for fifteen years. I thought I knew him quite well, which only goes to show how little of real importance ever gets exchanged in normal social intercourse. When he heard I was writing this book he volunteered to talk about his experiences of going to a prostitute as a client. I have been very touched by how, as soon as they know about my interest, men have wanted to open their secret cupboards. It is as if by proximity to prostitutes I have acquired something of their ability to contain the dangerous shadows that lurk within and there is an instant feeling of relief at being able to be real.

David began by filling in some childhood background to explain why his sexual development had been retarded and problematic. His father, having once attempted suicide by purposely crashing his car, finally succeeded in killing himself with a shotgun when David was 20. It was David who found him with his brains blown out. At the inquest it came out that his father had been awaiting trial on charges of gross indecency with a sailor in the back of a cab.

The shame and trauma of this tragedy had major repercussions in the family. For David it followed years of English public school sexual suppressions, perversions, homosexual experimentations and confusion. David had no clear idea where his sexual orientation lay. Apart from some schoolboy homosexual fumblings, he hadn't even managed to masturbate successfully by the age of 21 so he decided to get laid by a pro. It was a dismal failure as he chose the first hooker he saw on a street corner and she was cold, hard and mercenary, taking his money and fobbing him off. The same thing happened the next time.

Still a virgin, he made a respectable marriage to a woman with as many sexual problems as himself and managed to father two children before their ill-starred union fell apart. David found himself increasingly obsessed with the fantasy of cross-dressing. What he longed for was the opportunity to act out the fantasy in a safe environment. His attempts to go to prostitutes for this were also humiliating flops.

He told me of a strange and interesting dream that he had around this time: in it he dresses up in lovely, silky, sweet-smelling clothes. He looks like a beautiful woman when he has them on – not the grotesque, hairy transvestite he usually sees in the mirror. A man enters the room and makes ardent love to this desirable woman. David realizes that the man is also himself – a strong, potent, virile, manly man. The two conflicting sides of his nature become one.

David's homosexual explorations as an adult man, during the time of his second marriage, were also less than satisfactory. 'It was too easy,' he says. 'For me, homosexuality is the effortless option. To settle for what I know and understand would be the coward's way. But to confront the "other", the awesome, the fathomless, the unknown, is the challenge I want to face and it's very frightening.'

What came out of the conversation was his sense of deep disappointment in his encounters with prostitutes. There was always an enormous gulf between expectation and reality which only served to reinforce his isolation and sexual confusion. He longs for a true synthesis between his masculine and feminine natures. Obsessively and repeatedly acting out his cross-dressing fantasies is a joyless treadmill and ultimately he feels he can only find wholeness and peace from all the torments he has endured when he can understand them and break free of their tyranny. He still finds it terribly hard to admit his confusion, to ask for information, to share worries and to acknowledge failure. He still doesn't know what he really wants. Any relationships he has with women tend to founder on the rocks of pressure of performance. He is obviously very easily 'castrated' and tends to choose strongly castrating women for partners.

He has vainly tried to reconcile many outlandish and contradictory ideas about female sexuality – from wanton slut who can't get enough to prim, Victorian lady for whom sex is a distasteful marital obligation. He vacillates from one to the other and doesn't know which one to trust, which makes him nervous and fearful. He is both jealous and furious that women appear to have it so easy – they don't have to *do* anything. Men have to do all the work and carry all the anxiety, while women mock them by just lying there evaluating their prowess.

What he finds exciting is the stereotypical whorish look, lots of make up, tight trashy clothes, fishnet stockings, but the ladies he marries are elegant, uptight ball-breakers. He frets about the size of his penis and its unreliability. He worries about the low intensity of his sex drive and the infrequency of desire. He feels guilty about his fetishes and fearful that he will never be able to live up to some arbitrary 'norm'.

David is not an untypical punter and about as far-removed from the popular idea of a salivating, kerb-crawling brute as it is possible to be. He is a gentle father and a man of great artistic sensibility. Our culture does not assist any of us much in acquiring accurate sexual information. Men, in particular, seem to be victims of the myth that male sexuality is simple, straightforward and problem free. They are meant to be driven by lust and perfectly happy so long as they are getting enough. There is no room in this myth for ignorance, anxiety, lack of initiative, unreliable potency or homosexuality. The penises of popular mythology are impossibly large, rock hard and inexhaustible. They are battering rams forever trying to leap unfettered from behind straining flies. As Bernard Zilbergeld writes in his fine book, *Men and Sex*, 'Somehow the humanity of the penis has got lost.' The right prostitute would find David a very rewarding client. I was quite tempted to take him on myself. This is the side of the business I would enjoy.

* * *

Claire is absolutely a woman in every respect, apart from the fact that for fifty-five years she was a man, fathered three sons and has just become a grandmother. Her skin is soft, her voice a perfectly convincing alto, her gestures, body postures, pink dungarees and white sandals, soft blonde hair are all completely feminine. Only her big, strong hands betray her former identity. She was once a leading actor with the Bristol Old Vic and played Hamlet in a touring production. Now since her surgery only eight months ago, she produces a little magazine for the Gender Dysphoria Trust (formerly Shaft!) and devotes her efforts to trying to merge imperceptibly with the mass of womankind. No drag queen excesses for her. 'The greatest compliment anyone can pay me is not to notice me,' she said.

Claire has always been a prostitute even while she was married and occasionally used to do double-act displays as a man with Helen Buckingham in the days of Rossetti Garden Mansions. How significant that the whore was the first facet of her womanhood to find expression. In the Dark Ages, as she calls her pre-operative period, she once received some healing from a clairvoyant at a spiritualist church. The woman told her that she was most unusual because there seemed to be two people in her body. This insight was very helpful to her and a confirmation of what she had always known.

She described to me how during the operation the core of the penis is removed and a new vagina is formed from the skin of the scrotum. She doesn't lubricate like a woman and the inside of the vagina remains slightly hairy but apart from that it's perfectly serviceable. On a cruise ship recently she tried it out for the first time and picked up a man leaning over the railings in the classic time-honoured Bette Davis way. They went back to his cabin and Alfredo undressed her, apologizing for being rather small. ('He wasn't, he was perfectly sweet,' she said.) He wanted to enter her from behind so she bent over the bunk thinking, 'Oh God! He's going to find out. He's going to say, 'That's not a real one,' but he didn't. He pulled out just before coming and Claire's first thought was, Oh the dear man, he doesn't want to get me pregnant! Her second thought was that her hairy vagina had probably given him a bit of a shock.

After all the years of waiting, sex with a man proved a bit of an anti-climax. Claire has just entered into a lesbian relationship and finds another woman much more sensitive to her needs. Having been a heterosexual, albeit reluctant, male until last August she now finds herself in the puzzling predicament of not knowing which sexual preference she has, so she's experimenting. I thought both she and her ex-wife with whom she has remained on very good terms were immensely brave. Claire would like to publish an account of her life, but is biding her time until her youngest son, only 12 and still at boarding school, is old enough to be able to cope with the publicity and possible ridicule.

* * *

'If life gives you a lemon, make lemonade,' said Roz, pulling a wry face. I was talking to her in the foyer of a discreet hotel in Marble Arch where we sat taking tea and thin cucumber sandwiches. When I'd asked her on the phone how I would recognize her, she had said in a booming baritone, 'I'm 6 feet 3 inches and have a mane of red hair.' But nothing prepared me for her appearance. She is indeed 6 feet 3 inches, and twenty stone in weight, an unruly explosion of hormones dressed in a horizontally striped rugby shirt, voluminous black elasticated trousers, a black leather rocker's jacket and big square-toed lace-up policeman's shoes with a mop of matted cherry-coloured hair like a joke shop clown's wig, all topped off by a red beret worn flat on top.

She arrived in a breathless fluster being an hour and a half late, although she had phoned the hotel to warn me. She started by saying, 'How much has Sophia told you about me?' and when I said not a lot, she proceeded to talk for three hours barely pausing for breath and only moderately tailoring the saga to the questions I interjected.

Hers is an extraordinary story. He had been a bright, sensitive boy from a working-class family with one sister five years younger. Even from about the age of 10 or 11 he knew that he was trapped in the body of the opposite sex. There was no one in his childhood in whom he could confide his feelings of confusion and rage. In search of the alternative subculture, he made contact with the gay and transvestite clubs in his home town and during his teens found out about the possibility of having a sex-change operation.

He got good grades in his 'A' levels and decided to take up the offer of a place at Oxford, took a degree in English and did two years post-graduate work, but never completed his doctorate. Around this time, a friend, a 'post-operative' trans-sexual who'd had the operation at the age of 19, invited Roz to come with her to Chicago. By now Roz was living and dressing as a woman and had been taking female hormones for some time resulting in small breast development. He took a job as a topless waitress in a trans-sexual bar and soon learned about whoring from the other 'girls'.

They taught him how to do 'trick sex' (which usually only works with drunk punters). The technique is to strap the penis out of sight or invert it by pushing it up inside and then to wear a pubic wig to complete the deception. Punters are encouraged to have anal intercourse ('because it's my time of the month') or get fobbed off by being clenched between tightly gripped thighs. Apparently the punters that seek out trans-sexual prostitutes for sex play along with the subterfuge but know perfectly well what they are getting. They actually want the sexual ambiguity. Also, Roz theorizes, if something goes wrong and they can't get an erection or have an orgasm, it's easy to deflect criticism from their manhood and blame the whore for not being a proper woman.

I asked her what this headlong dash into prostitution straight from

Oxford was all about. Two reasons figured prominently. The first was immense guilt for having had a privileged education (Roz is also embarrassed about speaking with a posh Oxbridge accent), resulting in the desire to discharge some kind of debt to society by associating himself with an outcast subculture. The second was that identifying with the whore archetype and actually being *paid* to be a female sexual partner was a great affirmation of his/her womanliness. Also to share the scapegoating and social shunning endured by prostitutes gave credibility to her intention and proved her worthy to join the ranks of women. According to Roz, she was very successful at hustling despite not being exactly a raving glamour puss. She had a pretty poor opinion of most punters ('jerks'), but never felt bad about herself as a prostitute.

Roz had two sojourns in America; the first time she had to work merely to survive, the second time she was trying to save money towards the sex-change surgery she longed for. All the while she was mostly attracted to men, but never felt gay. Her specialities were threesomes with another prostitute, a little light sado-masochism and lesbian shows. Eventually, at the age of 33, after years of hormones, electrolysis to remove unwanted hair and other preparatory work, Roz had the operation. All kinds of dreadful things went wrong after the surgery – bladder infections, damaged urethra, suppurating skin grafts – and she nearly died. Her hormone production went haywire and this is when she put on six stone in weight and was forced to become celibate for years because the wounds refused to heal properly.

The saddest part of Roz's story is the apparent rejection she has suffered by the radical feminist movement with whom she yearns to be identified. Their ungenerous party line seems to regard all men as the enemy and trans-sexuals as highly suspect impostors, as unwelcome as any other male. Even the feminist publishing houses such as The Women's Press refuse to publish books by trans-sexuals, or so they told Roz when she tried to get her novel accepted, a novel about a trans-sexual hustling in Chicago in the 1970s.

The other great irony in Roz's story is that although since the operation she, too, has tried penetrative 'vaginal' sex with a man, in recent years she has become a 'lesbian identified trans-sexual' and no longer fancies men at all. She has just begun a relationship with a woman and no longer works as a prostitute, but earns her living as a publisher's reader, book reviewer and feature writer for a number of journals. If I found the twists and turns of her sexual roller coaster very confusing to try to follow, God knows how she's managed. There can't be many people who have had sex with a woman as a man, sex with a man as a man, sex with a man as a woman and sex with a woman as a woman. Her elderly parents, now in their seventies, have found it all very difficult, although Roz's Mum tries her best to be loving and understanding.

I was so moved by Claire and Roz's predicaments and by that of other pre- and post-operative trans-sexuals. Most of us have such a hard time anyway as women trying to integrate the various factions of our being. They started their quests so much further back down the line – as prisoners in the wrong body.

* * *

Roland, the gigolo, has suffered no such doubts about his gender. In fact his manhood has been his chief livelihood and earned him thousands of pounds in his time. 'Hi honey, I'm your blind date,' he said in a seductive, brown velvet voice when he rang me up. A friend had given him my number knowing that I wanted to meet him. I was rather glad my husband hadn't answered the phone. We made an assignation and my heart skipped a couple of beats when we met – he *is* an extremely attractive man. The son of Jamaican parents, he was born and brought up in London's East End. As he says himself, he grew up with a split personality identifying wholly with the white kids who were his friends. 'I was a Cockney, a likeable bloke, one of the lads, a true Englishman. I supported West Ham and had designs on being a professional footballer.'

Roland was selected for the Chelsea Boys team, but his parents, with traditional ideas about the value of education, disapproved and blocked his chances. Angry and determined to get back at his mother, he dropped out of school as soon as he could and got a job as an apprentice machinist for £8.50 a week. 'Naturally, most of my older friends were part-time villains with nice clothes and big cars. Their lifestyle seemed much more attractive, so I started hanging out with them in pubs and clubs, plotting, planning; I got caught up. The attraction was there, it was like a magnet. For me, looking back, I needed that. I needed the whole way of life and the rebellion it represented. People were always telling me I was bad right from an early age so I thought I might as well live up to it.

'The type of crimes we was doing wasn't major league stuff. I was never nasty, never hurt no one. We got our aggression out at football matches. I was part of the "Intercity Firm" and we used to organize to fight the other gangs of football supporters. I wasn't really keen on the serious warfare as I was starting to worry about how I looked and becoming interested in girls, but I did happen to get caught up in one serious fight where a bloke got stabbed. I was accused of being the ringleader and charged with attempted murder. I got two years Borstal which wasn't really a deterrent at all. A lot of people I knew were in there and I was proud to be one of them. It was a manhood badge. I could come out and say, "I been inside."

'Now that I've gone to college, got my degree, written my thesis on "Why do young blacks underachieve?", I can understand what motivated me. I'm not bitter, let's get that straight. I did what I did because I wanted to. I made a conscious decision.' He talks now with insight about how all cultures have their own adolescent male rites of passage: fighting, hunting, yelling, jumping up and down, proving themselves. In past times you could grow out of it, get a job, settle down. 'But in today's economic climate where there aren't the jobs and high qualifications are called for, a lot of my friends felt they couldn't cut the ice in the straight world and they got trapped in it.'

'When I came out of Borstal, I wasn't interested in being a villain any more. I could see myself getting killed or killing someone and doing life. I knew I was better than that; I'd known it from an early age. I'd experimented, but I was wise enough to move on. I got a job, started hanging out with black guys and going to clubs.'

Roland's first contact with a 'Sugar Mummy', a 'woman of substance', was at Ronnie Scott's, when he was 18. She was attracted to him, bought him drinks, took him home to her lovely flat. He stayed a few nights and she used to give him money and drive him to work in the mornings. One day she said, 'This is ridiculous, I want what I'm paying for with me all the time.' 'Fair enough,' thought Roland, and moved in. He gave up work and thereafter she supported him.

'At first I felt completely out of my depth, but I'm a quick learner. I had to conform to an image. She had a picture in her head of how she wanted me to be. She took me out and bought me expensive clothes. A lot of people don't know about this, they think women never pay for sex,' he laughed. 'I've got a very different story to tell. Mind you,' he added, 'there's not so much of it now with AIDS. A lot of women are scared. I'm talking about fifteen years ago and all the guys I was meeting were doing the same thing. We were status symbols. For me it became a way of life. I wouldn't go with a woman who didn't have money. If they wanted my company, they had to pay for it. I had no respect for women at all. Even if a woman smiled at me I'd find myself thinking, "I wonder how much she's worth." I never felt degraded and never thought of myself as a male prostitute. Gigolo is a much nicer word for it. There was certainly no social stigma attached. When people found out what I did, they'd come up and ask me how they could get into it! Lots of men secretly have fantasies about being a gigolo.

'It was a strange world. These rich women would all be down at the clubs trying to nick each other's men. They'd come up to you and say, "I can give you more money than you're getting now." It was like a chain reaction. Once you had a woman taking care of you, none of us stuck faithfully to the same one. Money flowed like water. If I dented my car I'd sell it and buy another one. Once someone shunted me and I just abandoned the car in Hyde Park!'

There were pressures, however, particularly relating to sexual performance. 'I was very cocky in the beginning, and could go all night,' said Roland, 'but as I got older.... There was one woman, for instance, who I really liked. She used to have good cocaine and she bought me a Merc, but she just wanted me for sex and I couldn't get an erection with her. I started to get fed up with being a puppet. One night when I went out against her wishes she changed the locks on me and I was left with nothing. All the gold, jewels, clothes, keys to the car were inside.'

Undaunted he moved in with a girlfriend who worked at a massage parlour. 'I have to admit I had double standards. It was all right for me to be doing what I did with other women, but I didn't want any girl I was involved with doing it with other men. She wanted to work for a big Madam named Scarlet – classy clients, international assignments – and I was really against it at first, but she went ahead anyway. The first £1,000 on the table convinced me and I found I could live with it! I didn't see this as pimping because, after all, it was her choice and I never put pressure on her or put her in contact with a client, but of course I was living off her money and it gives me cold shudders now to think what I've been party to.

'I used to go to Cannes where all the top working girls go in the summer. It was a *Who's Who* of pimps and gigolos. We'd sit there, all Italians and blacks, for three or four months of the year, lounging about, playing backgammon, making sure they didn't spend all the money. You wouldn't believe how much money they earned! All in all, I lived with working girls for seven years but it was a limbo land and I started to realize that I needed something that was going to make me a whole person. I didn't feel whole. I was half a man.'

The moment of truth came in 1983 when Roland became involved in a traveller's cheque fraud and got arrested. It was only the fact that he'd always been keen on sport and had recently won the British Championships in karate that the magistrate saw fit to fine him and give him a two-year suspended sentence. 'I'd have been an idiot if I hadn't seen it as a second chance. I made vows and promises to God that I would never do anything like this again and I haven't. I needed to do something constructive, so I started to teach at a youth club in Bethnal Green. I had no formal qualifications, but I talked to a youth leader there who recognized that I could relate to kids.'

Roland started as a voluntary worker and after a while they put him on the pay roll. He got up to the status of Deputy Leader and, with great courage because he didn't feel adequate to the academic demands, decided to go back to school. 'Nobody believed I could do it. It was a real struggle. I had to learn a whole new game, attitudes, jargon, way of speaking. I had to do English 'O' level plus a couple of others before I could even get on the degree course.' It took four more years, but three weeks before I met him, Roland graduated with a degree in Child Psychology.

'I couldn't have done it without my experience of the low life. It gave me a real understanding and a lot of my work now is showing kids they have options – they don't have to go into crime. The youngsters are all terrific sports people, but so many of them have a chip on the shoulder about being black. That's nonsense. Everybody I've ever had to deal with has been white and it hasn't stood in my way. All this grievance business is out of date, it's old hat, long gone years back. "Stop whingeing!" I tell them. "If you really want to do something, you can. There are so many college courses where you can take plumbing or something. They *want* working-class kids so take advantage of it."'

Roland is now working for the borough of Camden as a Senior Youth Worker in charge of seven employees. He's been partly responsible for setting up a flat for young people, a safe house for kids at risk. 'My advantage is that I've got street cred; I can play both ends of the spectrum. I sympathize and I empathize. I'm not that far removed from them. I get impatient, but I don't give up. Things take time. I just want them to know they have a choice.'

All through his wild life, Roland has tried to be honourable about sending money home to support his three children, aged 14, 7 and four. 'Their mother is a girl who I've known since school. She had my baby when I was 18 and she's the one I'm living with now. She's stuck by me through everything. You might find this hard to believe, but I'm very much into family – not like some of my friends. We'll get married – although she's not pressuring me, the kids are! She's my common law wife anyhow. I've always been honest with her. I had to do what I've done and I've got no regrets. In the long run it should make me a better father. Now that my own eldest daughter is reaching the age of rebellion, I really hope I can find a way to talk honestly about my experiences with her. I just want her to know that you can't sit around waiting for The Big One all your life. If you make it happen, you can do anything.'

One of the army of neatly-suited, invisible male prostitutes is Stewart, a thin, nervous, young gay man who lives with his dog in a wretched bedsit. We sat cross-legged talking on his bed while he held the dog in his arms and spoke in a scarcely audible voice with his eyes fixed intently on his shoes.

'I was all alone in London with no money so I looked through *Gay Times* and saw an ad for an escort agency. A guy interviewed me and asked if I'd done massage. I said I'd never done anything and only had one boyfriend in my life, but I got the job. The first time they sent me out I was a nervous wreck. I hated it but I got home with £70 in my hand and soon got used to it.

'Most of my clients were lonely, plump, unattractive men staying in anonymous hotels out by Heathrow Airport. Mostly well-off, public school, stockbroker types, they just wanted the company of someone younger, that's all. I'd go in a suit carrying a briefcase so I didn't look too conspicuous. I did run-of-the-mill massage and hand relief. Sometimes they didn't want anything. One oldish chappie, an American, just poured me a drink and sat me down for a chat. He wanted to talk about politics. Another guy I used to see was leading a completely double life. He only phoned the agency when his wife was out visiting, then he'd pick me up from the station in a Range Rover and take me back to this huge house right out in the country, very posh. He wanted me to sit there while he put a dirty tape on and masturbated. His kids were asleep upstairs!

'Yet another was a Conservative MP who was publicly very anti-gay, voting in favour of Clause 28 and everything just to keep in with Maggie. What a hypocrite! It used to make me sad thinking about all the lies and the loneliness. I didn't despise the punters, I mostly felt sorry for them and a lot of them were really nice people. Often I came away feeling quite pleased I'd made someone happy. The whole male scene is so invisible. It's just not known about. For every woman on the game, there's a man doing it too.'

Stewart made me a cup of tea and opened a tin of food for his dog. When he relaxed enough to smile shyly, his worried face was transformed by sweetness. He ruffled the dog's ears and got a few ecstatic wags in return. Then he clouded over again. 'I saw a kiddie about 15 in the public toilets the other day,' he said. 'He was watching me for a while, just standing there. Then he came over. "You can have me if you've got a fiver," he said. I was horrified. "You'd better be careful," I told him. "I could have been a copper for all you know. Why don't you join an agency? Be safe. Work like this under a subway and you'll get bloody beaten up."'

Dennis Nilsen murdered fifteen boys at his two London flats. Most of them were never even reported missing. Nilsen selected them from a pub, a well-known pick-up place for rent boys which happens to be directly opposite an emergency night shelter for homeless young people. Far from the image of distraught parents weeping by the telephone anxious for news, these kids are often 'throwaways' more than 'runaways'. Nobody cares what happens to them. They gravitate to the big cities, particularly the kids with enough gumption to leave their horrendous home lives and try to survive on their wits. They get a buzz from the freedom, the risk, the danger and the power. This can be quite addictive and is often accompanied by denial of what they are doing, making them even more vulnerable to everything from murder to porn.

It was to try to offer some refuge for kids like these that Richie McMullin, an ex 'rent boy', and Father Bill Kirkpatrick, a worker priest, co-founded Streetwise. Many of the young people who come to Streetwise have been physically, emotionally and sexually abused in their early childhoods. A typical example is Alex. When he was nine years old his father murdered his mother. His father was then himself murdered in prison. Alex was taken into care, placed in a home and sexually abused by a care worker who paid him with gifts. His already damaged self-concept was reinforced and shortly after he began to 'rent'. He is a prostitute and a heroin addict and lives in a squat. He joined Streetwise about a year ago. As Richie McMullin says, 'Alex finds it difficult to be touched in any way and seems not to know the difference between safe and unsafe touch. He protects his gentle centre with an overly developed aggressive posture.' Alex says Streetwise has been the reason why he hasn't killed himself. But now, just 19 years old, he has been diagnosed HIV positive.

'One consequence of the exploitation and ill-treatment these young people have suffered is a longing for revenge,' says Richie McMullin. 'They are often unable to enter the job market. They lack the basic qualifications, social skills, a permanent address, decent clothes, confidence, self-respect, a track record of previous employment, ambition or hope for their future. If they have HIV they are still further disabled. But they also know that they hold the most powerful and dangerous weapon they've ever had. Power, maybe for the first time in their lives. They can kill somebody just by being with them. It's like magic. They are walking time bombs.'

Streetwise accept the kids unconditionally, making it clear that they do not always accept their behaviour. In accepting the individual and not the behaviour they help them discover that they can be separate from and therefore make choices about their behaviour. They are trying to establish a therapeutic community for young male prostitutes to alleviate some of the despair and begin to contain the problem.

Richie McMullin knows all about the despair first hand. After the constant terror and humiliation of his own violent childhood, the first time a man was kind to him, bought him an ice-cream, took him to the cinema, stroked his leg – it was a revelation and felt good. He accepted the invitation to go with the man and learned an important lesson. 'He thrust some money into my hands. He was so pathetic and for the first time in my life I felt the thrill of having an adult in my power. He'd touched me, that was it, and was scared of being found out.'

Of his father he says, 'I never knew his love and I grieve for it still. Never once did I see him happy and laughing. Never once did he talk with me about anything, walk in the park, go into a shop. He would talk at me but never with me. He spoke through his belt and I never understood a word.' He talked about the contrast between the unreal, insane, brutal world of his father and the beautiful, real world which existed inside him. When a policeman came to his school one day telling the children to beware of strangers in luxury cars offering them sweets and money and to always remember that their families were the only places of safety, Richie was puzzled. Nothing could have been less safe than his home where his father played sadistic games with him and always tricked him into giving the wrong answer so that he could belt him again. He felt himself drawn to the world of these mysterious strangers.

'Vengeful relish' is how he describes his mood of that time. 'I'd make them pay. It was a crazy kind of disintegrated rejection which drove me. I was coming apart and in a strange way what I was doing would keep me together.' His parents never asked him where the money came from which was a relief, but it also angered him. In his heart he wanted them to ask so he could tell them the truth. But they never did. When awful things happened he always blamed himself and when he was anally raped by two men it only confirmed his view of himself as scum.

'Each time I went out I hoped and prayed that I'd find myself. A self I could live with. Then I could bring it home and *be* it. More often than not, however, I brought home a depressed, fucked-up Catholic rent boy. I almost welcomed the notion of going crazy because that would be one way of explaining my fucked-up life to myself. Death was another alternative, although I didn't want to die. I just wanted the pain to stop.'

At the end of the first part of his autobiography, *Enchanted Boy*, he writes, 'I'd come to realize that my need to have sex for money with men was because in a way they loved me, cared for me, paid attention to me, wanted me. These men supplied everything I'd ever wanted.'

TEN

Angela and Shirley work together from a little flat in Neasden. Ever since they were raided by the police last year – an unspeakably humiliating experience – they are careful to keep on the right side of the law which states that a woman can work alone with a maid, but two working girls constitute a brothel. For the time being Angela is the maid, Shirley the hooker. The Vice Squad officer who stitched them up, still comes round to see Angela for sex on a regular basis. In fact he was sorry afterwards and realized that he'd created a lot of unnecessary trouble for them. He has given his word they won't be bothered again if they stay within the letter of the law and are nice to him. They don't mind him, but bitterly resent the stupidity of this law which prevents them from earning much more money and making better use of the premises. They invited me over to spend an ordinary working day with them. They would show me the ropes so that I would be able to deputize as Shirley's maid if ever Angela has to take her son to hospital.

Angela recently had a total hysterectomy which left her feeling very sore and lacking in energy. This is why she is 'maiding' for Shirley. She is married to a big oafish guy who knocks her about and has two beautiful sons aged six and eight, one of whom is physically disabled and spends a lot of time in hospital. She and Shirley worked together for twelve years at the Wigmore Club before it closed down and they decided to set up this little flat with one other woman, Charlotte, who has now quit the business. Angela's husband still doesn't know what she does. In fact he chooses not to know as he is glad of the money she brings in. He is a warehouse manager and gambles most of his wages. Angela's money is essential for keeping the family going. It's a hard life but she has a great fighting spirit, always cracking jokes and bouncing bravely back from the latest disaster. Sometimes her veneer of bravado wears a bit thin. Just as soon as she feels up to it, she plans to go back on the game herself, maybe from another flat with her sister as her maid.

The maid's job is not at all glamorous. She mustn't compete with the working girl in any way. On the day I came Angela was looking very plain, dressed in tracksuit pants, a sweatshirt and baseball boots. She wore no make up and dark glasses. She'd had a lot of trouble with post-operative discomfort and her face looked rather drained. She smoked heavily, started on the vodka at lunch time and answered the phone in an irritable voice with a standard patter: 'Hello, can I help you? I'm afraid I don't know any of the details I just answer the phone for the young lady.' (She put her hand over the mouthpiece, 'Sometimes they try to get you engaged in conversation about vital statistics and what services are on offer just so they can have a free wank!') 'The charges are £20 for the basic massage and any extras are negotiated at the time of your appointment. The young lady is 25 years old, long red hair, very attractive. We could fit you in at 3 o'clock.' She can't say anything specific for fear it might be a Vice Squad trap.

At least two-thirds of the men who book are only playing with the fantasy and don't bother to turn up, so she overbooks. It's a delicate balance. Sometimes they all turn up and it's a nightmare – one in the loo, one in the living room, one in the cupboard. Shirley reckons to earn about £200 per day and gives Angela £45. Rent is £60 per day and they always take Friday off to have a long weekend. They advertise in the local newspaper: 'Massage – Ring such and such.'

The phone rang constantly. A lot of time wasters, but about twenty bookings, seven of whom turned up. Shirley processes them in approximately twenty minutes, giving either massage and hand relief, 'french' or sex. When they ring on the doorbell the maid lets them in, shows them into the bedroom and invites them to make themselves comfortable. Then Shirley goes in, finds out what they want, fixes a price, comes out to hide the money in a safe place, goes back in and does the job.

Shirley arrived about 12.30. She was wearing a jogging suit and trainers, but quickly changed into a black and pink skin-tight aerobics outfit with pink high heels. She released her beautiful Titian-coloured hair from its ponytail and it fell in a pre-Raphaelite cloud about her shoulders. In between each client she sprints into the bathroom for a quick douche in the bidet. Sometimes there's a half-hour break for a cup of tea or a sandwich.

The bedroom is warm and cosy. There is nothing to differentiate it from any other fluffy pink suburban boudoir, apart from the roll of couch tissue freshly laid on top of the bed to save changing the sheets too often, and a pink bulb in the bedside lamp. Incense was burning and a Bach violin concerto playing softly on the portable cassette player. Shirley uses baby oil or talc for the massage and there is a little drawer with condoms in for the blow jobs and sex. She always takes her clothes off ('It makes them come quicker') and practically never has any trouble. Most clients are extremely docile and do as she says. She decides the boundaries – no kissing, no cunnilingus, no anal sex. She enjoys being in control, unlike in her personal relationships where she feels she is never in control and intimacy is very frightening for her.

Most of the clients are very ordinary, regular working-class guys – 9-5 office workers, building contractors, postmen on their rounds, etc. One who arrived early and had to sit for ten minutes with us in the living room was a surveyor, a married man, carrying a portable phone from which he'd rung up in his car. He made small talk about his kids and his summer holiday plans, stroked Angela's dog and stared at his shoes until it was his turn. Shirley says she much prefers working with these ordinary men. The rich and powerful types at the Wigmore often treated the women with disrespect in direct correlation with their bank balances, ordering them about, deriving pleasure from humiliating them.

Shirley, originally from Yorkshire, is an extremely sensitive, intelligent and articulate woman of 41. She supported herself through college, taking a degree in English, by working at the Wigmore. She has been married and divorced and has a 13-year-old daughter at a boarding school in Hertfordshire. At the moment she is not in a permanent, personal relationship and hasn't been for some time. This gives her a lot of freedom, but can also be lonely.

Shirley is very interested in the healing arts, seeing prostitution as being an associated profession. She is an accomplished tarot reader and, as a sideline, gives workshops on femininity and sexuality. Her own personal psychotherapy and some rebirthing work have helped her 'come out' to a certain extent and begin to feel proud of herself as a person. A childhood history of religious brainwashing and guilt about sex and sin have made it difficult for her to get over her core belief of lack of self-worth. Her elderly parents have no idea what she does, think she works in an office, never discuss it or show any interest. She told me the first time she was able to stand up in a workshop in front of 127 people and say, 'I am a hooker and I'm afraid that you won't want to know me once you know that,' she found that everyone liked and accepted her just as much, if not more. Slowly but surely more supportive people have come into her life, very different, again, from the days of the Wigmore Club where a deliberately fostered climate of competition and rivalry kept the women from becoming too close to one another.

The more I talked to Shirley the more I liked and admired her. I hope she feels proud and dignified, at least some of the time. She is really trying, like Sophia, to become a whole woman and live all her aspects. I also hope that a gentler climate will at last begin to facilitate a much greater coming together of women into a genuine, supportive sisterhood devoid of judgements.

Angela first got into the business because one of her sisters introduced her to it to pay off some debts. Her sister has since married a millionaire ex-client and managed total amnesia about her past to the extent of rather hurtfully dissociating herself from Angela. They were extremely close and shared everything; now she feels quite lonely, unable to tell anyone what she does for all the reasons women have to remain clandestine. If only prostitutes weren't so stigmatized they would love not to have to live under the constant strain of the double life. Angela's father pretends not to know his three daughters have been on the game. She longs for the comfort and relief of being able to confide all the frustrations, humiliations, humour and sadness of the job to her husband but he doesn't want to know either. 'I love him, don't get me wrong,' she says, 'but I don't have much respect for him.' She doesn't have much respect for any man and thinks they're 'basically all wankers'.

Angela has a regular client, Sid, whom she has been keeping at bay with some difficulty since her hysterectomy, a repulsive old boy of 78 who only started coming to her after his wife died. 'He has a big bulbous nose with a permanent dew drop on the end of it and his cock is in exactly the same condition!' said Angela. According to her, Sid is the biggest bore on two legs and quite insensitive to boot. The day after her operation when she was feeling shocked and sick he came to visit her. The first thing he did was make a grab for her breasts saying, 'How are my little titties?' He is very wealthy and generous, paying all her court costs when she was busted. She was entertaining him at the time but, of course, there were no charges against him. All the culpability is on the woman's side. He also finances her car and summer holidays. She told him she was separated from her husband and now is hoist on her own petard. She can't get rid of him because he'd tell all. She hopes he will peg out before long, though preferably not in delicto flagrante.

Just occasionally she 'gets off' on the job, as she says. A 5′4″ Indian lorry driver with B.O. was the best lover she ever encountered. She held her breath and had a wonderful time whereas her own husband is a boorish lover and doesn't seem to listen when she tells him what she would like.

Of the men who came between 12.30 and 5 pm, most were processed in twenty minutes. One took less than ten minutes. It's fairly relentless round: a wank, one straight sex, a wank, a massage, another wank, one 'french'. In between, Shirley runs to the bathroom, cleans her teeth, has a quick gargle and a wash. Once she kept a guy waiting for ten minutes in the bedroom while she ate a tuna fish sandwich. She grumbled about blow jobs giving you jaw ache and the fact that the spermicide nonoxynol-9 with which all condoms are now impregnated tastes so disgusting, numbs your tastebuds ('You can't even enjoy a cup of tea afterwards') and ruined the tuna fish sandwich. They are absolutely strict about condoms for french or sex, but lament the fact that a better tasting stuff has yet to be invented. Shirley often gets fed up with the job and asks herself, 'What am I doing this for?' but she also said, and Angela agreed, that there is definitely something addictive about the life: the money, the power and control, the flexible hours, being your own boss. Any woman who worked for a pimp was crazy they reckoned.

Only one client ever defeated Angela. He was a judge, 'an evil old bastard and very weird!', who produced a cut-throat razor and asked her to make tiny cuts all over his body. 'When he took his clothes off, he was completely covered from the neck down in scars, thousands of them. Then when he was bleeding everywhere he wanted you to pour cologne on him! I just couldn't do it. It made me sick. This guy used to hold really kinky, occult parties at his house where he kept photos and files on everyone who came so he could never be blackmailed. He told me that whenever he hears the evidence in child abuse cases or sentences a woman to prison he gets an erection under his robes. Can you believe it? These are the people that run this country!'

A week or so after my introductory day in Neasden I received a telephone call from Angela saying, 'I've found a punter who will talk to you, but you've got to be here 9.30 Wednesday morning.' Who on earth feels like having fluffy pink sex in Neasden at such an ungodly hour? Or any hour. The whole place is so ordinary. I have always imagined the need to mark some boundary between the commonplace and the kingdom of desire. 9.30! Angela sees to this chap herself. Would he want to talk before or after? After, I reckoned. Anyhow, he was already there when I arrived, having a cup of tea in the lounge. A central heating engineer with his work overalls on, he was understandably bashful but friendly. It was immediately apparent why he probably feels more confident paying for sex since he was completely covered, at least on the bits of him I could see, by a disfiguring skin condition.

'I'll just take Alf through,' said Angela, delicately, 'and then you can talk after.' She left me manning the phone with a little script to read in case I got any enquiries. I did get one. 'Hello, can I help you? The basic massage costs £20 and any extra treatment can be discussed at the time of your appointment.' He booked in for 12 noon, but I realized after he'd hung up that I'd forgotten to give him the address. Must do better. I read the *Guardian* for fifteen minutes until Angela reappeared followed by Alf with a smile on his face. He wasn't exactly voluble, answering most questions with a monosyllable, but he was willing. He'd been married thirty-four years ago at the age of 21 to his childhood sweetheart, a home economics teacher, but ever since the birth of their last child, his wife has refused to have sex with him. She never enjoyed it anyway and only saw it as a duty. He endured the frustration for many years, but one day saw Angela's ad in the local paper. He came along for a bit of relief and has been coming ever since. He is extremely loyal to Angela and visited her every day when she was in hospital. 'He's not like a punter,' says Angela. 'He's a friend. He knows I'm a prostitute and he pays me, but I can tell him anything.'

'I think they should legalize it,' says Alf. 'What harm is it doing? I know people say it's wrong, but a bloke's got to have a bit of relief. Personally I think there'd be a lot less child molesting.' Alf has a son in his thirties, a married daughter and two grandchildren. He'd come twice a week if he could afford it but once, at £40, is all he can manage. He has a strong sex drive, he says, but sometimes his erection dies on him. 'We try hard, don't we Alf,' says Angela. 'Very disappointing, but never mind, love, it happens to all men sometimes.' She patted his arm sympathetically.

While we were talking Sid phoned – Angela's old sugar daddy – to say he was on his way over. Angela made a face. 'Alf, here, knows all about him and all about my husband and kids, but Sid doesn't know about anything. He thinks he's the only man in my life. He's a right pain. He's a monumental bore. He's jealous and he's got no sense of humour. For Chrissake don't let him see you here!' Alf got to his feet and went off to work just as Sid came in. Sid, a doddery old chap with Parkinson's disease, plonked himself on the sofa. More cups of tea all round and Sid launched into one of his interminable monologues while Angela, behind his back, cast her eyes heavenward in an expression of extreme martyrdom. A much more common hazard in a prostitute's life than physical danger seems to be terminal boredom.

Angela had ordered, as a jokey birthday present for her landlord, a 'multiflex, variable speed, flesh coloured, battery-powered vibrating dildo' from a sex catalogue and it had arrived in a plain brown envelope in the morning's post. I had to try hard not to laugh as old Sid, deadpan, put on his glasses and staggered over to the window with it to put the batteries in. With great hilarity we all had a feel of it once he got it going.

Luckily Sid didn't stay long and Angela decided that, since Shirley wasn't coming that day, she might as well try and get back in harness again. I felt very worried about her going back to work so soon, only four months after her operation. She was still sore and sat down gingerly. She showed me her scar which was red and tender looking. I didn't know how she could bear to subject herself to the demands of the job when she was still feeling very vulnerable and protective towards her body.

Altogether she saw ten clients and made £400. One dropped in unannounced, a tattooed plumber, married with four teenage children. He had a perfectly good relationship with his wife, he said, but he gets bored. He often just drops in to moan about the vicissitudes of a plumber's life, have a laugh, a cup of tea, a quick bonk, and do any handyman jobs that need doing in exchange. Angela was pleased to see him and obviously enjoyed the reciprocal arrangement. At one point two very smelly slobs came one after the other and Angela staggered out of the bedroom overcome with revulsion. I ran her a lovely hot bath and hoped it would soothe her a bit. I was quite distressed at the abuse she was allowing, but she didn't seem all that bothered.

I am haunted by the image of Angela, sitting stark naked after her bath drying herself in front of the gas fire; that careworn, ordinary 40-year-old woman's body just as it is for a few minutes, then back into the sexy knickers and high heels as the door bell rang again. This time I let the client in – a young Indian guy with a handsome face. At least he was appreciative and grateful. Another punter arrived and glowered at his knees in the sitting room until she was ready. 'Sorry to keep you waiting,' she said saucily, 'but I'm worth waiting for.' 'I hope so,' he grunted charmlessly.

In between the punters we talked about pregnancy, childbirth, miscarriages, children in hospital, hysterectomies, and the pain and loneliness of life when you only seem to give out love but never seem to get much back. Woman talk. She showed me a bounced cheque for £500 from the nephew of a famous millionaire arms dealer. The nephew was an idle, rich young man who had booked her for the whole day, 'and very hard work it was too, he was very demanding'. He had also booked for another whole day the following week and she'd turned down all other bookings thinking they were in luck, but they never saw him or his money again and cried with frustration knowing there was nothing they could do about it.

The following week Angela's little son had to go back in the hospital again. He was born with a congenital obstruction in his bowel and has had so many horrible operations in his life. Angela always stays in with him, so this provided me with my opportunity to do a stint as Shirley's maid. Shirley arrived for work about 11 am. Business hadn't been good that week and they were going to be hard pushed to pay the rent. She began the morning by going alone into the bedroom to meditate. Recently she has become interested in Buddhism and does the Nicheren Shoshu chant 'Nam Myoho Renghe Kyo' every morning. It is a meditation, a spiritual discipline and a preparation for the day. It acknowledges respect for the universal laws of cause and effect and affirms a willingness to make choices that will create maximum value for oneself and the environment. It helps one to become mindful of how we are constantly creating our own reality. Shirley is planning to come off the game before long although, as she says, it can be difficult to decide just when is the right time. She feels she has already got everything she needed from the job – self-awareness, understanding of life, the opportunity for discovering and expressing her own sexuality and friendships with some wonderful women.

The first client phoned and was round in twenty minutes – a young Asian named Raj who paid £50 for straight sex. Shirley got straight on the phone as soon as he'd left to discuss paint colours with the man who was decorating her flat. It seems as though the client was merely a hiccup in the day's events. She talked to me about how the job had been a way for her to exorcise and transform the violence in her life. She comes from a dysfunctional family with a morose, angry, violent alcoholic father and a mother whom she used to see as a poor, cowed victim, but now realizes was manipulative in her own way. From the age of nine she was sexually abused by her father, an RAF pilot, who used to come and get into bed with her after rowing with his wife. Shirley feels sure her mother must have known, but couldn't face the knowledge. Everyone in the family was scared to death of the tyrannical father and Shirley, as the eldest child, often took it upon herself to try and make things all right. She blanked out the abuse completely for years, recalling every detail of the sights and sounds, colours and smells up until the dreaded moment he got into her bed and after that, nothing. The memory finally came back in a therapy session only about three years ago bringing with it a pain so terrible she feared she would die of it. Afterwards she felt an overwhelming relief.

The doorbell rang and I showed client number 2 into the bedroom. This was Steve, a young, smartly dressed office worker. Another £50. Shirley came out after thirty-five minutes looking cross and fed up; lots of in/out thrusting had made her dry and sore. In the end she had to finish him off by hand.

Shirley has had a hard, sad life. Her childhood experiences of neglect and abuse led her into very disastrous relationships with men. She says she has never known how to relate to a man in any other way except sexually. She married an abusive man and after the divorce fell into a passionate and destructive affair with a Maltese guy, who sent her out on the streets. As she says, he was the catalyst but she knew it was her destiny. During the time she was streetwalking in Park Lane she was in a total self-destruct mode which may have been why she attracted a couple of horrific experiences. The first was when she got into a car with two men and they drove her out of town. One had a knife and said he was going to kill her. She has a nightmare image in her mind to this day of herself lying on her back with her legs up in the air, her clothes ripped and this maniac attacking the inside of her body while shrieking 'Watch me!' at his friend. They raped her repeatedly, stole her money and threw her out in the morning not knowing where she was. Another time she got in a car and the man started to drive out of London again. He drove and drove and didn't say a word. When she tried to ask him where they were going he snarled 'shut up!' She was very frightened. Finally he stopped the car in a remote place, had sex with her, didn't pay and threw her out face down in the mud at the side of the road. She was distraught and hysterical, wandering about on the motorway, until finally someone stopped and gave her a lift home.

In neither of these rape cases did she ever think to report it to the police. She somehow saw them as her own fault and no more than she deserved. She half-heartedly tried to commit suicide, then got heavily into drink and drugs.

Then client number 3, Edwin, a middle-aged businessman with a briefcase and an extremely ill-fitting wig, arrived. Shirley came out feeling sorry for him. 'He kept that awful wig on,' she said, 'while taking all the rest of his clothes off. He looked so pathetic I could hardly bear it and then he felt he'd let me down because it took so long for him to come.' Another £30.

Afterwards Shirley said that all the time she was in there servicing Edwin she had thoughts about how scared she is at the prospect of giving up the job. It is security, the only thing she knows. It's not just financial security, it's her identity. She knows where she is with it, knows what she's doing. She fucks, therefore she is. What will she put in its place? Now that she has her degree, she could do a social work diploma or a psychotherapy training. I said how important I thought it was to build on all the experience and understanding she has acquired through prostitution and not to disown it. It's not a question of turning over a new leaf, but using all this to create a unique place for herself in the world.

Client number 4, John, a young chap in jeans with a crew cut. Blow job, £35.

After he left, Shirley went into the bedroom alone again to do some meditation. Her father is now in an old people's home, suffering from brain damage caused by the alcoholism. He is a complete cabbage. Her mother is in the early stages of Alzheimer's disease which began shortly after Shirley confronted her one day with some home truths. She feels that her mother heard her, but almost immediately effected a rapid escape into the blameless state of senility. She has retreated to a place where nothing is her fault. Shirley is sad that it's too late for either of her parents to even be able to see that she is going to be OK, and that she forgives them. She had a powerful experience in therapy recently of feeling her heart open to her father and just fill up with compassion and forgiveness.

One of the hateful parts of the job is being a mere body in the eyes of so many of the men that use her – an object, a collection of orifices to be plugged and poked. 'All we are is FUCK BUCKETS!' screamed one of the women at the Wigmore after a particularly depressing day, and although Shirley was very shocked by the expression she also says she needed to hear it said out loud because it's true. She feels both physically and psychically invaded by male energy, so much so that it's very difficult to summon enough of her own energy to do anything else. Most women find prostitution damaging not only because it is socially unacceptable and therefore leads to being ostracized, but because it is an abuse of the feminine. As Shirley says, 'Although, on the face of it, you seem to be ultra-feminine, it's actually the masculine side of you which is out there controlling, making money, in charge. The dreamy, soft, open, enfolding side often has to be shut down for protection. Many people use their bodies in their jobs – they have to be physically present – but they don't feel invaded in the same way.' No woman, she believes, could do this job and not feel invaded.

It's a horrible feeling not to be seen or heard as a whole person and in spite of all the good and positive things the job has given her there remains that bleakness. 'It's been my hell,' she says, 'but through it I will be transformed.' Her new found spiritual awakening has made her very attracted to the idea of going to India to stay for a while on an ashram and then having a period of celibacy in order to make a break with the old life and a transition to the new. She believes that her karma in this life is to understand and to deal with addiction. She has been addicted to violence, to valium, to speed, to slimming pills, to cocaine and to alcohol. She is now addicted to whoring and finding it very hard to replace it with anything she wants more. She said she has always been afraid that if she ever gave up whoring she would be 'on the run' from it. It would pursue her, always trying to devour her. I said what about looking at it the way Sophia does, as something you are *choosing* to do for the time being. There are no rules, no absolutes. Being a whole, beautiful person includes the part that is the whore and you can love that part too. It's not a struggle between good and evil, acceptable and unacceptable. It's doing what feels right for you easily and naturally. The challenge is to live in harmony with what is loving and respectful for yourself. Other things being equal, being truly honest at that level then allows you to make the choice whether to work as a prostitute or not.

In her book, *Women, Sex and Addiction*, Charlotte Kasl writes: 'From the moment we acknowledge our addiction and state our willingness to do something about it, we start to release our inner light – the light of truth, the holy source within us. We start our homeward journey.'

Hour after hour we sat talking in the stuffy little parlour with the gas fire on. At least twenty people phoned to make appointments, but only a quarter of those showed up. Client number 5, Lawrence, was a short, fat man, well-dressed, middle-aged, with a dapper little goatee beard. Hand relief, £30. We hung on for another half-hour after he left, but the last booking didn't arrive.

It seemed so insulting and humiliating for Shirley to be just sitting there looking pretty and sexy and ready while nobody knew or cared enough to even bother to cancel. At least the men who did show up wanted her for something, were pleased to see her. At least she got a reaction from them, even if it was only a load of spunk, but to be merely an empty dustbin, waiting, was unendurable. I felt very indignant on her behalf. It is impossible to read or write while waiting because the atmosphere of tension, anger and ennui is so highly charged. Sometimes when she and Angela are there on their own they shout and yell until they are hoarse just to release the frustrations. And when she drives her car, Shirley often screams and swears at the top of her lungs when no one can hear her.

In two more weeks Shirley plans to finish working. She recognizes all the pitfalls of giving up an addiction of this magnitude. Being on the game, 'fucking my life away', is like a drug with the omnipresent possibility of dying from an overdose. The constant succession of anonymous partners was a headlong rush into oblivion, annihilation, self-destruction, but to change you really have to want to live. Aminah Raheem in her book, *Soul Return*, writes, 'Even in the midst of our fragmentation something pushes us towards being whole. Jung claimed that we carry an "archetype of wholeness" within us which is always at work to bring us toward fullness and self-realization.'

When we become lopsided, eventually the abandoned part cries out for attention. Signals from the neglected parts of the body, mind or emotions will be given – through desires, phobias, dreams, hunches, or symptoms – which demand care. If they are ignored for too long they become increasingly insistent, progressing towards self-destructive habits, accidents, or disease. Shirley and I have come from opposite directions to listen, to hear and to exchange. We held each other in an embrace of profound empathy as women knowing that we share so much, celebrating our journey, our friendship and the place where our paths intersected.

ELEVEN

Charlotte, who used to work at the Neasden flat with Angela and Shirley, has become a good friend. She is so wonderfully blunt and honest and makes me challenge assumptions all the time. She was still working when I first met her at a whore's party and I was struck by both her looks and her attitude. An artistic, pretty woman – you'd take her to be a university lecturer or perhaps a doctor – she was dressed in a simple skirt and poloneck jumper with heavy silver jewellery made by herself. She wore her thick brown hair pinned off her face with a plastic crocodile clip, giving her an appearance ten years younger than her 42 years. We only talked briefly on that occasion, but she said that being a hooker (which she didn't become until she was over 30) had helped her discover and liberate her own sexuality. She liked the job and was very fond of and grateful to the men who were her clients. I wanted to ask her more about that so we arranged to meet again.

Charlotte comes from a family where there was no physical abuse as such, but her father was a cold, emotionally distant man. 'He was all right when we were both little children,' she said with a wry laugh, 'but somehow, after the age of nine or 10, he couldn't or wouldn't relate to me and just never noticed me.' In the early seventies, after a few years of trying to make it as an actress and then doing a secretarial course, she joined a spiritual community in India. Inhibitions about nudity, about expressing her feelings and about asking for what gave her pleasure gradually evaporated in the warmth of the sun and the prevailing ethic of spirituality through sexual awakening. Among other things Charlotte discovered the freedom and release of being able to share with a man the experience of pleasuring herself. On returning to England she made the decision to act out a fantasy she'd had since her teens which was to become a prostitute. 'Sexuality can be a site of oppression, of course,' she said, 'but it can also be a terrain for the development of a woman's positive and liberating desires, feelings and ideas.'

She got a job at the select Wigmore Club where she worked discreetly for years. The place was full of judges, barristers, politicians, aristocrats and people in the entertainment business. Her enjoyment of performing in front of men made her a very popular hooker and enabled her own sexual emancipation. Unfortunately for Charlotte, when some adverse publicity from the tabloid press kept the clients away, the club had to close. Charlotte then joined forces with Angela and Shirley and they worked quietly and independently from the little flat in Neasden, until the police bust earlier this year. Charlotte was deeply shocked and depressed by the experience of appearing in the dock in front of a courtroom full of strangers, listening to a list of items found in the flat being read out: underwear, dog-collar, canes, condoms, etc. It could hardly be described as evidence of a criminal offence, but they were heavily fined. The whole sorry tale of the trial of Cynthia Payne showed English sexual hypocrisy at its most blatant. She offered a much-needed service at reasonable rates, with reductions for pensioners, in a friendly atmosphere. Elderly men were cheered and disabled men catered for. All involved were consenting adults, no nuisance was caused, no neighbours complained but Madame Sin was heavily fined and sent to prison. According to the law the men had committed no offence, as indeed they hadn't but where was the women's offence? For Charlotte it was the spur she had been subconsciously waiting for to close this chapter of her life, although after seven quite fulfilling years leaving prostitution has been harder than she thought. Apart from the money, the three-day week and the flexible hours which allowed her time to make her jewellery, there was also that element of addiction to 'the life' which is compounded by the near impossibility of maintaining normal friendships and romantic involvements alongside it.

Charlotte is currently focusing all her energies on trying to consolidate a relationship with her young lover, an Italian waiter, who knows nothing of her past. She would love to be able to tell him, but doesn't want to risk losing him. She thinks he would not be able to cope with the knowledge, although he has often told her stories of encounters he has had with prostitutes in the past when he was a sailor, in particular one girl who was lovely to him when he was ill in hospital in Brazil. She came each day with flowers and presents. He, from his own personal experience, knows that a whore is a woman with many facets and yet he will occasionally explode about 'putanas' and condemn them all as sluts. His part in the commercial transaction is, of course, above reproach and perfectly normal for a man who is only doing what comes naturally.

Although my generation of women have escaped the worst excesses of sexual conditioning, I reflected on the attitudes that have forged me and shaped society's view of female sexuality. In the long history of the sexual control of women, the nineteenth century found women, particularly middle-class women, trapped in sexually passive and suffocating roles by a social climate that emphasized polite and decorous behaviour and especially stressed virginity and chastity. Any woman who stepped out of line was either hysterical or deviant.

Susan Edwards' informative book, *Female Sexuality and the Law*, makes pretty horrific reading. Apart from the usual social and legal constraints, medical practitioners, gynaecologists, mental health physicians among others inhibited, prohibited and regulated female behaviour by defining what was appropriate sexual, social behaviour. Gynaecological disorders were frequently diagnosed and horrific punitive treatments prescribed for masturbation, sexual fantasies and 'nymphomania'. Right up until 1900 and beyond clitoridectomies were performed for 'sexual excess', leeches were applied, women declared insane and given electrical shocks to their genitals to 'cure' them. Many were indecently assaulted by doctors advocating 'genital massage'. 'Women were consistently presented as unstable, irresponsible and hysterical. Women's experiences of sexual intimidation, assault, rape or incest were defined as arising not from real events but from either imagined sexual longings (wish fulfilment) or sexual excess (extreme provocation from the woman).' Much of this thinking still lingers today in the 'she asked for it' style of reasoning.

In sharp contrast to the idealized sexually passive, innocent woman was the woman of sexual experience – the unchaste or fallen woman – who might range from the daring, unmarried woman with a lover to the prostitute. She was either loose, bad, mad, or wanton – a temptress, a seducer. 'Since desire for sex was supposedly non-existent,' writes Susan Edwards, 'therefore women who showed any interest in it were grossly abnormal or totally lacking in morals and the desire defined as malfunction or disease or innate "badness".' The awful Contagious Diseases Act of 1866 gave unprecedented powers to the police to detain any woman suspected of being a prostitute against her will in hospital requiring her to be medically examined – forcibly if necessary – without consent. This law hit working-class women particularly hard and was a further weapon in the control of women. The law was founded on the erroneous principle that unchaste women carried and transmitted VD, whilst the men who consorted with them only contracted it.

As recently as 1959 the defending counsel in a rape case introduced evidence to show that the woman was 'wanting in chastity and common decency'. And in 1975 the defence counsel, again in a rape trial, introduced evidence to the effect that the complainant had a conviction for prostitution *fifteen years previously*, thus creating a slur on her character and credibility.

'Understandings of women in our culture,' writes Dr Edwards, 'have proceeded from conceptions of their sexuality.' She concludes, 'The oppression of women arises fundamentally from the control over sexual expression and the patrolling of the boundaries of thought on the nature of sexuality in women.... This control is achieved by a variety of means, one of which is the criminal justice system formally enshrining and codifying the attitudes to women which permeate our culture. They are used as a means of coercion to obtain conformity with norms and mores.'

Many women now live in terror that other people will discover their secret sexual desires. They are afraid of their imaginations, of how they might paint themselves inside a sexual drama, of what will surface if they let themselves go. They are constrained by what is acceptable and alarmed by the strength of their fantasies. As Charlotte said, 'I used to be angry and afraid of the feelings that were alive in my body. I felt driven between my wish to be a decent, reasonable woman and my equally powerful wish to throw all my beliefs and upbringing away and explode into my own sexual raving.' Maybe not in the South Sea Islands, but certainly in our culture it is hard to be a woman and be sexual too. Women like Charlotte are showing that we can dare to create a synthesis and live with the danger of our real desires.

Jess Wells, in her angry book *The Herstory of Prostitution*, bravely reveals the manner of her own awakening sexuality:

I used to masturbate to fantasies of being a prostitute. It was a very dark secret. I was the woman of Lina Wertmuller's films. The big one, bold and swishing her way to the toilet, howling with laughter, her kimono whipping off massive breasts.... The one who throws her half-stockinged leg into the air and sits smack in the middle of the old man's lap. 'C'mon honey, let's fuck. So put a little cream in my box, milkman' ... Or the women of what's-his-name the Italian ... The film where she stands near the sea at a construction site and rubs herself up and down the wall like a cat. She stares at them, announcing herself, her sexuality, in up-front, no-doubts language, 'I am here. I am my sexuality.' ... The only women I ever saw enjoying sex were in films, and the only women enjoying sex in films were prostitutes.... My fantasies were not of exploitation or the desire to be bought, but were of an inner voice of sexuality demanding to be heard.

I felt a great sympathy for these words. They echo many of my own innermost feelings and those of countless non-prostitute women I have spoken to, trapped in the good-girl archetype. If a woman was courageous enough to try and define her own sexuality it was easy to dismiss her as unfeminine, a castrating bitch, a filthy slut or a threat to the established order. Most women still find it incredibly difficult to risk disapproval and to assert themselves sexually.

One evening over dinner, Charlotte tossed a gauntlet in my path by saying that it was all very well spending a few sessions at Amber's bondage parlour and 'maiding' in the Neasden whorehouse, but if I really wanted to understand the work I should try for myself, a slice of life in the average day of a prostitute, six to 10 ordinary punters one after the other at the flat.

I lay awake for ages that night wondering what I really felt about the idea. The attraction of prostitution is the ego boosting one of knowing that a man wants the pleasure of your body so much he's willing to pay. As a 'respectable' 50-year-old grandmother the chances of being a lust-inspiring sex goddess are not likely to come my way for all that much longer! My protestations that I'd left it all about twenty years too late were brushed aside. Lots of men would adore me, said Charlotte; I'd fulfil all their older woman fantasies. So that would be one aspect – sexual power. Another aspect would be the more romantic, earth-mother one of 'the healer'. Many is the time that I've worked with a person, channelling and focusing healing energy and unconditional love into him and realized what a short step it would be to include sexual ministrations in the package, if it were appropriate. And not just for men either. It always seems a shame that a woman can't go and have a no-strings-attached healing/erotic massage from a skilled professional of either sex.

The financial contract makes the whole thing nice and tidy; no further emotional connection is expected. So what if I did a day's work and saw six to 10 clients? After thirty-two years of marriage, I didn't even know how to put a condom on a man. I'm conditioned to fear all the horrendous 'risks' of prostitution, but I actually know that practising safe, protected sex with a punter is a very low risk activity compared with an impetuous, unprotected fling with a lover.

How would I feel about the money? I've always had trouble charging for anything, being one of life's natural volunteers. It would be good for me to set a price on what I think I'm worth. All the things I've ever done well in my life have been things that society doesn't value much in monetary terms. (Nurses have that problem too – the hooker interviewed in the New Statesman told how she got paid £2.50 an hour for doing 'manual evacuation' i.e. putting on rubber gloves and removing stools from a constipated patient when she was a nursing sister. Now she gets paid ten times that for digital manipulation on her own terms! 'Knowing that some men are handing over half their week's wages gives your work value.' she said.)

What about doing it for charity? I quite like the fantasy of doing a sponsored whore-in and making the money available to the English Collective of Prostitutes to help women who aren't free to make the choices I can make. I, like Connie, would love to see a sort of safe house where women can be helped to make such choices. There would be no moral judgements, no coercion and access to viable alternatives if they wanted to get off the game. But in my heart of hearts I knew that was a cop out. It would be a way of trying to keep my own hands clean. Getting paid for sex is the whole point. I've spent too much of my life appearing good and sweet on the outside and having a secret, sleazy part on the inside. It's time I owned up.

But could I really bear to sit there in my frilly knickers for hour after hour waiting to be chosen, stood up by spotty-faced telephone engineers and arm-pitty office workers who don't even bother to phone and cancel? No, I couldn't. And I'm not nearly brave enough or quick witted enough to walk the streets. Domination work looks superficially like a doddle but, as I've already found out, unless you are really turned on by it, like Amber, the head games are exhausting. The men suck you dry, emotionally, because they have an unquenchable hunger. Creating and performing their fantasy means being alert and watchful all the time.

No, it would have to be on my terms not theirs. My fantasy would be to run a sort of wholistic whorehouse – massage, healing, sex, and counselling in aesthetically pleasing surroundings with crystals and candles where the prostitutes, both male and female, gave a genuine, caring service and mutual respect was the order of the day. I discussed this possibility with Charlotte and Shirley. Could a whore work in a different way? I know, for example, that Shirley is fed up with marketing 'a young lady, 25 years of age' and would like to be the person she is with all the maturity and experience that brings with it. However she felt that ultimately it would still come to the same thing on a psychic level – too many men, too much male energy invading your body. Even if you weren't selling an impersonal product – a 25-year-old fantasy woman, disembodied lips, vulva, breasts – but the services of a highly skilled real person, you would still feel overwhelmed and vandalized. Charlotte thought I was being naive. It wouldn't work because most men who come to a prostitute don't want all this sweetness. It isn't erotic. They're looking for everything a wife is not. Naughty, clan-destine, off-limits sex is exciting. Whores are vehicles of flight, refuges from the married state and all its responsibilities. When you provide everything for a man you become the lover, the wife, the mother. For a man who visits a prostitute, lust is separate from affection, desire estranged from love.

I asked an old friend, a successful, distinguished man in a public position, what he thought of the idea. He shook his head. 'What men want from a prostitute is unemotional sex. The kind you can shower off afterwards and leave behind like a game of squash. Prostitutes provide what I call "male sex",' he said, '– brief contact, high-impact, impersonal, business-like – whereas "female sex" requires commitment, finesse, relationship, courtship. If, for whatever reason, one is not satisfied at home, it's so *convenient* to go to a prostitute. It's a straight-forward transaction; it doesn't require involvement or responsibility. One doesn't have to buy all those flowers, take the woman out to dinner, massage her ego as one would have to do in a regular relationship. One has only so much time and energy. Your wholistic brothel would be too *nice*. It might begin to break down my carefully constructed compart-ments. Men always distinguish two types of women – the solely maternal and the exclusively sexual – the women you marry and whores. The thing about a prostitute, in the male imagination, is that she loves cocks, she's always ready. She doesn't have to get up in the night to feed the baby. She has no other feelings than sexual ones. She's never tired, bored or ill. You just pay your money and fuck. Realism is detumescent. As the old Yiddish aphorism goes: "When the prick stands up the brain gets buried in the ground."'

Even Byron, the archetypal romantic and womanizer, divided women into virgins and anonymous 'animals'. Men seem to have a strong drive for a liaison devoid of intimacy where there is absolutely no pressure to reveal their own or have to acknowledge another person's humanity. The psychoanalyst Melanie Klein talks about the difficulty a baby has in reconciling the good, loving, nourishing mother with the bad, punishing, withholding mother and how this ambiguity is often resolved by splitting the mother into two parts. As an adult he can still carry this split image within him. He falls in love with the good, pure woman whom he desexualizes but he projects the fear, hatred and erotic power onto the figure of the whore: bad mother, the desirable but dreaded whore; good mother, the yearned for and idealized healing madonna. For a prostitute, or a wife for that matter, to try to create a synthesis of both these archetypes and refuse to be a party to be split would be to create utter confusion.

I couldn't see a way that I could rise to Charlotte's challenge. If I was going to sample 'the life', I still wanted to remain true to myself. It looked like the end of the story but it wasn't quite ...

I am writing this the day after my first experience of prostitution. Last night I got paid £200 for being a whore. It feels very strange to write those words and to say them out loud and to let the significance of them hang in the air. The odd thing is that although I feel proud, I'm suddenly aware of what it means not to be able to tell anyone. So many people would give me a hard time. The only person I could talk to quite openly and honestly was Shirley. The main feeling I have is one of tremendous sisterhood, love and solidarity with the beautiful women I've met on the game. The actual job was no different from something I might have done for free twenty years ago.

Sophia had rung me a couple of weeks ago in a mischievous frame of mind, suggesting she set the whole thing up with a regular client she has been seeing on and off for ten years. I will disguise his identity and just say he is the son of a billionaire shipping magnate, who was sexually crippled very early in life by being sent to an English public school where he became fixated on matrons and nannies and bottoms. He is quite a sweet chap with a highly developed sense of the elegant and the subtle. Not for him the crudities of anything hasty or explicit, the great erotic turn on is in imagining what is going to happen and to luxuriate in the anticipation.

The evening began with Sophia and I preparing ourselves over at her place for the night's work. I can see that the addictive part of prostitution could be in the ritual of getting dressed up, putting on make up, fantasizing about the hunt and the moment of capture – all pretty basic, primitive stuff. Not to mention knowing that the male will be drawn to your sexuality like a magnet, a moth to the candleflame. What power! Something I've got is so irresistible that men would part with their wages for it. That feeling of power along with the excitement of living on the edge must be one of the hardest things to give up. Dolores made the parallel with a dangerous sport – even when it is frightening or disagreeable, prostitution provides an intensity, a high, a distraction perhaps from buried pain.

We arrived in a taxi, under cover of darkness, and were shown in by the valet. Bruno awaited us with studied casualness in a designer track suit with a bottle of chilled Chablis in the drawing room of his beautiful Highgate house. He talked non-stop, nervously, firstly about what a good Catholic he is and how important religion is in his life. I don't know what the church would have to say about the amount of energy he devotes to fornication and lewdness but, as he made sure we knew, he prays and goes to confession so presumably he's managed to square all that away quite comfortably. Then he recounted, blow by blow, his most recent sexual exploits with women, particularly his long suffering regular girlfriend. It was a very boring monologue and brought home to me how hard earned the money is. It's not the *sex*, it's the *men* that are such hard work. Accustomed to paying for people to listen to him and laugh at his jokes, he was completely self-centred. Never would he know or ask or care that my child is going into hospital next week for a serious operation, that I'm even a mother at all, that Sophia's best friend just died of AIDS, that we have joys and sorrows, hopes and fears.

For the sexy bit of the evening the idea was that we would play cards in the bedroom. Sophia has to wrack her brains to dream up erotic scenarios to suit his rather arrested sexual development and she had written out some naughty forfeits on screwed up bits of paper. The loser of each round had to pick one out and perform it (kiss someone's boots, strip down to your underwear, show your bottom, get a spanking, etc.). Luckily for me, I never lost once but it drove him wild. He was having such a good time and acting like an over-excited six-year-old at his birthday party. To round it all off, Sophia and I gave each other a few light smacks on the bottom while he got to watch. The thought of how embarrassing this would be for me was the greatest possible turn on for him and whichever governess had wielded her power over him way back when was well and truly avenged once again.

All this dragged on until 2 am when he stuffed £200 down each of our bras and we got a taxi back to Finsbury Park. In fact I didn't feel the slightest bit embarrassed or degraded. Bruno was so pathetic and harmless that it felt more like putting someone out of their misery and I quite enjoyed larking about with Sophia. Not an experience I would care to repeat too often, though. If I had to be a sex object out of necessity or poverty I would hate it and become extremely depressed, but *choosing* to be a sex object sometimes is quite erotic. To be honest I also enjoyed the power of knowing the effect I was having. Although he appeared to be calling the shots because he was paying the money, actually Sophia and I had total control. At any time we could have pulled the plug on the fantasy and really demolished him. It's because whores don't call the guy a sick pervert or a pathetic wanker and walk out that they stay in business.

Bruno told us during his monologue that his aspiring family had sent him away to England to a boarding kindergarten at the age of three and during the holidays he was looked after by a foster mother who was cruel to him. His controlling use of women now is a transparently obvious way to express his anger and impotence. If he was an ordinary man without money to burn he would probably be in therapy, raging against the mother who abandoned him and howling for the little boy whom nobody cared for. He certainly could do with it. As it is, he can pay huge sums of money to tell his life story to whores and lose the pain of remembering for a little while by acting out his erotic fantasies.

So, I had crossed some invisible barrier and become a whore, whatever that means. I told my husband. Having indulged some of his indiscretions before now, I reckoned he owed me an indulgence. 'I thought your curiosity would probably get the better of you,' he said mildly. I don't think he thought I'd changed much, except that I might have become a bit bolder, sexually, than I was before I started this exploration. As Sophia said, acknowledging the whore in myself doesn't necessarily mean going on the game. It can mean having the kind of sexual relationship I want with the man of my choice.

The following Saturday, Sophia and I met up to go shopping with some of our immoral earnings. She took me to some amazing shops, including Transformations in Euston, a shop for transvestites and transsexuals which stocks stilettos in enormous sizes, corsets, lifelike silicone breasts and accessories. I wanted to buy a very tarty red basque but nothing actually fitted a woman's shape – they were all made for men. The other customers were such ordinary guys and they looked at us with wistful envy being able to be women without even trying. I'd somehow imagined lots of Dame Ednas and *Cage Aux Folles* artists, but they were nothing of the sort. Apart from a few saucy costumes, such as French maids' uniforms complete with frilly panties and a few sequinned cocktail frocks, most of the clothes were unremittingly drab and consisted mainly of 1950s suburban housewives' floral rayon, pussy-cat bow blouses and knee-length, sensible, polyester skirts, the sort of thing that might be worn by an ex-nun. They all want to look like their mothers!

Then we went to the Skin Two Warehouse in Ladbroke Grove which stocks every type of fetish wear you could possibly imagine and plenty you couldn't – rubber miniskirts, handcuffs, shiny vinyl rain-coats, leather underwear, thigh-high boots with impossible heels like stilts, masks, studded dog-collars. The place was full of weedy chaps carrying plastic shopping bags furtively breathing in the heady aroma of rubber. I would never have had the nerve to go in there on my own but with Sophia it was just tremendous fun and I felt that lovely con-spiratorial silliness I used to enjoy so much in my teens. She bought some erotic books and I bought an outrageous leather garment with a zip up the front which I hoped my husband would enjoy.

A little while after our whoring episode I invited Sophia to my house for supper. I wanted to give her something precious of mine to mark the profound connection we had shared. It had seemed like an initiation and a bond and I wanted to thank her for trusting me. I have a heavy carved jade pendant which used to belong to my mother. It is in the form of the serene face of an old woman and has always seemed to me an object of great symbolic strength. A necklace for a goddess. I knew at once that this should be the gift. What I didn't know was that she, too, wanted to give me something to celebrate the closeness between us. She brought me a wonderful African ceremonial bowl which rests on a three-legged stand carved out of a single piece of wood. It was a chalice fit for a medicine woman. We exchanged our tokens of unconditional love and respect in a little ceremony that required no words and we hugged each other – connecting to the positive life force energy in us and around us, delighting in the synchronicity of life's coincidences and the humour of life's paradoxes. We are kindred spirits, wise women, friends, sisters, healers, whores, goddesses. Helping each other to recognize and grow into our power, beauty and wholeness. The process of becoming whole is not about being perfect, but about the warmth and safety of knowing your body and soul are truly connected. It is about staying centred in your power, accepting your humanness, and opening your heart to love.

Sophia also introduced me to a translation of a mysterious ancient text. Called 'Thunder, Perfect Mind', it is a long poem full of paradox and antithesis delivered by a woman. I was excited both by its forcefulness and by its continued relevance. Here are some extracts from it:

Thunder, Perfect Mind

Look upon me, you who reflect upon me
and you hearers hear me.
You who are waiting for me, take me to
yourselves.
And do not banish me from your sight.
And do not make your voice hate me, nor your
hearing.
Do not be ignorant of me anywhere or any time.
Be on your guard.

For I am the first and the last.
I am the honoured one and the scorned one.
I am the whore and the holy one.
I am the wife and the virgin.
I am the mother and the daughter ...

Do not be arrogant to me when I am cast out
upon the earth,
and you will find me in those that are to come.
And do not look upon me on the dung heap
nor go and leave me cast out,
and you will find me in the kingdoms ...

In my weakness, do not forsake me,
and do not be afraid of my power ...

I am the one who has been hated everywhere
and who has been loved everywhere ...

I am control and the uncontrollable.
I am the union and the dissolution.
I am the abiding and I am the dissolving ...

I am lust in outward appearance,
and interior self-control exists within me.
I am the hearing which is attainable to
everyone
and the speech which cannot be grasped.
I am a mute who does not speak,
and great is my multitude of words.

Hear me in gentleness, and learn of me in
roughness.
I am she who cries out,
and I am cast forth upon the face of the
earth ...

For many are the pleasant forms which exist in
numerous sins,
and incontinences,
and disgraceful passions,
and fleeting pleasures,
which men embrace until they become sober
and go up to their resting place.
And they will find me there,
and they will live,
and they will not die again.

In trying to find out what love has to do with it, the most important
lesson for me was to have faith in the process of learning as I went
along. The whole quest has been a process of discovery about my own

confusion and my own coping strategies for life. The sexual arena is the place where so much of our compulsive and addictive behaviour gets acted out. Sometimes the revelations have been painful, sometimes shocking.

After my disturbing experience of working at Amber's dungeon, I decided to go and get some therapy myself to help me understand the maelstrom of emotions and issues it brought up for me. I had to take an inward journey into the chaos, fear and loneliness inside. Many early childhood experiences and programmings that I had never even been aware of began to make themselves known. Things began to swim up from the deeper recesses of my unconscious mind, struggling to reach the light.

I had to face my life-long denial of things that had been done to me, and the pain of having taken *so long* to become conscious and begin to recover. I truly believe that my cancer was the beginning of my journey to consciousness. It was the life-threatening jolt I needed to break through my watertight armouring. When I asked it, 'who are you and what are you saying to me?' it answered in a very clear voice, 'I am an angry, hungry child.' From that moment, just a year ago and right in the middle of writing this book, I knew my task was to listen very carefully to the wiser part of me that wanted to tell the truth. The dense part, the fearful part, has always wanted to stop up my ears but the cancer shouted at me, 'change or die!'

This journey of discovery and spiritual awakening has brought me blessedly close to the people I've met in the course of the research. I believe the only thing separating me from a prostitute is a difference of degree. Prostitution is the institution which allows all of us to hide from our internal conflicts about sex; it enables us to project the shadow outwards. Prostitutes act out the pain and confusion for the rest of us and pay the price of society's scorn. So many of our issues are parallel and so much of our healing depends on each other. Our pride and wholeness as women, as human beings, as children of the universe will take us to our full potential for love and power. Whether my life be a long one or a short one I want to make today the best that it can be – the way it always should have been – and feel comfortable and secure in my own heart.

I would like to understand the Whore in me as the archetype which represents true sexual power, confidence and integrity. I want to own her, embrace her and celebrate her. She is the one who brings the goddess's love into the human dimension. Complete in herself, she is a fit mate for a god.

She is different from the wounded child to whom sex with another wounded child provides a seductive illusion of power – a validation of her womanhood. Lacking the true ability to nurture themselves and possessing only the most fragile sense of personal identity, prostitutes stay on the game addicted to the fix. The job inspires the same excitement and hatred that the needle has for the junkie, the bottle for the alcoholic. Like any behaviour that is used to anaesthetize pain, it becomes addictive. They promise themselves they're going to quit but they don't. I've met so many women who say, 'I've been going to come off the game for ten years but I'm still here'. It is safer to take off your knickers and let your body get on with it so that painful things like communication and vulnerability can be kept at bay by the illusion of power and control.

'I'm not there when I'm having sex with a punter,' said Lorraine, the heroin addict with the teardrop tattoo. 'I mean, like, I'm *gone*. I'm somewhere else. I can make my mind fly off to a fairytale land of unicorns and rainbows where I'm always a little girl in a pale blue dress.'

FURTHER READING

Bailey, Paul, *An English Madam*, Jonathan Cape, London, 1982

Bell, Laurie, *Good Girls, Bad Girls*, Women's Press, Toronto, 1987

Carter, Angela, *The Sadeian Woman*, Virago, London, 1979

Delacoste, Frederique and Priscilla Alexander, *Sex Work — Writings by Women in the Sex Industry*, Seal Press, Seattle, 1989

Edwards, Susan, *Female Sexuality and the Law*, Martin Robertson, Oxford, 1981

Edwards, Susan, *Women on Trial*, Manchester University Press, 1984

French, Dolores, *Working — My Life as a Prostitute*, Gollancz, London, 1989

Gilbert, Harriett and Christine Roche, *A Women's History of Sex*, Pandora (RKP), London, 1987

Harding, M. Esther, *Women's Mysteries*, Rider, London, 1982

Kasl, Charlotte Davis, *Women, Sex and Addiction*, Ticknor and Fields, New York, 1989

McMullen, Richie, *Enchanted Boy*, G.M.P., London, 1989

Perera, Sylvia Brinton, *The Scapegoat Complex*, Inner City Books, Toronto, 1986

Pheterson, Gail, *A Vindication of the Rights of Whores*, Seal Press, Seattle, 1989

Pomeroy, Sarah B., *Goddesses, Whores, Wives and Slaves — Women in Classical Antiquity*, Schocken Books, New York, 1975

Qualls-Corbett, Nancy, *The Sacred Prostitute*, Inner City Books, Toronto, 1988

Raheem, Aminah, *Soul Return*, Privately printed, California 1987

Roberts, Nicky, *The Front Line — Women in the Sex Industry Speak*, Grafton, London, 1986

James Robinson ed. *Thunder, Perfect Mind* translated by members of the Coptic Gnostic Library project for the Institute for Antiquity and Christianity, E.J. Brill, Leiden, Netherlands, 1984

Vance, Carole S., *Pleasure and Danger — Exploring Female Sexuality*, RKP, Boston, 1984

Welldon, Estela V., *Mother, Madonna, Whore*, Free Association Books, London, 1988
Wells, Jess, *A Herstory of Prostitution*, Berkeley, California, 1989
Wilson, Annie, *The Wise Virgin*, Turnstone Books, London, 1979
Wilson, Colin, *The Misfits — A Study of Sexual Outsiders*, Grafton, London, 1988
Zilbergeld, Bernard, *Men and Sex*, Fontana, London, 1980

More books from Optima

Women in Wartime
by Jane Waller and Michael Vaughan-Rees

The unsung heroines of the Second World War were the women who were left behind. Isolated from the action, fearful for the lives of their menfolk and hopeful for a future at peace, they adapted well to a rapidly changing world.

This book provides a full commentary on home life during those wartime years. Drawing on an unrivalled collection of contemporary women's magazines, the authors have extracted features, fashion tips, morale-boosting stories, mottoes and recipes to present a panoramic view of women's shifting roles.

Emotional reactions, the practicalities of working and maintaining a home, relationships with Allied troops and, of course, love, leisure and fashion are all included, together with advertisements and readers' letters from the war years. As never before, the portrait that emerges of women in wartime is one of immense courage, good humour and ingenuity.

ISBN 0 356 12887 3, Price (in UK only) £9.99

Growing up in the Fifties
by Terry Jordan

Television, teenagers and rock'n'roll
Beatniks, 'Ban the Bomb' and CND
The Coronation and Commonwealth immigration
The New Look • The Cold War and Suez
Elvis and Buddy Holly • James Dean

Were the Fifties just nondescript years, a bland transition while the world caught its breath between the excitements of World War II and the Swinging Sixties? *Growing up in the Fifties* proves the Fifties had more to offer than longer skirts and an end to rationing. As the deprivations of the post-war period receded, most people had 'never had it so good' and youth culture was busy inventing itself.

In this collection of seven interviews, girls now grown tell the stories of their childhoods and teen years with perception and humour. Their detailed memories of a daily life, so different from today's, provide a rich background for understanding the events and social attitudes which shaped the decade, the role of women in it, and the individual women they were to become.

ISBN 0 356 15553 6, Price (in UK only) £5.99

Conversations with Mothers and Daughters
by Celia Dodd

What is it about the bond between mother and daughter that stirs up such powerful emotions? At best, it's an enviable source of enduring support, at worst it's a flashpoint of tension and disappointment. In conversation with Celia Dodd different generations of women, from teenagers to great-grandmothers, talk frankly and often with great emotion about their personal experiences of the relationship, and the influence it has had on their lives. Abandoned daughters, runaway teenagers, daughters who care for invalid mothers, women who have lived through anorexia, the menopause, or estrangement, share the insights their different experiences have given them.

The impact of the 'New Man', working mothers and the super-woman on the relationship are also assessed. As parental roles blur and women gain greater confidence outside the home, new role models are emerging to inspire generations of daughters to come.

Whether they speak from a Yorkshire mining village, a Glasgow tenement, the home counties, or London's Asian communities, these mothers and daughters all bear witness to the power and influence of the first, and often the most important, relationship in a woman's life.

ISBN 0 356 12891 1, Price (in UK only) £5.99

Eating Your Heart Out
by Julia Buckroyd

For those who endure the vicious cycle of eating disorders, misuse of food has become the way in which they express their emotional hunger and signal their distress, whether this is through obsessional dieting, compulsive eating, bingeing and vomiting, or anorexia. For women in particular, increasingly at odds with an emphatically marketed standard of slimline beauty, food can become a secret form of self-punishment.

Eating Your Heart Out examines those areas of distress demonstrated in this way, covering both traditional and feminist ideas about sexuality and society, conflicts about success and competition, and complexity of family relationships. Not since the publication of *Fat is a Feminist Issue* have the implications of eating disorders been so comprehensively assessed.

Julia Buckroyd, an experienced counsellor, has written a thoughtful and challenging book that focuses on the underlying causes of, and provides new insight into, behaviour that is symptomatic of unhappiness.

ISBN 0 356 17088 8, Price (in UK only) £5.99

Experiences of Abortion
by Denise Winn

However compelling the reasons, however right the decision may feel, few women undergo abortion lightly. Whether or not they have regrets about it – and most women have mixed feelings – abortion arouses strong emotions which need to be acknowledged.

In this book, women of varied circumstances talk about their experiences of abortion – how they felt when they discovered they were pregnant, what was involved in the decision to have an abortion, their feelings about it immediately afterwards and also much later. Their stories show that anger, sadness, confusion, grief and relief are all perfectly natural and normal reactions, that they come in many different forms and should be allowed expression. It is hoped that by reading this book other women will be helped to come to terms with their own experience.

ISBN 0 356 14140 3, Price (in UK only) £4.99

Experiences of Hysterectomy
by Ann Webb

Although many women later claim that having a hysterectomy was the best thing they ever did, initially they may have mixed feelings, feeling that the loss of their womb will affect their femininity and sexuality, their identity as women.

In this book, written in association with the Hysterectomy Support Group, different women talk about their emotions both prior to and after undergoing surgery. Perhaps through the sharing of experience women will be helped to express their own feelings and feel more able to cope with them.

ISBN 0 356 14141 1, Price (in UK only) £4.99

Miscarriage
by Margaret Leroy

Miscarriage can be a deeply distressing experience yet little information on the subject is available. A woman's questions may go unanswered and her friends, and even her partner, may not seem to understand her feelings.

This book draws on the experience of the thousands of women a year who contact the Miscarriage Association. It provides comprehensive medical information and emotional support for women and their families. Topics covered include:

- What happens when you miscarry
- What are the causes and what can you do to help
- How you and your partner may feel
- How friends and relatives can best offer support
- How to give your next pregnancy every chance of success

ISBN 0 356 12888 1, Price (in UK only) £5.95

All Optima books are available at your bookshop or newsagent, or can be ordered from the following address:

Optima, Cash Sales Department,
PO Box 11, Falmouth, Cornwall TR10 9EN

Please send cheque or postal order (no currency), and allow 60p for postage and packing for the first book, plus 25p for the second book and 15p for each additional book ordered up to a maximum charge of £1.90 in the UK.

Customers in Eire and BFPO please allow 60p for the first book, 25p for the second book plus 15p per copy for the next 7 books, thereafter 9p per book.

Overseas customers please allow £1.25 for postage and packing for the first book and 28p per copy for each additional book.

WITHDRAWN FROM HAVERING COLLEGES
SIXTH FORM LIBRARY

H.S.F.C   Library Services

48073

'What's this?'

'Read it, please, *nkosana*.'

Emmanuel tore the envelope open and extracted a folded piece of paper with two lines of text written on the lined face. He read the words out loud. '*The captain had a little wife. This wife was with him at the river when he died.*'

'You were the one who sent me to King's farm,' Emmanuel said. He recognised the hand. It made sense now. The person who'd left the note ran like no-one he'd ever seen; ran with a relentless stride that had left him gasping for breath. Captain Pretorius and Shabalala stirred the hearts of the old people as they crossed the length and breadth of the Pretorius farm without stopping, without drinking. Like so many white men, Emmanuel thought, I was beaten by a warrior of the Zulu *impi*.

'What happened that night on the riverbank? I'm not going to tell the Pretorius family or the other policemen. So go ahead and just say it.'

Shabalala paused as if he couldn't bear to put into words the things he'd kept bottled up for so long. 'The captain and the little wife were together on the blanket. Captain was shot and fell forwards. The little wife, she struggled from under him and ran on the sand to the path and then the man pulled the captain to the water. This is all I know.'

'Christ above, man. Why didn't you tell me straightaway?'

'The captain's sons. They would not like to hear these things. None of the Afrikaners would like to hear this story.'

The Pretorius boys were the unofficial lawmakers in Jacob's Rest. Anton and his burned garage were an example of the rough justice they meted out to offenders. What chance did a black policeman stand against the mighty hand of the Pretorius family?

'I understand,' Emmanuel said.

Shabalala had to live in Jacob's Rest. Writing unsigned notes was the simplest way for him to help the investigation and stay out of harm's way. It was better and safer for everyone involved if a white out-of-town detective was the one to uncover the truth about the captain.

'Detective Sergeant.' The Zulu constable motioned to the back of the house. 'Please.'

Emmanuel followed Shabalala through the neat sitting room into the kitchen. A black woman stood near a table. She looked up with a concerned expression but did not make a sound.

Shabalala led Emmanuel through the back door. They took seats at either side of a small card table. In the yard behind Shabalala's house there was a chicken coop and a traditional *kraal* for keeping animals overnight. Behind the *kraal* the property fell away to the banks of a meandering stream.

Both men looked towards the distant hills as they talked. The serious business of undressing Captain Pretorius could not be done face to face.

'Do you know who the woman is?'

'No,' Shabalala said. 'Captain told me of the little wife but not who she was.'

Emmanuel sank back in his chair. He'd had about enough of Willem Pretorius's firewalls. Why didn't he boast about his conquests like a normal man?

'What did he tell you about the girlfriend?'

'He said he had taken a little wife from among the coloured people and that the little wife had given him . . . um . . .' The pause lengthened as Shabalala sought the most polite way to translate the captain's words.

'Pleasure? Power?' Emmanuel prompted.

'Strength. The little wife gave him new strength.'

'Why do you call her little wife?' He'd seen the photographs and there wasn't one thing in them that his own ex-wife Angela would have agreed to do.

'She was a proper little wife,' Shabalala stated. 'The captain paid *lobola* for her, as is the custom.'

'Whom did he pay the bride price to?'

'Her father.'

'You're telling me a man, a coloured man, agreed to exchange his daughter for cattle?' He leaned towards Shabalala. Did the Zulu policeman really believe such a far-fetched story?

'Captain told me this is what he did. He had respect for the old ways. He would not take a second wife without first paying *lobola*. This I believe.'

'Yes, well. I'm sure the white Mrs Pretorius will be delighted to hear her husband was such a stickler for the rules.'

'No. The missus would not like to hear this.' Shabalala was deadly serious.

The sound of a woman's voice singing in a far-off field carried back on the breeze. Spread out before them, a great span of grassland ran towards distant hills. This was one Africa, inhabited by black men and women who still understood and accepted the old ways. Five miles south in Jacob's Rest another Africa existed on parallel lines. What made Willem Pretorius think he could live in both places at the same time?

'We have to find this woman.' Emmanuel pulled the Mozambican calendar from his pocket and laid it out on the small table between them. The time for secrets was over. 'She was the last person to see Pretorius alive and maybe she can tell us what he was doing on these particular days.'

Shabalala studied the calendar. 'The captain was in Mooihoek on the Monday and Tuesday before he died but he did not leave the town on the other days.'

'What do you think those red markings mean? Did he go somewhere for a few days each month?'

'No. He went to Mooihoek to buy station supplies and sometimes to Mozambique and Natal with his family, but not every month.'

'These markings mean something.' Emmanuel sensed another dead end coming up. 'If Pretorius was doing something illegal . . . smuggling goods or meeting up with an associate . . . would you have known?'

'I think so, yes.'

'And was he doing anything like that?'

Shabalala shook his head. 'Captain did not do anything against the law.'

'You don't think the Immorality Act counts?' Emmanuel was amazed by the tenacious respect Shabalala still held for his dead friend. Of all the people in Jacob's Rest Shabalala had earned the right to be cynical about Willem Pretorius, the lying, adulterous white man.

'He paid *lobola*. A man may take many wives if he pays the bride price. That is the law of the Zulu.'

'Pretorius wasn't a Zulu. He was an Afrikaner.'

Shabalala pointed to his chest just above the heart. 'Here. Inside. He was as a Zulu.'

'Then I'm surprised he wasn't killed sooner.'

There was a shuffle at the back door and the round-faced, round-bottomed woman from the kitchen carried a tea tray onto the *stoep* and set it down on the table.

'Detective Sergeant Cooper, this is my wife, Lizzie.'

'*Unjani*, mama.'

Emmanuel shook hands with the woman in the traditional Zulu way, by holding his right wrist with his left hand as a sign of his respect. The woman's smile lit up the *stoep* and half the location with its warmth. She was a fraction of her husband's height but in every way his equal.

'You have good manners.' Her greying hair gave her the authority to speak where a younger woman would have stayed silent. She gave the calendar a thorough look-over.

'My wife is a schoolteacher.' Shabalala tried to find an excuse for his wife's inquisitive behaviour. 'She teaches all the subjects.'

Lizzie touched her husband's broad shoulder. '*Nkosana*, may I see you in the other room for just a moment, please?'

There was an awkward silence before the Zulu policeman stood up and followed his wife into the house. It didn't do well for a woman to interrupt men's business. The murmur of their voices spilled out from the kitchen. How Captain Pretorius arranged the purchase of a second wife was not as important as finding the woman herself. She was the key to everything.

Shabalala came back out onto the *stoep*, but remained standing. He tugged on an earlobe.

'What is it?'

'My wife she says this calendar is a woman's calendar.'

'It was the captain's. I found it at the stone hut on King's farm.'

'No.' Shabalala fidgeted like an awkward schoolboy. 'It is a calendar used by women to . . . um . . .'

Shabalala's wife stepped out from the kitchen and picked up the calendar. 'How silly can a grown man be?' she asked Shabalala with a click of her tongue. She pointed to the red-ringed days. 'For one week a month a woman flows like a river. You understand? This is what this calendar is saying.'

'Are you sure?'

'I am a woman and I know such things.'

Emmanuel was stunned by the simplicity of the explanation. It would never have occurred to him in a hundred years of looking. The calendar was about the woman and her cycle, not an elaborate puzzle of illegal pick-up dates and activities. The camera, the calendar and the photos were all linked to the shadowy little wife, whoever she was.

'Thank you,' he said, then turned to Shabalala. 'We have to find the woman before the Security Branch beats a confession from the man in the cells and then throws all the other evidence out the window.'

'The old Jew,' Shabalala suggested. 'He and his wife also know many of the coloured people.'

'He won't speak,' Emmanuel said. 'But I know someone who might.'

Emmanuel crossed the street to the burnt-out shell of Anton's garage and Shabalala set up watch in the vacant lot next to Poppies General Store. If Zweigman took flight during Emmanuel's talk with Anton, the black policeman had orders to follow and observe from a distance.

Emmanuel entered the work site and the coloured mechanic looked up from the wheelbarrow of blackened bricks he was cleaning with a wire brush. Slowly, a sense of order was being imposed on the charred ruins of the once-flourishing business.

'Detective.' Anton wiped his sooty fingers clean with a rag before shaking hands. 'What brings you to these parts?'

'You know most of the coloured women around here?' Emmanuel didn't waste time with preliminaries. If he didn't get anything from the mechanic, then he'd move on to the old Jew.

'Most. This got something to do with the molester case?'

'Yes,' Emmanuel lied. 'I want to find out what set the victims apart from the other coloured women in town.'

'Well . . .' Anton continued moving bricks to the wheelbarrow. 'They were all young and single and respectable. There are one or two women, I won't mention names, who are free and easy with their favours. Molester didn't go after them.'

'What about Tottie? You know anything about her private life?'

'She hasn't got one. Her father and brothers have her locked down so tight a man's lucky to get even a minute alone with her.'

'No rumours about her taking up with a man from outside the coloured community?'

The mechanic stopped his work and wiped the sweat from his brow. His green eyes narrowed. 'What you really asking me, Detective?'

Emmanuel went with the flow. There was nothing to gain now from being shy or subtle. 'You know any coloured man who practises the old ways? A man who might take a bride price for his daughter?'

Anton laughed with relief. 'No dice. Even Harry with the mustard gas would never swap his daughters for a couple of cows.'

It was highly likely the deal, any deal with native over-tones, was done in secret to avoid the scorn of a mixed-race community that worked tirelessly to bury all connection to the black part of the family tree.

'Has any coloured man come into money that can't be explained?'

'Just me.' Anton grinned and the gold filling in his front tooth glinted. 'Got my last payment a couple of days ago but I don't have a piece of paper to prove where it came from.'

The secretive Afrikaner captain and the coloured man who'd bargained for sexual access to his daughter were not likely to advertise their venture in any way. Only a traditional black man, steeped in the old ways, would talk openly about the bride price paid for his daughter.

'Okay.' Emmanuel abandoned the line of questioning and backtracked. 'Have there been rumours about any of the women in town or out on the farms taking up with a man from outside the community?'

Anton carefully selected a charred brick and began scrubbing in earnest. 'We love rumours and whispers,' he said. 'Sometimes it feels like the only thing that keeps us together.'

'Tell me.'

'If Granny Mariah hears I repeated this, she will hang my testicles out to dry on her back fence. I'm not exaggerating. That woman is fierce.'

'I promise she won't get that information from me.'

'Couple of months back . . .' Anton chose to talk to the brick in his hand, 'Tottie let slip to some other women that she thought the old Jew and Davida were close. Too close.'

'Any truth in it?'

'Well, Davida was over at the Zweigmans' house all hours of the day and night. She walked in and out whenever she pleased and it didn't seem right, one of us being so comfortable with whites.'

'Did anyone ask her what she was doing there?' He couldn't connect the heated exchange of bodily fluids with the shy brown mouse and the protective old Jew. His relationship with her seemed paternal, not sexual.

'Reading books, sewing, baking, you name it, she always had an explanation for being there.' Anton worked a lump of ash out of the brick's surface with his fingernail. 'I was sweet on Davida at the time. We went walking and I even got some kisses in but she changed, Davida did. It was like she went into a shell once the talking started. She wasn't like you see her today, all covered up and quiet. The girl had some spark back then.'

'Really?'

'Oh, yes. Beautiful wavy hair down to the middle of her back; all natural, not straightened. At socials she was the first one up to dance and the last one to sit down. Granny had her hands full with her, I'll tell you.'

The description didn't remotely match the cloistered woman hiding under a headscarf. But the fact that the shy brown mouse once had long black hair did make her a possible match for the model in the captain's photographs. What was her body like under the shapeless clothes that hung from her like sackcloth?

'What happened?' Emmanuel asked.

'I still can't figure it,' Anton said. 'She got through the molester thing okay and then one day the hair is all gone and she won't walk with me anymore.'

'When did this change take place?'

'April sometime.' Anton threw the damaged brick into a wheelbarrow. 'Zweigman and his wife nursed Davida through a sickness and when she came out, well, nothing was the same as it was before.'

April. The same month Captain Pretorius discovered the German shopkeeper was actually a qualified surgeon. Did Zweigman reveal the extent of his medical skills during treatment of Davida's mysterious illness? And if that were the case, how had Willem Pretorius found that out? The shy brown mouse was the only common link between the two men.

'Thanks for your help, Anton,' Emmanuel said and held his hand out to end the informal interview. 'Good luck with the clean-up.'

He wanted to run through the connections between Willem Pretorius and Davida Ellis with Shabalala so he could clarify the links in his own mind. First, Donny Rooke sighted the captain behind the grid of coloured houses on the night he was murdered. Then Davida appeared at the stone hut. Somehow *Celestial Pleasures* had travelled from Zweigman's study to Pretorius's locked room as well. The elements were beginning to connect.

'Detective.' Anton stayed half a step behind him. 'I wasn't joking about Granny Mariah. She'll never forgive me if I cause trouble for her granddaughter.'

Emmanuel didn't know how to tell the mechanic that Davida's troubles were likely to run far deeper and wider than a rumour spread by an ex-boyfriend. If the shy brown mouse proved to be the principal witness in the murder of a white police captain, everyone in South Africa was going to know her name and her face.

Granny Mariah and Davida were at work in the garden, planting seeds into long rows of freshly turned earth. The older woman's green eyes widened at the sight of the white policeman and his black offsider walking across her garden on a spring day.

'What do you want?' She straightened up and put her hands on her hips.

'I need to speak to Davida.' Emmanuel remained calm and pleasant in the face of Granny Mariah's hostility. There wasn't much a non-white woman could do once the force of the law turned against her.

'What do you want with her?'

'That's between Davida and myself.'

'Well, I won't have it. I won't have you coming in here and making trouble for my granddaughter.'

'It's too late for that,' Emmanuel said. He felt sorry for the fiery woman and admired the strength she showed in the face of overwhelming odds. This was a battle they both knew he was going to win.

'Granny . . .' The shy brown mouse stepped forward. 'It's all right. I'll talk to the detective.'

'No. I won't have it.'

'He's right,' Davida said quietly. 'It's too late.'

The brown-skinned matriarch held onto her grand-daughter's hand and squeezed tight. 'Use the sitting room, baby girl,' Granny Mariah said. 'It's more comfortable.'

'We'll talk in her room.' Emmanuel walked to the small white building at the edge of the garden and opened the door. Inside the old servants' quarters he pulled up a chair from which to survey the interior of the room. The wrought-iron bed and bedside table were instantly familiar from the photographs. On the floor closest to the pillows was a neat stack of leather-covered books taken from Zweigman's library. All that was missing was a giant slab of white meat lying resplendent on the bed.

Davida entered the room and the images Emmanuel had seen after getting back from Lourenço Marques flashed through his mind. The fall of long dark hair across her face, the jewel hardness of her erect nipples against the white sheets, the sleek lines of her legs ending in a thatch of dark pubic hair . . . and Willem Pretorius ready to taste it all.

'Did you know Captain Pretorius?' he asked.

'Everyone knew him.'

'I mean did you know him well enough to, say, have a talk with? That sort of thing?'

She turned to face the window, her fingers toying with the lace edge of the curtains. 'Why are you asking me these questions?'

'Why aren't you answering?'

'Because you already know the answer. That's why you're here.' Her breath made an angry sound as it escaped her mouth. 'Why must I say it?'

'I need to hear it from you, in your own words.'

'Okay.' The shy brown mouse turned to him and he glimpsed the fighting spirit of Granny Mariah alive and well in her. 'I was sleeping with Captain Pretorius in that bed right there. You happy now?'

'"Sleeping with" as in napping or "sleeping with" as in fucking?'

'Most nights we did both.' She was defiant, ready to burn all the remnants of herself as a good woman. Emmanuel liked the angry Davida a lot better than the milk-and-water version she peddled to the world.

'I'm wondering why a mixed-race woman would get involved with a married white man whose family lives just a few streets away. Do you like taking risks, Davida?'

'No. It wasn't like that.'

'How was it?'

'I didn't want to.' She scraped curls of flaking paint off the windowsill and rubbed the residue between her fingers. 'He didn't want to.'

'He forced himself, did he?' Emmanuel didn't try to hide his scepticism. How long did it take Willem Pretorius to raise the white flag and surrender to the pleasure of the wrought-iron bed? A day, a week, or possibly a whole month?

'He tried,' Davida insisted. 'First with abstinence and then with the photos, but those things didn't work.'

'Tell me about the photographs,' he said.

She'd volunteered the information without knowing he was in possession of printed copies. Maybe it made her feel better to admit to the things in her life that had been locked in the internal vault. Being a model in pornographic photographs was an illegal activity sure to have her barred from membership in the League for the Advancement of Coloured Women.

'Captain said if he had some photos to look at, then he wouldn't have to touch me. He said looking at pictures was a lesser sin than committing adultery.'

'I see.'

The differences between the two envelopes of photographs was stark. The first pictures were naive and gentle, the second explicit and untamed. Some time between shooting roll number one and roll number two, sin had won the battle for Captain Pretorius's soul.

'But the photographs didn't work and the two of you ended up committing adultery? Is that right?'

'Yes.' Her voice dropped to a whisper. 'That's what happened.'

'What was your relationship like?'

'I already told you.'

'So, Captain Pretorius would have sexual relations with you and leave immediately afterward? There was nothing more to it?'

'No. Captain liked to stay and talk for a while afterward.'

'How would you describe your relationship with him? Good?'

'As good as it could be.' She shrugged her shoulders. 'There was never going to be wedding bells.'

'Then why did you do it? Anton or any of the other coloured men in town would have been more suitable choices, wouldn't they?'

She made a sound of disbelief low in her throat. 'Only a white man would ask a question like that and expect an answer.'

Emmanuel felt he was seeing her for the first time. The meek coloured girl he could deal with, even ignore, but this furious sharp-eyed woman was something else altogether.

'What's the question got to do with my being white?'

'Only white people talk about choice like it's a box of chocolates that everyone gets to pick from. A Dutch police captain walks into this room and I say what to him? "No, thank you, Captain sir, but I do not wish to spoil my chances for a good marriage with a good man from my community, so please *ma baas* take yourself back to your wife and family. I promise not to blackmail you if you promise not to punish my family for turning you away. Thank you for asking me, Mr Policeman. I am honoured." Tell me, is that how it works for non-white women in Jo'burg, detective?'

Emmanuel felt the truth of her words. It was as if she'd slapped him hard with an open hand. He sat forwards and considered the implications of what she'd said. A secret and illegal affair with an Afrikaner certainly delayed any chance of getting married or of beginning a serious relationship with someone in her own race group. Jacob's Rest was too small to cover that level of illicit activity. Davida Ellis was stuck in limbo: an unmarried mixed-race woman tied to a married white man.

'When was the last time you saw Captain Pretorius?'

The rush of colour brought on by her tirade ebbed away, leaving her curiously ashen.

'The night he died,' she said.

'Where?'

'He came here to the room. He said for me to get my things because we were going out to the river. I didn't want to go but he was angry and said we were going.'

'What was he angry about?'

'He caught Donny Rooke spying on him and had to give him a hiding as a warning. I cleaned the captain's hands with a cloth before we left because he'd split the skin on his knuckles.'

That was one up for Donny and confirmation that Pretorius leaned hard when he had to. It was unlikely that Donny, the outcast, could have organised an assassination and a foray into Mozambique to cover his trail after the beating he'd taken. Donny wasn't nearly smart enough or strong enough for that.

'You didn't want to go out that night?'

'No.' She fell back into her old ways and concentrated on her hands while she spoke. 'I never liked going outside with the captain. I was scared that someone would see us.'

'Pretorius had no such worries?'

'He said it was okay now that he knew who was spying on him and the river was his favourite place to . . . you know . . . to go.'

Emmanuel remembered his impression of the crime scene and the distinct feeling that the victim might have been smiling when the bullet struck. Not so far off the mark, then.

'Captain Pretorius thought someone was spying on him before he caught Donny that night?'

'He said he knew there was someone out on the veldt and that he was going to catch him.'

'When did he first tell you that someone was spying on him?'

'Three, four weeks or so before he died.'

'He thought that man was Donny?'

'Yes. That's what the captain told me.'

What on earth would lead Willem Pretorius to believe that Donny Rooke, of all people, was capable of cunning undercover surveillance? The watchful presence was still out there in the dark, and it sure as hell wasn't Donny.

'What happened then?' He believed everything Davida had said so far and wondered when she'd slip and try to cover up a hole in her story. Everyone had something to hide.

'We went to the police van and I got under the blanket in the back. We drove to Old Voster's farm. Captain got out and checked to see if everything was okay. He didn't come back for a long time and . . .' She took a deep breath. 'I got scared, but then he came and said it was all clear, so we went down to the river.'

She was breathing harder now, her chest rising and falling in an unsteady rhythm. She was like this in the stone hut. Scared to death.

'Go on.'

'Captain spread the blanket out and then . . . well . . . that's when it happened. Two popping sounds and he fell forwards just like that.'

'Captain Pretorius was standing by the blanket and you were sitting down?' Emmanuel asked. Something was missing from her description of the events.

'We were both on the blanket.' She stared out the window like a prisoner watching a flock of birds soar above the barbed wire. 'We were . . . he was . . . you know . . .'

'Davida, turn around and look at me,' he said. 'Tell me exactly what happened on the blanket. Don't leave anything out. I won't be angry or shocked.'

She turned back to him but didn't lift her gaze from the middle button of his jacket. After what she'd done in the photographs, it was amazing to see a blush work its way up her neck, darkening her skin.

'Captain was doing it to me from behind.' Her voice was a reedy whisper. 'He finished and was doing up his buttons when I heard the two popping sounds. I didn't know what it was and then the captain fell forwards and I couldn't move. He was on me, lying on top of me. I tried to move but he was on top of me.'

'What did you do then?'

'My heart was beating so loud that my ears were ringing.

I was crying, too. Trying to get out from under the captain. That's how come I didn't hear him until he was behind me.'

'Who?'

'The man.'

'What man?'

'The man with the gun. He kicked my leg and said, "Run. Look back and I'll shoot you." I pushed myself out from under the captain and I ran. I fell over on the kaffir path and my necklace snapped but I didn't stop to look for it. I got up again and I ran until I got back home.'

'This man. What language did he use?'

'English. With an accent.'

'Tell me about the man. Did you see any part of him?'

'I was facing away and the captain was behind me. I didn't see him. I only heard him telling me to run.'

'From his voice,' Emmanuel said, 'what would you guess? White, coloured, black, or Indian?'

'A Dutchman,' she answered straight off. 'A proper Afrikaner.'

'Why do you say that?'

'His voice. A Boer used to giving orders.'

That description matched ninety per cent of the men who'd attended Willem Pretorius's funeral. It was the same as finding a match for a man wearing khaki work pants or overalls. He was sceptical. Wasn't it a little too improbable, and convenient, to have a phantom Afrikaner descend from the sky to absolve her of involvement in the captain's murder?

'Did you know the man, Davida?'

'No, I didn't.'

'Was it a coloured man? Someone from town?'

She looked up now, alert to the change in atmosphere. Her eyes were the colour of rain clouds.

'It was a white man,' she repeated. 'He spoke to me like I was a dog; like he enjoyed giving orders.'

'Did you know the man, Davida?' He hit the question again and waited to see where she went with it.

'I told you. No.' Her voice was pitched high with frustration. 'I don't know who it was.'

Emmanuel studied her face; strikingly pretty now that she'd ditched the novice nun pose and he could see her clearly. 'He did you a favour, didn't he? The man. No more posing for illegal photos. No more lifting your skirt every time Pretorius came calling.'

'That's not right. I didn't want to hurt the captain.'

'Why not?' Emmanuel countered. 'Sleeping with you is against the law. Making pornographic photographs is also against the law and yet he forced you to do both those things. That's right, isn't it? You couldn't say no to an Afrikaner police captain.'

'That's true.' The rain clouds burst and she wiped the tears from her face with a quick hand. Crying for a dead Dutchman in front of an Englishman. Could there be a more ridiculous thing for a mixed-race woman to do?

'You had feelings for him,' Emmanuel said. He'd seen the photograph she'd taken of Pretorius. Davida and the captain shared more than just a mutual physical pleasure.

'I didn't love him.' She was angry about the tears and the cool way he watched her struggling for control. 'But I didn't hate him, either. He never did anything to hurt me. That's the truth.'

'There's plenty of ways to hurt someone without raising a hand to them.' Emmanuel's own anger came in a flash and he let ten per cent of it out to breathe. 'What will happen when you testify in court and everyone in South Africa hears about the photos and the fact that you were a white policeman's *skelmpie*? Will that feel good or will that hurt? No matter. You can always remember how considerate Willem Pretorius was when he led you down the road to nowhere.'

'You're cruel,' she said.

Emmanuel stayed quiet for a moment. He'd gone too far. 'I'm sorry,' he said. 'Let's get back to the riverside. Is there anything else you can tell me about the man who shot Captain Pretorius? Anything at all will help.'

It took her a while to recover from the terrifying spectre of the courtroom and the public fallout from the murder trial.

'He was quiet,' Davida said. 'Like a cat. I didn't know he was there until he was right behind me.'

'You were frightened and crying,' Emmanuel reminded her. 'Hearing anyone would have been hard.'

'I know but . . . it was like the time the Peeping Tom grabbed me. I didn't know he was there until right before he jumped. It was like that.'

'Was the killer's accent the same as the man who grabbed you?' Emmanuel asked. No matter which way the case turned, the molester was always there, like a shadow.

'They both sounded strange.' She looked directly at him, the connection clicking into place. 'Like someone putting on a voice.'

Well, if she was lying about the man at the river, he couldn't fault her performance. She appeared amazed not to have made the link before now between the killer on the riverbank and the molester.

Emmanuel digested the new information. It supported his theory that the captain's murder was tied to small-town secrets and lies and not part of an elaborate communist plot to derail the National Party government.

He stood up and brushed the creases from the front of his trousers. Two days ago he'd believed Davida was a shy virgin who shrank from the touch of men not of her own 'kind'. That perception was now a confirmed pile of horseshit and he was forced to give serious credence to her version of events regarding the captain's murder. He no longer trusted his instincts when it came to the captain's little wife.

Was that because, as the sergeant major suggested, there was something in her that stirred him? Emmanuel avoided looking at the wrought-iron bed and resisted the flood of uncensored images that came to him in a rush. Of all the times for his libido to rise from the dead, this would have to be the worst. Davida Ellis was a mixed-race woman and a key witness in the murder of an Afrikaner policeman: the devil's very brew.

Emmanuel turned his back on the bed and faced the window where she stood. 'When did you take up with Pretorius? Before or after the molester stopped?'

'After. The first time the captain came into this room was to interview me about the attacker. That was the end of December.'

'Do you remember being asked anything unusual by the captain?'

'Well . . .' She considered her answer. 'Everything about the interview was strange. Not like with Lieutenant Uys, who asked three questions and then chased me out of the police station.'

'Strange in what way? Tell me about it.'

'Captain came here to this room by himself.' She let that breach of protocol sink in. 'He asked me to sit down on that chair and close my eyes. I did and then he asked me to think about the man who'd grabbed me. He asked a lot of questions. Was the Peeping Tom bigger or smaller than me? I said bigger but not by that much. What was his skin like? Rough or smooth? I said smooth with only a little roughness, like a man who works with his hands now and then. Did his skin smell of anything in particular? Coffee, cigarettes, grease, or soap – any of those things? I said no but his hands did smell familiar. Captain told me to keep my eyes shut and try to remember. Where had I come across the smell before?'

'Did you remember?'

'I said that Anton's hands smelled the same way. Like crushed gum leaves.'

'You think Anton's the Peeping Tom?'

'No,' Davida said. 'Anton's hands are rough, like sandpaper, and his arms are hard with muscles. The man who grabbed me had soft hands and a smaller body than Anton's.'

He didn't ask her how she knew those intimate details about Anton. Presumably she did a lot more than take the air when she went out walking with the lanky mechanic.

'How did Captain Pretorius react when you told him about the smell on the molester's hands?' There was no mention of the gum leaf smell in the record of interview typed up and filed after the captain's informal visit to the old servants' quarters. There had to be a reason for the omission.

Davida shifted uncomfortably, and then seemed to realise that both her reputation and the captain's were lost beyond any hope. Head up, she spoke to Emmanuel directly, in much the same way as Granny Mariah had outside the church. 'My eyes were closed. I didn't see his face but I know he was pleased. He stroked my hair and said, "You're a clever girl to remember that, Davida." I opened my eyes and he was half-way out of the door.'

What was it about the town of Jacob's Rest? The heat, the isolation, or maybe just the proximity of the race groups appeared to make the exercise of power over others irresistible. Emmanuel himself had almost touched Davida's wet hair outside the captain's stone hut because he'd tasted the thrill of knowing that she was under his command and would keep his secrets safe. Wasn't that feeling of power just an extension of the white *induna* fantasy that the National Party was now enacting into law?

'Did you ever tell Anton about the connection with the Peeping Tom? Ever ask him what the crushed gum leaf smell was?'

'Captain came back here three or four days later and it was hard to talk to Anton after that. I don't know what the smell was and the captain never mentioned it again.'

'Did you always call him "Captain"?'

The bold act evaporated and Davida went back to looking at the magic spot in front of her right toe. 'He liked to be called Captain before and during and then Willem afterward.'

Yes, well. A relationship with a morally upstanding Dutchman with a taste for pornography and adultery was bound to come with a dizzying level of complications and arcane rules. Emmanuel glanced around the room and took note of the hastily made bed and the dust motes dancing over the painted concrete floor. Seemed that Willem got all the neatness he needed at home and then came to this room to wallow in the mess and untidiness.

'Did you visit Pretorius at the stone hut?' he asked. The stone hut that was kept as fastidiously clean as the locked study in the immaculate Cape Dutch house but without the help of a maid.

'Yes, I did.'

'When you'd finished calling him Captain Pretorius and then Willem, did you clean for him?'

She looked up now, grey eyes sparking with indignation. 'I'm not a maid,' she said.

No, she wasn't a maid and not overly fussy about house-keeping on the whole. Somebody had cleaned the stone hut to a hospital ward level of cleanliness. The only thing missing was the astringent smell of pine antiseptic. 'Was the captain fussy about the interior of the hut? You know, did he have a place for everything and everything in its place?'

'No. He didn't care so much about keeping neat.'

'Not in this room and not at the hut,' Emmanuel said. In every other respect Willem Pretorius had kept himself very neat indeed. The immaculate white house with his immacu-late white wife, the starched police uniform and spotless undershirts were all outward indications of his clean and spotless soul. Flip a coin and you got the shadow Willem, slumming naked in an unmade bed with a smile on his face. Why was the stone hut so clean? The captain hadn't been expecting any visitors.

'What were you doing at the hut?' Emmanuel asked.

'Getting the photos.' She was nervous now, her shoulders straightening as she pulled herself out of her slouch. 'I didn't want anyone to find them.'

'Did your mother clean up the hut, Davida?'

'No.'

'What did your father think about your relationship with Captain Pretorius? Did he approve?'

That threw her and she cupped a hand to her flushed cheek. 'What are you talking about? My father died when I was a child. In a farm accident.'

'I thought Willem Pretorius arranged for a bride price to be paid to your father in exchange for you?'

'Wh – what? Where did you get that from? That's a lie.'

'Which lie are we talking about? The one about the bride price or the one about your father being dead?'

Davida quickly hid her fear and confusion in her shy

brown mouse persona. 'I told you the truth about Captain Pretorius and myself. I even told you what we were doing when he got shot. Why would I lie to you now, Detective Sergeant Cooper?'

'I don't know.' He noted the correct use of his title. 'But I'm sure you have your reasons.' He walked to the door, conscious of Shabalala waiting outside and of the gathering speed of the investigation. He had to make the connection between the molester and the captain's killer real enough to stand up in court. He needed evidence.

'Are you going to take me to the station?' she said.

'No.'

The Security Branch and the Pretorius brothers were the last people he'd expose her to. She was safe so long as she remained an anonymous coloured woman working for an old Jew in a shabby local store. Once she'd been revealed as Captain Willem Pretorius's doxy the knives were going to come out and the punishment for her transgressions would be fierce.

'What do I do?' She sounded lost now that everything about her secret life had been exposed.

'Stay here. You can help your granny in the garden but don't leave the property until I get back and tell you it's okay to move around.'

'When will that be?'

'I don't know.' He pulled the door halfway open, then stopped. 'What happened back in April?'

'How do you know about that?'

'I don't. That's why I'm asking.'

She hesitated, then said, 'I had a miscarriage. Dr Zweigman made sure everything was cleaned up and healed but the captain thought he killed the baby. They had a fight about it. I never talked about Dr Zweigman with the captain after that and I never talked about the captain with Dr Zweigman, but we all knew.'

'I'm sorry,' Emmanuel said and stepped out of the room and into the garden. He was sorry to have ever heard of Jacob's Rest. He was also sorry to discover that the disconnect switch, the one that allowed him to endure the grisliest murder investigations without getting emotionally involved, no longer worked.

'Crushed gum leaves . . .' Emmanuel said to the mechanic after he and Shabalala had made their way back to the garage. 'What do you use on your hands that has that particular smell?'

Anton rummaged in a wooden bucket and pulled out a tin can stamped with an impression of a slender leaf with jagged thunderbolts spiking out from it. 'Degreaser. Us mechanics use it to clean up. It gets the dirt up from around the nails and between the fingers.'

'Who would use this particular cleaner?' Emmanuel prised opened the top and sniffed the thick white slurry. The gum leaf smell was intense. 'Just mechanics, or anyone fixing machinery?'

'Well, it's not cheap, so it wouldn't be used by someone fiddling around with their bicycle or bore pump. The only other place I've seen this stuff in town is at the Pretorius garage.'

'Is that where you get your supply?'

Anton laughed. 'Good heavens! Can you imagine Erich Pretorius letting me buy anything from his place? No, I get my little sister to bring back two or three cans when she comes home from Mooihoek for the holidays. She's at boarding school there. She was only down this weekend because of the funeral.'

'Would you notice if a can was missing?'

'Definitely. I string my supply out over the year. Like I said, it's expensive. December's supply has got to last to Easter, then I have to stretch the next one to August.'

'December and August?' Emmanuel gave the can of precious cleaner back to Anton and pulled out his notebook. Something was nudging his memory. 'Why those months in particular?'

'School holidays,' Shabalala said. 'My youngest son comes home also at these times.'

The molester was active during two distinct periods: August and December. Emmanuel gave his notes a quick check. That was right. He checked specific dates with Anton. The attacks occurred during the holidays and at no other time of year. The attacker might be partial to schoolgirls. Or on school holidays himself.

'Gentlemen.' Zweigman appeared holding a container of his wife's butter biscuits as an entrée into the conversation. 'My wife will be upset if I do not deliver these as promised.'

'The molester? What made you think it was a white man?' Emmanuel said.

'I have no proof. Just a feeling that the colour of his skin is the reason why he was not caught and brought to trial.'

'Okay.' Emmanuel included all three men in the conversation. 'Let's assume the molester was a Dutchman. Are there any white men that you know of who are only here in town for the big school holidays?'

Zweigman, Anton and Shabalala all shook their heads in the negative. Emmanuel moved on. 'Which white boys were at boarding school last year? I'm talking about boys over the age of fourteen.'

'The Loubert boys, Jan and Eugene,' said Anton. 'Then there was Louis Pretorius and I believe the Melmons' son Jacob. I don't know about the Dutch boys out on the farms.'

'What about Hansie?' It was a ludicrous thought but Emmanuel had to cover all the bases. Whittling down the suspect list by scraping together pieces of information on white schoolboys was a primitive science at best.

'Training,' Shabalala answered. 'The constable was at the police college during the last half of the year.'

'The boys who were away at school last year? Did any of them ever get caught on the kaffir paths after dark?'

'Louis and the Loubert boys,' Anton replied. 'They were using the path to obtain . . . um, things that the captain thought were unhealthy.'

'Liquor and *dagga* from Tiny? Is that right?'

'*Ja.*' Anton lifted his eyebrows in amazement. 'I thought only Captain Pretorius and the coloured people knew about that. It was kept pretty quiet.'

'Small town,' Emmanuel said. 'Which of those three boys would have access to the cleaner?'

'Louis for sure,' Anton answered again. 'The boy is always messing around with engines and fixing things up. He's good with his hands and Erich lets him have whatever he wants from the garage.'

'Was Louis home for the August and December holidays?' Emmanuel asked Shabalala.

'Yes,' Shabalala said. 'He came back for all the holidays. The missus does not like him staying too long away.'

That was three out of three for Louis. He knew the kaffir path almost as well as a native; he was home for the holidays; and he had easy access to the eucalyptus-scented cleaner.

Those facts alone warranted an interview even though the idea of the boy as the molester still seemed ludicrous.

Emmanuel went back to the bit about Louis being good with his hands. On the first day of the investigation Louis had given the distinct impression that his father was the mechanical whiz. He'd said as much.

'I thought the captain was letting Louis help him fix up an old motorbike,' Emmanuel said.

'Other way around. The captain was helping Louis. There's not much that boy doesn't know about engines but the captain was always asking for help after he'd stuffed something up.'

'You think Louis is capable of finishing that Indian motorbike without help?'

'Completely.' Anton placed his precious supply of antigrease cleaner into the wooden bucket. 'Beats me why he went to bible college when he should have been working at his brother's place. Being a mechanic suits him a hell of a lot better than being a pastor.'

'Yes, but it doesn't suit his mother.' Mrs Pretorius had a pretty clear idea about her youngest son's future: a future free of oil stains and overalls.

'The school holiday inquiry is an interesting one,' Zweigman broke in politely. 'But that does not explain why the attacks stopped in the middle of the Christmas holidays and have not recurred.'

'You're right, December twenty-sixth was the last reported attack. That still leaves how much of the holiday?'

'The first week of January,' Shabalala replied so softly that Emmanuel turned to him. The Zulu constable looked just as he had on the banks of the river the moment before they pulled Captain Pretorius from the water. His face carried sadness too deep to be expressed with words.

'The Drakensberg.' Emmanuel remembered Hansie's drunken ramblings out on the veldt. When had the captain sent Louis 'a long way away' after discovering the drinking and *dagga* smoking? 'Is that where he was, Shabalala?'

'*Yebo,*' the Zulu man said. 'The young one, Mathandunina, was taken by the captain on the first day of January to a place in the Drakensberg mountains in Natal. I do not know why.'

Emmanuel scribbled van Niekerk's name and phone number and a query onto a page in his notebook, tore it out, and handed it to Zweigman.

'Call this number and ask this man, Major van Niekerk, if he has an answer to this question. Constable Shabalala and I will be back within the hour. If not, look for us in the police cells.'

It was five past twelve and Miss Byrd was sitting on the back steps of the post office, chewing on a canned meat sandwich made with thick slices of soft white bread. She was startled to see both the detective sergeant and the Zulu policeman walking towards her.

'The engine part that Louis Pretorius is waiting for? Has it come in yet?' Emmanuel said.

'It came the day before his father passed. Tragic, hey? Captain not getting to ride the motorbike after all the hard work he and Louis put into it. To be so close and not . . .'

'I thought Louis was coming to the post office every day to check for the part?'

'No.' Miss Byrd smiled. 'He calls in to collect the mail for his mother. He's very considerate that way, a very sweet young boy.'

'Yes, and Lucifer was the most beautiful of all God's angels,'

Emmanuel said. He and Shabalala walked back onto the kaffir path. They started as one towards the captain's shed. He'd told the Zulu constable about the attack in the stone hut and the mechanical rattle he'd heard just before passing out.

'Looks like he dismantled the bike after he finished it, so no-one knew he had transport.' Emmanuel took a guess at the sequence of events. 'I'm willing to bet that Pretorius didn't know anything about the engine part arriving from Jo'burg.'

'He said nothing of it to me.'

They picked up the pace and jogged in unison across the stretch of veldt that swung around the back of the police station and curved past the rear fence line of the houses facing onto van Riebeeck street. The noon sun had burned away the clouds to reveal a canopy of blue.

'You don't have to come in,' Emmanuel said when they reached the shed door. 'Right or wrong, this is going to cause big trouble.'

'That one inside.' Shabalala hadn't even broken a sweat on the run. 'He is the only one who knew which kaffir paths the captain was running on. I wish to hear what he has to say to this.'

Emmanuel gave the door a shove with his shoulder, expecting resistance, but found none. The door swung open to reveal the darkened interior of the work shed. He stepped inside. Both Louis and the motorcycle were gone. Emmanuel walked over to the spot where the Indian had been resting on blocks and found a large oil stain but nothing else.

'The little bastard's taken off on his motorbike. You have any idea where he could have gone, Shabalala?'

'Detective Sergeant –'

Dickie and two new Security Branch men wrestled the Zulu constable from the open doorway. Lieutenant Piet Lapping entered wearing a sweat- and ash-stained shirt and rumpled pants. Lack of sleep had made his craggy face look like a bag of marbles stuffed into a white nylon stocking.

'Lieutenant Lapping.' Emmanuel smelled the anger and frustration coming directly off Piet's sweat-beaded skin and concentrated on remaining calm. The Security Branch couldn't nail him for anything. Not yet.

'Sit down.' Piet indicated the chair in front of the hunting desk. Dickie and his two bulldozer pals followed and took up positions at either side of the door. Emmanuel did as he was told and sat down.

'Dickie.' Piet held out his hand and took a thin folder from his second in command, which he held up for closer inspection. 'You know what this is, Cooper?'

'A file,' Emmanuel said. It was the information folder delivered by special messenger on the day he'd gone to Mozambique.

'A file . . .' Piet paused and rummaged in his pants pocket for a cigarette. 'Sent especially to us by district headquarters. Have you seen this particular file before, Cooper?'

'No, I have not.'

Piet lit his cigarette and allowed the flame from his silver lighter to burn longer than necessary before snapping it shut with a hard click. He placed the file gently onto Emmanuel's lap.

'Take a good look at it. Open it up and tell me if you see anything unusual about the contents.'

Emmanuel cracked the yellow cover and made a show of checking the inside before closing the file and resting his hands on the folder.

'It's empty.'

'Hear that, Dickie? It's empty.' Ash from the lieutenant's cigarette fell onto the file but Emmanuel did nothing to remove it. 'It's obvious to me now that Cooper was promoted quick smart because he's sharp. He's got it up here, in the *kop*, where it counts. Isn't that so, Detective Sergeant?'

Emmanuel shrugged. They weren't having a conversation; Lieutenant Lapping was running through the standard text-book interrogation warm-up that demanded the interrogator make at least some attempt to extract information via voluntary confession. Beating suspects was hell on the hands and the neck muscles and from the look of him Piet was coming off a heavy night in the police cells.

'I'm not angry.' The lieutenant went down on his haunches like a hunter checking a spoor trail. 'I just want to know how the fuck you managed to extract the contents of a confidential file while it was under lock and key.'

Up close, Emmanuel saw the blue smudges of exhaustion under pockmarked Piet's eyes and smelled the gut-churning mix of blood and sweat coming off his person. It was a rank abattoir fug overlaid with the mild lavender perfume of a common brand of soap.

Emmanuel did his best not to pull back from the Security Branch officer. 'Maybe district headquarters forgot to include them,' he said.

Piet smiled, then took a deep drag of his cigarette. 'See, with any other team of police I'd buy that explanation. But this is my team and my team doesn't make mistakes.'

'I'd go back to district headquarters and see who typed the report and posted the file,' Emmanuel suggested.

'Done all that,' Piet replied almost pleasantly. 'And what I found was this: you, Detective Sergeant Cooper, were the person who helped the messenger sign the folder into the police box when it arrived in town.'

'I was being polite. One department of the police is supposed to help another department, isn't it?'

'My first thought is that your close friend van Niekerk

tipped you off about what was in the folder. You knew the file was coming and somehow you managed to lift the contents. Did one of those spinsters at the post office let you into the police box? We've been too busy to ask them in person but I think an hour alone with me will get them to open up, so to speak.'

The Security Branch operatives laughed at Piet's turn of phrase and Emmanuel sensed the group's anticipation at the possibility of questioning two country maids. Affable, trusting Miss Byrd with her fondness for feather hats. Five minutes in Lieutenant Lapping's company and she'd be broken for good.

'Why are you chasing postal clerks? I thought you had a communist in the bag, ready to confess. Did something go wrong at the station?'

Piet's dark eyes were dead at the very centre. 'The first thing you will have to accept, Detective, is that I am smarter than you. I know you took those pages and I will find out how. I will also find out why.'

'No confession, then? What a shame. Paul Pretorius was certain it would only take and hour or two for the suspect to open up, so to speak.'

Piet smiled and the dark centre of his pupils came alive with a bright flash of intent. 'I promised Dickie that he could work on you if the time ever came, but I've changed my mind. I'm going to enjoy seeing you crack myself.'

'Like you cracked the suspect at the station?' Emmanuel said. A Security Branch officer he might be, but Lieutenant Lapping had superiors to report to, generals and colonels hungry for a victory against enemies of the state.

Piet blinked hard, twice, then got to his feet and strode to the doorway. He put his hand out and Dickie placed a brown paper envelope in it with a look that sent a chill down Emmanuel's back.

What the hell did they have? It was good. It had to be. Keep calm, he told himself. You've been through a war. You've seen things that killed other men and you survived. What was there to be scared of?

'You know what's in here?' Piet held the envelope at eye level.

'I don't have a clue.' Emmanuel found that he sounded calm despite the sick rolling of his stomach. What the hell was in the envelope? Had they somehow got a new background report on him in the last fourteen hours?

Piet opened the envelope and extracted two photos, which he held up with schoolmarmish precision. 'Tell me, Cooper, have you seen these images before?'

There wasn't time to slip the mask of indifference back into place. He tried to make sense of it, to see all the angles at the same time, but he couldn't get past the stark black-and-white images of Davida Ellis first with her legs spreadeagled and then stretched out on the bed like a cat waiting to be stroked. His copies were halfway to Jo'burg, safely packed under a layer of pink plastic rollers in Delores Bunton's luggage. Unless . . . unless the Security Branch had somehow intercepted his courier.

'So . . .' Piet ground his cigarette out with the heel of his shoe. 'You have seen them before.'

'Where did you get them?'

'We found them exactly where you left them. Under your pillow.'

Was Piet telling the truth or just trying to catch him out in a lie? He had no idea and that was just the way the Security Branch boys liked it. Until he knew exactly where the photographs came from he was going to play for time and information.

'What were you doing in my room?' he asked. 'You looked through it the other day and didn't find anything.'

'Some fresh information came to light.' Piet signalled to Dickie, who took the photos, but remained standing by his partner's side. 'Information concerning your personal tastes.'

Dickie made a tutting sound and leered at the images of the woman. 'That's two laws broken right there, Cooper. If it was a white woman or a light-skinned one we might have turned a blind eye but this . . . this is serious business.'

'Where did you get the information from?' Emmanuel asked. It seemed that both Dickie and Piet were playing the personal angle. They were tying the photographs to his alleged perversions and not to the homicide investigation. Good. That meant the bundle of photos he'd sent off on the 'Intundo Express' bus were safe. The feeling of triumph passed quickly. He was still in hot water, caught in possession of banned materials.

'Who told us about the photos, Dickie?'

'A little bird,' Dickie replied as if the expression was something he'd just made up off the top of his head.

Emmanuel glanced at the photos. If his copies were safely on their way to van Niekerk in Jo'burg, then these images must have come from the safe in the captain's stone hut. It was the only logical explanation, and all the connections he'd made this morning pointed to the thief being the captain's youngest son.

'Was it pretty boy Louis who told you where to find the photos?' Emmanuel kept his eye on Dickie to see if the name and the description triggered a reaction. What he got wasn't a subtle clenching of the jawline but a teeth-baring snarl.

'How you can even mention his name after what you –'

'Dickie!' Piet interrupted. 'I know this kind of activity upsets you but you must remove your personal feelings from the work. We are miners and it is our job to find the seam of gold in the dirt. You cannot let the dirt bother you.'

Activity? The word stuck with Emmanuel. What activity would upset Dickie enough to warrant professional counselling from his superior officer in the middle of questioning? The answer made Emmanuel sit up straight. How deep was the hole the angelic-looking boy had dug for him?

'Louis says I molested him?'

'What exactly are you doing here in the shed, Cooper?'

'Gathering evidence.' Emmanuel stemmed the rising panic. The blond boy had set a stunning trap baited with banned images and topped it off with an accusation guaranteed to outrage every red-blooded male in Jacob's Rest.

Dickie snorted. 'A pervert looking for a pervert. That's a good one.'

'Go back and stand with the others,' Piet instructed his partner with a flex of his knotted shoulder muscles. 'I'm too tired to question Sergeant Cooper and instruct you in the finer points of the work.'

'But –'

Piet gave Dickie a look that sent him lumbering back to his corner, from where he glared at Emmanuel as if it was his fault that he'd been relegated to the sidelines.

'Well, which one is it?' Emmanuel asked. 'Do I enjoy looking at dark girls or chasing white boys?'

'They're not mutually exclusive. You could have used the photographs to stimulate the interest of a boy who would otherwise find you unattractive. You get my drift?'

'Why the hell would I choose to show an Afrikaner boy photographs of a coloured woman in order to arouse him? What kind of sense does that make?'

'Maybe those are the only photographs you could get hold of.'

'We're policemen. Either one of us could get pictures of a white girl doing everything except fucking a gorilla.

The cops and the criminals always have the best stuff, you know that.'

'You're right.' Piet patted his shirt pocket and extracted a squashed cigarette pack. 'But that doesn't take Louis Pretorius's complaint away. A jury won't think about the finer points, like the race of the woman in the photos. The fact that it's a coloured woman will only get you more prison time.'

Why had Louis exposed himself so openly? He must have known that planting the photos would finger him as the person who'd stolen the evidence from the stone hut and yet he'd done it anyway.

'Did Louis swear out a formal complaint against me in writing?' Emmanuel asked. How serious was Louis about keeping him hemmed down and out of action?

'Yes.'

'Show it to me,' Emmanuel said.

The Security Branch men were in the middle of breaking the biggest case of their careers. Where did they find the time to pen a formal report on the matter of an English pervert attempting to corrupt an Afrikaner country boy? Small potatoes compared to getting a confession from a Communist Party member tied to the premeditated murder of a police captain married to Frikkie van Brandenburg's daughter.

'You don't get to ask us for anything,' Piet said.

'Then arrest me and charge me,' Emmanuel said clearly, to make sure there was no confusion. He didn't believe they had more than Louis's verbal complaint and that wasn't enough to hold a fellow white policeman behind bars. Right at this moment he had better things to do than provide a break for the exhausted Security Branch officers.

'You know what I think?' Piet said. 'I think the file you stole had the dirt on you and your pal van Niekerk, on your mutual affection and your shared interest in boys. Penny to a pound, that's the reason he tipped you off about it.'

'Why don't you call district headquarters and get them to tell you exactly what was in the file, or is it a bad time to admit you lost it? No confession and no file. Your superiors will be pleased to hear that.'

There was movement at the door and Dickie shuffled aside to let the moon-faced policeman in the badly cut suit into the shed.

'*Ja?*' Piet gave the newcomer permission to speak.

'It's been an hour, Lieutenant. You said to find you and alert you of the time.'

Piet checked his watch with a weary shake of his head. Where did the minutes go? 'You are free to leave, Cooper, but before you go I should warn you about something.'

Emmanuel waited for the threat. He wasn't about to play second fiddle in Piet's grand orchestration of events by asking him to specify the nature of the warning.

'Louis came to the station and complained to his brother about your . . . attentions. You're lucky we were there to stop Paul Pretorius and the rest from coming after you straight away. I can't make any promises regarding your safety because we have more important things to attend to at the moment.'

The Security Branch officers had regained some of their spark. They were letting him go because he was a minor impediment to the smooth running of their investigation. An hour to shake the tree for the information about the missing file contents and Louis's allegations was all they'd allowed while Moon Face kept watch on the real prize back at the police cells. God knows what position they'd left the young man from Fort Bennington College in while they took a quick break: strung up by his thumbs or suffocating in a wet post office canvas bag?

'Has it ever occurred to you,' Emmanuel said, 'that the man at the station hasn't confessed to the murder because he isn't the killer?'

Piet turned on him. 'The kaffir was at the river at the same time and the same place as Captain Pretorius. We have the right man and by nightfall we'll have a signed confession. What have you got, Cooper? Some sad pictures of a coloured whore and a whole family of Afrikaner men ready to skin you alive. You were only on the case because Major van Niekerk was desperate for a piece of the action and now it is time for you to fuck off and let us get on with our jobs. You are way out of your depth. Understand?'

'Perfectly,' Emmanuel said. How would he end the day: beaten and kicked to shit by the Pretorius brothers or with the killer behind bars? A betting man would lay two to one on a beating. The only unknown factor was the time and the severity of the punishment.

The shed emptied. The wide stretch of the veldt spread all the way to the horizon. How was he going to find one boy in all that space?

The call, a series of short whistles followed by a soft coo, was nothing Emmanuel had ever heard before. He stepped onto the kaffir path and the birdcall repeated with a loud insistence that caught and held his attention for a second time. A thick tangle of green scrub stirred and Shabalala materialised from the underbrush like a phantom. The Zulu constable stood to his full height and waved towards the bush with an insistence that seemed to say 'run like hell', so Emmanuel did. He ran across grass and dirt, followed now by the sound of male voices in the captain's garden. He was level with the wild hedge when Shabalala grabbed him and threw him down to the ground.

Emmanuel tasted dust and felt his shoulder spasm with pain as he was held down on the ground by the Zulu's powerful hands. 'Shhh . . .' Shabalala put his finger to his lips and pointed in the direction of the captain's shed.

Emmanuel peered through the slender gap Shabalala had made in the bush cover. The Pretorius brothers were in the empty shed, searching for the English detective who'd tried to corrupt their baby brother. Henrick and Paul were the first ones out onto the kaffir path, rifles slung across their backs in a show of armed strength.

'Fuck.' Paul spoke the word with venom, his frustration evident in the hard set of his shoulders.

'He can't have gone far.' Henrick was calmer. 'Take Johannes and go round the hospital and the coloured houses. Erich and I will go this direction past the shops. We'll meet up behind Kloppers.'

'What if he's not on the kaffir path? What if he's gone bush?'

'Englishmen from the city don't go bush,' Henrick said. 'He'll be in town, hiding somewhere like a rat.'

Johannes, the quiet foot soldier of the Pretorius corps, stepped out of the shed with his hands sunk deep into his pockets. 'The motorbike. It's gone but I don't see how. Louis is still waiting for the part to come from Jo'burg.'

'We're not looking for the fucking motorbike.' Paul turned his frustrations onto his brother. 'We're trying to find that detective.'

'Well, he's not in the shed.' Erich joined the musclebound trio. 'He must have heard us coming and taken off into the veldt.'

'If he's out there, he won't last long,' Henrick said. 'First we'll check the kaffir path and then the Protea Guesthouse.

If we don't find him, we'll have a sit-down and decide which houses to search.'

The brothers split up and moved along the grass path in opposite directions. Only Johannes appeared uncertain as to the purpose of their mission. He gave the empty shed one last puzzled glance before following Paul in a quick march towards the Grace of God Hospital.

The hunting party began their first sweep of the town. The Pretorius boys had taken the law into their own hands and no-one was going to stop them.

'How am I going to find Louis and dodge his brothers at the same time?' Emmanuel wondered aloud. The size of the town made it impossible to escape the Pretorius family and the unbroken stretch of veldt made it unlikely that the boy could be found without an army of searchers.

'We will find him,' Shabalala said.

Emmanuel turned to the Zulu policeman; Shabalala needed to know exactly how deep the water was before he stepped into it. 'Louis has told his brothers that I interfered with him. It is not true, but the brothers believe him and if you are caught with me they will punish you also.'

'Look.' The black man shrugged off the warning and pointed to a shallow dip carved into the ground and camouflaged by the thick brush. Inside the hollow was a can wrapped in oilskin cloth. He pulled out the package and handed it over for inspection. Emmanuel unwrapped the can and sniffed at the still damp oilskin wrapping.

'Petrol,' he said. 'Louis's?'

'I think the young one kept it here to fill his motorbike. The can is empty.'

'Mathandunina is planning to travel,' Emmanuel said. The border was just a few miles away. If Louis slipped across to Mozambique it would take months to track him, and that's if the Mozambican police decided to cooperate. 'Can you point the direction Louis is headed in?'

'I can find where the young one has gone,' Shabalala said without arrogance. 'I will go to the shed and follow the tracks. You must follow me out here on the veldt. It is not good for you to be on the path.'

'Agreed.'

Shabalala walked to the deserted shed and stood for a while, examining the prints in the sand. He turned in the direction of the Grace of God Hospital and set off at a measured pace. Louis hadn't taken off in a haze of petrol fumes and churned grass like an impulsive teenager blowing off steam. He had stuck close to the outer edge of the town for some reason. And, Emmanuel figured, there had to be one: everything Louis had done so far was planned and thought out. The boy was slippery enough to fool his own father about the motorbike – an impressive task when you considered just how secretive and two-faced the captain had been. Like father, like son.

Emmanuel picked up his pace to catch up with Shabalala, who followed the trail to the edge of the sports club playing fields. They crossed from the white side of Jacob's Rest to the rows of coloured houses and then the paths that led north to the black location. Where the hell was Louis going?

The buildings of the hospital came into view. Emmanuel and Shabalala sidled past the morgue and the non-whites' wing. It was the same stretch of the kaffir path where the captain had parked when he came to pick up Davida Ellis for their last outdoor frolic – and where Donny Rooke had had the bad luck to be at the same time.

The distinctive line of gum trees that marked Granny Mariah's property was visible up ahead and to the left. A memory stirred and Emmanuel moved faster. He had good reason to know this place as well. It was here, within sight of that back fence, that he'd encountered the watchful human presence breathing in the darkness.

Shabalala stepped off the kaffir path and headed into the veldt at a right angle so that he was almost directly in front of him.

'What is it?' Emmanuel asked when he reached the spot where the Zulu constable was crouched down to inspect an area of disturbed earth.

'He has come off the path and parked his motorbike here.' Shabalala pointed to markings in the dirt that wouldn't make sense to anyone but a tracker. 'The young one parked and then walked back in that direction.'

They looked towards the line of gum trees. The back gate to Granny Mariah's garden swung back and forth on its hinges in the breeze. Thoughts of the Pretorius brothers' vigilante rule vanished and he and Shabalala ran to the kaffir path and the open gate.

One step into the yard and Emmanuel spotted Granny Mariah lying in a furrow of turned earth, the blood from the gash in her forehead feeding the newly planted seeds in a steady red stream. He ran to her side and felt for a pulse. Faint but there. He turned to Shabalala, who was wisely locking the gate behind him.

'Go out the front door and get the old Jew. Tell him to bring his bag and his wife's sewing kit with him.'

Shabalala hesitated.

'Go out the front,' Emmanuel insisted. The coloureds of Jacob's Rest would just have to deal with the shocking sight of a black man leaving and entering Granny Mariah's house in plain sight. 'The Pretorius boys are still on the kaffir paths, so you have to use the main streets. Get back as quickly as you can without causing a commotion.'

'*Yebo*.' The Zulu constable disappeared into the house and Emmanuel took off his jacket and rolled it under Granny Mariah's battered head. He felt her pulse again. No change, so he went to search the old servants' quarters, already certain he would find it empty. He put his head in and looked for signs of Davida before checking under the bed to make sure she wasn't hiding there.

'Davida? It's Detective Sergeant Cooper. Are you here?' He opened the wardrobe. A few cotton dresses and one winter coat with fake tortoiseshell buttons. He walked out to the garden, where he soaked his handkerchief in the watering bucket and gently wiped Granny Mariah's bloodied face. This mess was exactly what the information in the molester files pointed to: an escalation of violence leading to deprivation of liberty and God knows what else. The captain had only delayed the inevitable by sending Louis off to a farm in the mountains and then on to theological college, where, it would seem, the Holy Spirit had failed to dampen the fires of sin burning within him.

Granny Mariah groaned in pain but remained unconscious. Just as well. The disappearance of her granddaughter would be a heavy burden for the normally resilient old woman to shoulder in her weakened state. She'd be lucky to get her head off the pillow in the next few days.

Zweigman hurried into the garden with Shabalala trailing close behind. The white-haired German got to work quickly, his expert hands checking vital signs and determining the range and extent of injuries.

'Bad. But, thank God, not fatal.'

'How bad?'

'A laceration to the scalp which will require stitching. Severe concussion but the skull is not fractured.' Zweigman the surgeon took control. 'We will need to move her inside so I can clean her up and begin closing this wound. Please, go into the house and locate towels and sheets while Constable Shabalala and I move her to a bedroom.'

Emmanuel followed orders and soon Zweigman was setting up. He snapped open his medical bag and placed bandages, needles, thread and antiseptic on a dresser closest to the double bed where Shabalala had laid Granny Mariah.

Emmanuel signalled to Shabalala to move out to the garden. They stood at the back door and in view of the bloodied row of turned earth.

'Davida is gone. The captain's youngest son has taken her. There can be no other explanation,' Emmanuel said.

'I will see.' Shabalala examined the markings on the ground. He worked his way slowly to the back gate, unlocked it and continued out onto the veldt. Why, Emmanuel wondered, did he find it necessary to have the Zulu constable confirm the obvious? Was it because he still didn't trust his instinct where Davida was concerned and therefore couldn't rid himself of the niggling feeling that maybe, just maybe, Davida and Louis were somehow in this together? Two star-crossed lovers bound together by the cold-blooded murder of Willem Pretorius. But that conclusion was no more far-fetched than the teenaged boy turning out, in all probability, to be the molester.

Shabalala re-entered the garden and locked the gate behind him. His expression was grave. 'It is so,' he said. 'The young one has taken the girl with him and they have gone on the motorbike.'

'Did he take her or did she go with him?'

Shabalala pointed to scuffled lines in the dirt. 'She ran but he caught her and pulled her back to where the old one was lying in the dirt. After that, the girl went with him quietly.'

'Why would Louis show his hand before we'd even questioned him?'

'We must find Mathandunina,' Shabalala said with simple eloquence. 'Then we will know.'

Finding Louis would be a massive task requiring man-power and time – two things he didn't have and was unlikely to get any time soon.

'What direction did he go in?' Emmanuel asked, visualising the enormous stretch of grassland that surrounded Jacob's Rest on all sides and spread out across the border into Mozambique. He brought himself back to the blood-soaked garden. He had to work with what he had: a Zulu–Shangaan tracker and an enigmatic German Jew. Things could be worse; he could have been left with Constable Hansie Hepple.

'Towards the location. It is also the way to *Nkosana* King's land and the farm of Johannes, the fourth son.'

'Where would a white boy on a motorbike go with a brown-skinned girl he's holding against her will?' The whole thing carried the stamp of disaster. Surely Louis saw that?

'Not to the location.'

'Or to his brother's farm. Wherever he goes, Louis is going to attract attention. My guess is he's going to have to keep well hidden until he's –'

'Done with her.' Zweigman finished the sentence from where he stood in the dim hallway, his shopkeeper's shirt and trousers stained with blood from the operation. 'That is what you were thinking, is it not, Detective?'

'I don't know what to think. As far as I can see, the whole abduction makes no sense.'

'Maybe it makes perfect sense to Louis Pretorius.' Zweig-man reached into his pocket and pulled out a piece of paper, which he handed over. 'Your major said to pass this on to you as soon as possible.'

Emmanuel unfolded the lined sheet and read the informa-tion. Deep in the Drakensberg Mountains of Natal was a farm, a retreat, known as Suiwer Sprong, or Pure Springs, where high-bred and wealthy Afrikaners with close ties to the new ruling party sent their offspring to be 'realigned' with the Lord. Shock therapy, drug therapy and water therapy were some of the ways that 'realignment' was delivered from the hands of the Almighty to the suffering few. A Dr Hans de Klerk, who'd trained under the pioneering German eugenicist Klaus Gunther prior to the outbreak of the Second World War, was head of the set-up.

'A nut farm with a religious bent. Is van Niekerk sure of this?'

'Your major sounds like a man who is sure of many things. He is certain that this place in the Drakensbergs is the only institution that a family such as the Pretoriuses would use to seek treatment for a psychological illness.'

The family should get their money back. Whatever therapy Louis underwent hadn't stuck. A few weeks back in Jacob's Rest and Louis had fallen into his old habits in a more dangerous way than before.

Emmanuel considered the steps that had led to the abduction and assault. Louis wasn't unbalanced enough to overlook the fact that Davida Ellis was the only one who could tie him to the molester case and to the murder of his father. With Davida out of the way, all that stood between him and freedom was the word of the English detective he'd accused of trying to seduce him. It was a clever plan, well executed. So far.

'This abduction may not be as irrational as it looks.' Emmanuel recalled the information from the molester files. Reading them had given him the feeling that the perpetrator was headed for a violent culmination to his fantasy life. 'Louis gets to finish what he started in December and he gets to eliminate the only person who can connect him, however vaguely, to the murder of his father.'

'If that is the case,' Zweigman observed quietly, 'he will keep her alive until he has enacted his fantasies.'

'I think so.' Emmanuel didn't want to delve into the German's statement. He turned to Shabalala. 'Where could Louis go and hide out without being found? It has to be a place large enough to hold two people. I don't think he'll go to the captain's hut. It's not secret enough. Is there a cave or maybe an old hunting shack?'

The Zulu constable glanced up at the sky for a moment to think. Then he quickly picked up a long stick and drew a crude map in the dirt. He made three crosses at almost opposite ends of each boundary.

'There are three places on *Nkosana* King's farm that are known to me. The captain and I hid here many times when we were boys. The young one, Louis, has also been to these places with his father when the land was still with the family.'

'Can we get to all three in an afternoon?'

'They are far from each other and this one, here, we must go to on foot. It is a cave high on the side of a mountain and the bush is thick around.'

'The other two?'

'This one is an old house where an Afrikaner lived by himself. It is falling in but some of the rooms have a roof over them.'

'What's it like? The area around the house?'

'Flat. The house is sad, like the white man who used to live in it.'

'That's not the place.' Emmanuel pictured the crime scene at the river, the sweep of land and sky shimmering with a quintessentially African light. It was a beautiful place to die. Louis and his father both shared a taste for forbidden flesh and they might have been sufficiently alike to prefer courting women in an outdoor setting. There was nothing like the raw beauty of nature to arouse an Adam and Eve fantasy in which the apple was eaten to the core and the racial segregation laws were nonexistent.

'To which one of these places would you take a girl to show her the view?'

Shabalala pointed to the location of the mountain cavern. 'From the ledge in front of the cave you can see the whole country and a watering hole where the animals come to drink. It is a place to stir the heart.'

Just the sort of isolated and romantic spot a deranged Dutch boy might take a woman on her final outing. The Afrikaner love of the land was as tenacious as the influenza virus.

The cave was a long shot. But it made sense. The boy hadn't torn out onto the veldt with a captive girl without a specific place to hide already in mind. And Louis wasn't going to hide on a working farm trampled over by labourers and herds of cattle. King's personal fiefdom, once the Pretorius family home, had plenty of open space and very few people to spoil the illusion that South Africa was, in fact, empty when the white man arrived. Louis could hide there for a long while without drawing attention.

'How far on foot to this place?' Emmanuel asked.

'We must park and walk for maybe half an hour to the bottom of the hill and then fifteen minutes to the top.'

Emmanuel rounded it up to one hour. The Zulu–Shangaan tracker covered more ground in a shorter period of time than anyone he'd ever met, and that included soldiers running like hell from the fall of mortar shells.

'We should check the cave. An isolated and sheltered place on a deserted piece of land seems right for what Louis most likely has planned. I've got nothing to back up my case. It's just a feeling. That's all.'

'Your instinct and Constable Shabalala's knowledge of the land are all you have, Detective, so you must move and move quickly,' Zweigman said. 'The men at the police station will not drop even one pen to set out in search of a dark-skinned girl.'

'Not unless she's a communist,' Emmanuel said and turned to the towering black man standing at his side. Without Shabalala's help, the wheels were going to fall off the already shaky wagon.

'We'll need to get my car and head out to King's farm. Are you still with me?'

'Until the end,' Shabalala said.

They chanced the main streets in the hope that the Pretorius boys were still prowling the kaffir path. All was clear when they eased onto Piet Retief Street and moved past the white-owned businesses. The garage was open, but under the temporary management of an old coloured mechanic who shouted orders at the black petrol pump attendants from his spot in the shade. No sign of Erich the flamethrower or his big brother Henrick at Pretorius Farm Supplies, either.

A Chevy farm truck carting the wide, rusty disks of a plough provided enough cover to get them past the police station and onto the dirt road to the Protea Guesthouse. Emmanuel and Shabalala crossed the raked and tidy yard. Sun sparked off the silver hubcaps of the black Packard. A twig snapped and the Zulu constable tensed, catlike. Another twig snapped and he released a pent-up breath.

'There is someone behind the big jacaranda tree,' he said. 'We must leave this place quickly.'

The car was parked beyond the jacaranda and there was no way to get to it without one of them being caught in the ambush. He couldn't risk losing Shabalala.

Emmanuel checked their line of retreat. It was clear. He nodded at Shabalala and they ran fast and low towards the whitewashed fence and the dirt street freshly sprinkled with water to keep the dust down.

'Go, go!' Paul Pretorius was in full commando mode, calling out orders to his second in command.

Johannes stepped out from behind the fence and took up position in the middle of the driveway. Emmanuel heard the sound of Paul's boots crunching on the loose gravel behind him. Shabalala split off to the right of Johannes. Emmanuel split off to the left and together they ran a full press towards the startled fourth son. The Pretorius boys expected him to be alone and their haphazard ambush reflected the bone-deep belief that an English detective in a clean suit was easy prey.

'Stand your ground,' Paul Pretorius called out.

Brutal rounds of boarding school rugby training and bruising matches on forlorn country fields surged from the dark pit of Emmanuel's memory as Johannes moved to block his path. Left hand out, he pushed hard against Johannes's chest and heard the satisfying crunch of the fourth son's body hitting the dirt road. It was the first time that the tutelage he had received at the heavy hands of Masters Strijdom and Voss had amounted to anything.

'This way.' Shabalala sprinted towards Piet Retief Street and across the sweating asphalt to the kaffir path opposite. A shout from the direction of Pretorius Farm Supplies was enough to push them onto the grass path in record time. Now they had the whole Pretorius clan after them.

'Here.' Shabalala pulled back two loose palings in a splinter-faced row of pickets and they crawled into a squat yard with a smokehouse at its centre. The garden boy, milky-eyed with a bony face and ash-white hair, looked up with a start.

Shabalala put his finger to his lips and the old man went back to weeding the flowerbed as if nothing unusual was happening.

'Peter?'

'Yes, missus?' the garden boy answered and Emmanuel and Shabalala moved behind the smokehouse for cover. They leaned against the corrugated iron wall and waited for the appearance of the Pretorius boys or the nosy white missus.

'What's that, Peter? I thought I heard something.'

'Just the wind, missus.'

'Okay.' The voice grew fainter as the missus moved back into the sitting room. 'You make sure those weeds are gone, hey?'

'Yes. All gone, missus.' Peter's milky eyes darted up to check the position of the white detective and his third cousin by marriage, the police constable, Samuel Shabalala.

'Keep going. Down that way.' The sound of Henrick Pretorius's voice kept Emmanuel pinned against the smokehouse wall. One call from the gardener or the missus and that would be the end of the rescue mission. Shabalala rested and Emmanuel took his cue from the black constable and relaxed his clenched jaw. The pounding of footsteps diminished, then disappeared as the Pretorius boys continued the chase.

'My car's no good,' Emmanuel said. 'If they have any brains they'll have slashed the tyres or left someone sitting on the bumper to guard it.'

'We must find another car. There is one close by.'

'Where?'

'The police station.'

'The police station? How are we going to manage that, Constable?'

Shabalala moved to the front of the smokehouse and indicated a brick dwelling with coloured glass panels set into the front door and a wagon wheel fence along its wide *stoep*.

'The young policeman. He lives with his mother and his sisters. That is his house.'

'You want Hansie to get the car?'

'I can think of no other person who can get the police van from the front of the station.'

'God help us.'

Emmanuel crossed the street with Shabalala and knocked on the front door with two clear raps. Through the coloured glass panels he saw the young policeman make his way down the corridor. The door swung open and Hansie peered out with a sullen expression on his face. His blue eyes were rimmed with red and his nose glowed a dull pink from constant blowing.

'I got the necklace.' He sniffled. 'I got it back just like you said, Detective Sergeant.'

'Good work.' Emmanuel stepped into the corridor and forced Hansie back a few feet. Shabalala closed the door behind them. 'I need you to get me one more thing, Constable.'

'What?'

'The police van,' Emmanuel said. 'I need you to go to the station and collect the police van.'

'But Lieutenant Lapping gave me the day off. He said I didn't have to come in till tomorrow.'

'I'm putting you back on duty.' Emmanuel made it sound like an instant promotion. 'You're the best driver on the force. Better than most of the detectives I work with in Jo'burg.'

'Honest?' The compliment perked the boy up enough to forget about the necklace and the day off.

'Honest.' Emmanuel looked directly at Hansie in order to gauge just how deeply his words were sinking in. 'I want you to go to the police station, get the van, and drive it back here. Can you do that?'

'*Ja.*'

'If anyone asks you where you're going, tell them you are looking for a stolen . . .' His city knowledge hit against the reality of country life. What was there to steal in Jacob's Rest?

'Goat,' Shabalala supplied. 'You are looking for a stolen goat.'

'Have you got that?'

'I'm looking for a stolen goat.'

'Go straight to the police station and come straight back here with the van.' Emmanuel repeated the instructions, hoping some of the information stuck in Hansie's muddled brain.

'Yes, Detective Sergeant.' The boy straightened his uniform and quick-marched towards the front door with wind-up-toy precision. Everything – Louis's apprehension, Davida Ellis's safe return, and the service of justice – all rested in the hands of eighteen-year-old Constable Hansie Hepple. A feeling of dread assailed Emmanuel.

A skin-and-bone blonde girl, her hands and apron covered in sticky bread dough, appeared. Blue eyes, darker and denser than her brother's, glimmered with a faint internal light.

'That was a pretty necklace,' she said in Afrikaans. 'Hansie cried when he had to take it back and his sweetheart was angry with him. Ma's gone to the store to get bicarb of soda to settle Hansie's stomach.'

'We have got to find an alternative way out of here. This is no place for men like us to end,' Emmanuel said to Shabalala.

They pushed through the rough country, drawn on by the looming mass of towering rock and clouds. In an ancient time, long before the white man, the mountain must have had a spiritual significance. Emmanuel felt the pull of it as he struggled to keep tabs on Shabalala's agile navigation through the monotonous blur of branches, thorns and termite mounds.

Fifty-five minutes and one brief break later, they reached the foot of the mountain and encountered a solid rock wall softened here and there by tufts of grass and stunted trees growing from crevices carved by centuries of wind and rain. As natural formations went, it had a handsome but unfriendly face.

'How do we get up?' Emmanuel leaned back against a sun-warmed boulder that nestled beside the mountainside like a schoolboy's marble. It was good to have a break; to feel the air coming in and out of his lungs without the fiery afterburn caused by lack of oxygen.

'We go around and then up,' Shabalala said, and Emmanuel noted with satisfaction that the Zulu constable had broken a sweat on the cross-country trek.

'Is the goat on the mountain?' Hansie asked, after drinking deeply from his water canteen. The boy policeman's face had progressed from white to pink and then finally to a coal-fire red that rivalled a split watermelon for sheer depth of colour.

'I hope so,' Emmanuel said as he followed Shabalala around the base of the massive rock outcrop. They walked for five minutes until they came to a deep crease in the mountainside. Shabalala pointed to a path that wound upward and disappeared behind a windblown tree with branches bleached like bones.

'Up here.' Shabalala led them onto the skinny dirt lane, slowing now and then to check a clump of grass or a snapped twig.

'Any sign of them?' Emmanuel asked as he scrambled over

loose rocks and exposed roots. Louis and Davida could be a hundred miles in the opposite direction.

'There are three paths to the cave. I can say only that they have not come along this way.'

'Maybe they haven't come here at all.' The fear that had tugged at him since speeding out of town and heading to the mountain was now lodged like a splinter in his gut. He'd made a meal of the scraps thrown to him throughout the investigation and now he was about to find out if all the hunches and conjecture amounted to anything.

Shabalala stopped at the intersection of three paths that joined up into one and examined the ground and the surrounding loose stones. 'They are here,' he said.

A moment of relief washed over Emmanuel. He moved quickly up the path, his exhausted muscles fed by adrenaline. Louis had a good three-hour lead on them and God knows what had happened to Davida Ellis in that time.

The grass trail ended at a wide, flat rock ledge that jutted out over the steep fall of the mountainside and offered a breathtaking view of untamed country running to all points of the compass. A martial eagle, white chest feathers flashing starkly against the pale sky, circled on a warm air current in front of them. Far below on the plain, a watering hole sparkled in the late afternoon sunlight. It was as Shabalala said, a place to stir the heart.

'There.' The Zulu constable pointed across the ledge to the dark mouth of the cave hollowed into the rock face.

'Detective Sergeant . . .'

'Shh . . .' Emmanuel silenced Hansie. 'Wait behind this bush and guard the path. If anyone comes, call out to me. Understand?'

'*Ja*. Call out.'

'Good.' Emmanuel unclipped the holster at his hip, the first time he'd done so since arriving in Jacob's Rest, and pulled out his .38 standard Webley revolver. With Shabalala at his side, he ran low and fast across the rock ledge with his ears straining for the sound of voices or the click of a rifle bolt sliding back. An eerie silence followed them into the cave.

Emmanuel did a visual sweep of the interior and holstered his weapon. The cave was a scooped out oval, large enough for a Voortrekker Scout troop to hold an all-night sing-along inside. Diffused afternoon light illuminated an unsettling domestic scene. A thin bedroll made up of a sheet and grey blanket was laid out in the middle of the space and next to it, a lantern and a bucket of water. A container of rusks, strips of dried beef, and two enamel plates and cups lay on a flat stone. An open Bible, a box of candles and a coil of rope were placed on an empty rucksack, that served as an altar.

'Where are they?' Emmanuel said. The cave was set up to imitate a living place, a place to sleep and eat and do who knows what with the Bible and the rope. The teenager had every intention of spending the night and possibly longer holed up in his private chapel.

'I will see.' Shabalala checked the tracks on the floor and stepped out of the cave to investigate further. He returned quickly.

'They have gone along the narrow way to a place with a waterfall. It is spring. The water will be flowing.'

'Can we follow?'

'It is narrow. There is space for only one person to walk at a time. I can take you.'

'Let's go,' Emmanuel said. 'I don't want to take the chance of finding a second corpse in the water.'

Emmanuel swung in behind Shabalala and they approached the mouth of the pathway, which disappeared like the tail of a snake into the mountainside. A low, sweet voice singing an Afrikaans hymn stopped them at the entrance. A few swift steps and he and Shabalala were crouched behind a spiked bush with the teenaged constable, who was hot-cheeked and flustered.

'What is it?' Hansie asked.

'Whoever steps out from that pathway, you are not to make a sound,' Emmanuel said. 'Understand? Not even a whisper.'

Davida Ellis stumbled onto the flat rock ledge in her bare feet with her arms wrapped protectively around her midriff. She was soaking wet and her pale green dress clung to her brown skin. Drops of water splashed onto the rock surface and formed a small puddle at her feet. She shivered despite the mild spring heat.

Louis Pretorius appeared, stripped naked to the waist with a rifle slung across his shoulder like a native scout. He continued singing and dried his face and hair with a handkerchief, which he returned to the pocket of his damp jeans. The words of the Afrikaans hymn circled high into the clouds, as if on a fast track to the Almighty. Louis had the face and the voice of an angel.

He finished his song and laid his hand lightly on Davida's shoulder. She flinched but he didn't seem to notice her reaction to his touch. He spoke close to her ear. 'I will sprinkle clean water on you and you will be clean. Ezekiel 36:25. It feels good to be cleansed and made new, doesn't it?'

His hand moved to her neck, his fingers brushing the delicate bones of her oesophagus. 'God hears better if we speak out loud and raise our voices to Him.'

Emmanuel made ready to sprint across the rock ledge if the boy's fingers encircled Davida's throat.

'Agghh . . .' Hansie released a scandalised breath that travelled across the open space and bounced off the hard rock surfaces. He might as well have thrown a stone. Louis tensed and swung his rifle across his chest so it nestled firmly in his hands. His finger rested on the trigger and aimed the gun's barrel towards the bush.

'Come out,' he called in a voice that was close to friendly. 'If you don't I'll unload this chamber into the bushes. True as I stand here.'

'Don't —' Hansie jumped to his feet, his hands raised in surrender. 'Don't shoot. It's me. It's Hansie.'

'Who's with you?' Louis asked. 'You're not clever enough to have made it here on your own.'

'Not clever? What —'

Emmanuel and Shabalala stood up. Emmanuel didn't want Louis to panic and send Davida on a shortcut to the Lord God via the sheer drop just two feet to his left. And he sure as hell wasn't going to let Hansie Hepple conduct the negotiations for release of the hostage.

'Detective Sergeant Cooper.' Louis greeted him with a nod of his head as he would someone he'd met on the street corner or the church steps. 'I see you got out of the jam I fixed for you. And you brought along Constable Shabalala for company. What brings the three of you out to the mountain?'

'We could ask you the same thing.' Emmanuel kept his tone friendly and noted the supremely self-confident way the bare-chested boy handled his rifle. He looked born to the ways of the bandit. Davida shivered next to him.

'This is a long way to come for a shower, isn't it, Louis?' he said and tried to appraise Davida's condition. She stared at him with the mute shock he'd seen many times on the faces of civilians caught in the crush of two warring armies. Her eyes pleaded for rescue and restoration.

'I am acting on God's command. I don't expect you to understand what it is I do here today, Detective.'

'Explain it to me. I want to understand.'

'And He shall wash away the sins of the world.' Louis circled a hand around Davida's arm and jerked her against his hip. 'I have purged the dirt from her physical being with pure water and stones and now I will cleanse her soul of the sin that has made her an impure vessel.'

'Last time I checked you weren't the Lord God. You were Louis Pretorius, son of Willem and Ingrid Pretorius of Jacob's Rest. What qualifies you to clean anyone's soul but your own?'

'And He hath put a new song in my mouth, even praise unto our God: many shall see it, and fear, and shall trust in the Lord.'

In a trade-off of scripture verses, Emmanuel was sure he would lose out to Louis. The young Pretorius boy was so tightly wrapped in his holy vision that he didn't even recognise that what he'd done to Davida and her grandmother was sin itself. For Louis, it was all holy bells and whistles backed up by a chorus of angels.

'But . . .' Hansie was having trouble keeping up with the conversation. 'That girl is a darkie. What are you doing up here with one of them?'

The fire in Louis's eyes was bright enough to rival his grandfather Frikkie van Brandenburg's incendiary glare. 'When I was a child, I spoke as a child and when I was grown I put away all childish things. You, Hansie, are one of those childish things.'

'What are you talking about?' Hansie asked. 'You're not supposed to be washing or doing whatnot with one of them. It's against the law and I know that your ma won't be happy to see you standing so close, either.'

'My mission does not concern my earthly family or you. God called me and you are standing in the way of His works.'

'Let me get this straight.' Emmanuel tried to gauge the depth of Louis's delusion. 'God, the redeemer of souls, has called you to the theft of pornographic images, lies, assault, and the kidnapping of unclean women? When did you get this calling, Louis? At Suiwer Sprong or afterwards at the theological college?'

Louis's pretty face seemed to distort. 'Everything I do is in the service of the Lord.'

'Did the Lord call you to molest those women last year?'

'That was the work of the devil. I broke free of his chains and have been cleansed of all my sins.'

'Is this how they drove the sin out of you on the farm? With outdoor showers and fear?' Van Niekerk had listed 'water therapy' as one of the cures being offered at the quasi-religious nut farm. What methods had the German-trained Dr Hans de Klerk used to purify the Pretorius boy?

Louis blinked hard. 'Everything that was done to me was in the service of the Lord. I was lost and now I am found.'

Emmanuel felt an unexpected stab of pity. Louis was brought up by his mother to believe he was the light of the world, but he'd inherited his father's taste for life outside the strict moral code of the *volk*. He was torn in two, lost, and made more dangerous by a spell of 'realignment' deep in the Drakensberg Mountains.

'Was your father an impure vessel, Louis?' Emmanuel asked. He was interested in Louis's attitude to the captain's hypocrisy.

'Pa was led astray by the work of the devil, same as me.' The boy looked over at the Zulu constable. 'My pa was a good man, hey, Shabalala? A godly man.'

'I believe it.'

'I'm not disputing your pa's goodness,' Emmanuel said, 'I'm just wondering how hard he struggled with the devil. You went away to the farm and conquered the devil, but your father stayed on, and well . . . he let the devil win a few nights a week. For almost a year.'

'Captain Pretorius wasn't in league with the devil!' Hansie's voice rose three octaves higher. 'You didn't know him. He was clean inside and out.'

'No man is clean inside and out.' Emmanuel returned his attention to Louis and kept his tone even and nonconfrontational. 'You know what it is to struggle with the devil, don't you, Louis? You want to be holy and yet here you are on top of a mountain with a terrified woman, a gun, and a piece of rope coiled on your Bible.'

'This woman is the root of all the problems.' Louis curled his hand tightly around Davida's forearm until she gasped in pain. 'She is the one who needs to be cleansed of her carnal nature.'

'Like you cleansed your father at the river?' Emmanuel tested the connection between the molester and the murderer. An unbalanced boy with a sighted rifle and delusions of godhead was a dangerous animal. 'That's what you did, isn't it? You arranged a face-to-face meeting with the Almighty and then you dragged his body to the water to cleanse him of sin. Is that how it happened?'

'I don't know what you're talking about.'

'You killed your father to cleanse him, didn't you, Louis?'

'Of course not.'

'You knew he wasn't going to stop sinning, so you helped him break free of Satan's trap. I understand that. I understand how it happened.'

Louis loosened his grip on Davida's arm and levelled a

damning stare at the English detective. 'I loved my father. When the devil had me in his claws, my father prayed with me and together we found a way out. I would never raise a hand to him. He saved me.'

'You didn't shoot him at the river?'

'No. Honour your mother and your father so your days may be long on the earth. That's God's promise.'

'But you spied on your father when he was alive. That wasn't an honourable thing to do, was it?'

'Witnessing.' Louis let go of Davida's arm and pushed the messy blond hair from his forehead. 'I had to witness the depth of his wrongdoing to understand just how far he'd strayed from the path of righteousness.'

'You didn't enjoy it?' Emmanuel saw Davida slump back against the rock face and draw great mouthfuls of air into her lungs. She was still shivering and probably in shock. 'You got no pleasure from watching your father having sex with one of the women you'd messed with the previous December? How many times did you witness your father straying from the path, Louis?'

'I can't remember,' the boy muttered.

'Surely once was enough? You see your father with a brown-skinned woman and you know, don't you? You know that a sin is being committed without having to come back a second and a third time.'

'I was witnessing. I didn't enjoy what I saw.'

'Truly?' Emmanuel had the tiger by the tail and he had every intention of shaking it until it coughed up a lung. 'I think you were doing something that began with W, but it wasn't witnessing. You got as much pleasure as your father did, only from a distance.'

'Shabalala.' The bare-chested boy appealed to the black policeman. 'You know my family. We are from pure Afrikaner blood. You are from pure African blood. This business has come about because of those with impure blood among us. Is that not so?'

'Your father was pure. The woman is pure. When they were together, there was no wrong in them.'

'You can't believe that.' The boy was thrown by Shabalala's calm and forgiving statement. 'She's the reason my father went astray and was killed. The fault is in her.'

'That one there. She was your father's little wife and I tell you again, there was no wrong in them. The captain made the arrangement for her in the old way and did not intend any disrespect to come to her during his lifetime and even now after he has gone.'

Louis blushed at the Zulu constable's criticism but didn't lower his weapon. 'Your native ways are not for the *volk* to live by. Our God does not permit the tainting of our bodies or our blood with those from a lesser sphere. It is written so.'

Davida, still shaking, had inched her way along the rock wall and was now out of arm's reach of the teenage prophet.

Emmanuel stepped forward and drew Louis's attention to him. 'Did you ever offer your father the chance to come here and cleanse his sins in the waterfall?' he asked.

'No.'

'Why not?'

'There was never a good time to bring it up. I didn't know how to tell him that I knew what he was doing.'

'Well . . .' Emmanuel said. 'How about after he'd finished and both of you were satisfied and feeling good about the world? You could have met him out on the kaffir path and exchanged notes before praying together.'

'You are a foul-minded Englishman. It's a pity my brothers didn't catch you and teach you a lesson.'

Emmanuel shrugged and stared over the rock ledge to the vast sweep of country beyond. Davida was inches from the cave mouth and safety. 'By their deeds shall ye know them.' He dragged out a biblical quote from the deep vaults of memory. 'What's a jury going to make of an Afrikaner boy out here with a kidnapped coloured girl? Do you really believe your brethren will understand that you washed her body to cleanse her and spied on your father having sex with her in order to bear witness to the Lord?'

'God is my guide and my staff. It is not for man to pass judgement on what I have done.'

'Things are different now, Louis. When you got rid of your father you got rid of the one person who was willing to break the law to protect you.'

Louis's finger was tight on the trigger. 'I had no hand in what happened to my father. He was struck down before his time and I pray to the Almighty that he sees into Pa's heart and forgives his transgressions.'

'Louis . . .' Hansie's vacant blue eyes brimmed with tears of frustration. 'Tell the detective sergeant this is all a mistake. You didn't touch those coloured women and Captain didn't do like what he says . . . with the sex and the devil and the little wife.'

Louis smiled, truly the most beautiful of God's angels. 'You know what my pa told me once, Hansie?'

'No.'

'That you cannot know God until you have wrestled with the devil and the devil has won.' He turned to Davida to illustrate his point and found her gone. The rifle swung easily in the boy's hands and he raised it to his eye and took aim at the cave mouth where the woman appeared as a dark fleeting shape. His legs were spread in the classic marksman pose that gave stability to the torso and increased the likelihood of hitting the mark.

'Drop the weapon, Louis!' Emmanuel shouted across the rock ledge, handgun squarely on target. 'Drop it or I will shoot you.'

The shadow disappeared from the cave mouth and Louis slowly lowered his rifle to his hip. His fingers twitched around the barrel but the gun stayed put.

'Do not move.' Emmanuel's voice was clear and authoritative as he closed the distance between them. 'Drop the gun to the ground and kick it towards me. Now.'

Louis loosened his grip and the rifle clattered across the ledge where Constable Shabalala picked it up and swung it across his back. The captain's youngest son sank down into a crouch and stared out across the miles of brown- and green-speckled veldt. It was midafternoon and the light had a soft and yielding quality that made the scrub appear hand-painted on the canvas of the Earth.

'Now,' Louis said, 'she will never be saved.'

Emmanuel signalled to Shabalala to stand guard while he checked the cave.

'Davida.' He called out her name and stepped into the interior of Louis's bizarre mountain home. She sat near the cave entrance with her knees drawn up tightly underneath her. Emmanuel crouched next to her but didn't touch her despite the fact that her body shook with a bone-rattling intensity. She'd had enough of white men trying to help her for a lifetime.

'It's okay. You're safe now,' he said. Her skin was scratched with fine red lines from the wash-down Louis had given her with rocks and pure spring water. 'Did he hurt you any-place that I can't see, Davida?'

'Not like you think. Not that way.'

'Can you tell me what happened?'

'No, not now. Did you find my granny?'

'Zweigman is with her. He says she's injured, but she's going to be all right. You know he'll take good care of her.'

'Good. Good.' She started to cry and Emmanuel retrieved the grey blanket from the made-up bedroll. He held it out for her to see.

'Can I put this on you? You need to get dry and warm before we make a move.'

'Outside. I'll put it on outside. I don't want to stay in here.'

They left the cave and she huddled near the entrance; her instincts telling her to stick close to shelter. Emmanuel wrapped the blanket around her shoulders and noticed that she didn't look across to where Louis was under guard.

'It smells of him,' she said. 'Like flowers on a grave.'

'You'll need to keep it on until you're warm, then we'll head back to Jacob's Rest.'

'I'll go when you go,' she said and rested her chin on her knees to watch long wisps of white cloud stretch across the sky. Emmanuel walked over to Shabalala and stood by his side. The Zulu constable looked weary, as if this end to things was more terrible than he had imagined.

'What now?' Louis asked over the sound of Hansie's snivelling. 'Are you going to arrest me?'

'I've got no choice,' Emmanuel said. 'You are charged with assault and kidnapping. Both are criminal offences and you will have to stand trial.'

'My mother . . .' There was a glimmer of fear in Louis's eyes. 'She'll know all the ways the devil has led me astray.'

'Most likely, yes.' Emmanuel checked the position of the sun. It was time to get moving if they wanted to make it back to Jacob's Rest before nightfall. The police station was still out of bounds. They'd have to use Zweigman's store as a holding cell for Louis at least until Davida Ellis was safely returned home. After that he'd have to make a dash for Mooihoek with the captain's youngest son in custody. The Pretorius boys would skin him alive and boil his bones for soup if they caught him in the company of their sweet little brother.

'You're going to put him in prison?' Hansie was shocked.

'That's generally where people accused of assault and kidnapping end up, Hepple. That is the law.'

'But it's not right putting a white man in jail over one of them. It's not decent.'

'What's decent or not is for a judge to decide. Collect the evidence, complete the docket, and present the case in court. That's my job. And yours, too.' Emmanuel checked Davida to see if she'd stopped shivering. The long march back to the car was going to be difficult with Hansie, Louis, and a traumatised woman in tow.

'I'll get her,' he said to Shabalala. 'You get Mathandunina.'

They split off to their separate duties but didn't get far. The distinct sound of a safety catch releasing caught them midstep. Emmanuel turned to see Hansie standing, tear-stained and snotfaced, with his Webley revolver aimed right at his midsection. A bullet in the gut administered by a dull-minded Afrikaner boy was a lousy way to die.

'Constable Hepple.' He used the title to remind the teen-ager that he was an officer of the law. 'Put the gun down, please.'

'No. I won't let you take Louis to jail.'

'What should we do with your friend, Constable Hepple?'

'Let him go.'

'Okay,' Emmanuel said and left Hansie to fill the sudden power void.

'Go,' the boy policeman urged his friend. 'Go. Run.'

The bare-chested prophet was crouched down, staring out

across country, as if mesmerised by the colours of the veldt spread out below him.

'Louis.' Hansie's voice was loud and raw in the arena of rock and cloud. 'What are you doing? Go.'

The teenaged boy stood up and walked to the very edge of the rock platform, where he spread his arms out wide to feel the wind blowing in from the bush lands. He turned back to face the cave, his hair bright as a halo.

'This is a holy place. Can you feel it, Detective? The power of God so close.'

'I can,' Emmanuel said.

'You're right, Detective. I should have brought my father here and tried to save his soul. If I'd done that he'd be alive today.'

'It wasn't your job to save him.' Emmanuel could feel the pull of gravity dragging on Louis's heels, threatening to suck him over the edge and into the void. 'A man is responsible for the health of his own soul. You did nothing wrong.'

Louis smiled. 'The sin is that I didn't try. I left him adrift in a sea of iniquity.'

'It's hard for sons and fathers to talk. You said yourself that it was difficult to bring up the topic of what your father was doing.'

'I didn't want him to stop. You know there were evenings when, right after Pa had finished, I'd lie out on the grass and look up at the stars. What happiness I felt inside, knowing that he and I were alike. I was my father's son, not Mathandunina.'

Hansie lowered his revolver so it was now aimed somewhere between Emmanuel's pelvis and his kneecaps. There was still no room to make a sudden move towards Louis, who remained perilously close to the cliff. Constable Hepple was too dull of mind to understand that the threat to his boyhood friend came entirely from within.

'Remember, Shabalala?' Louis switched to Zulu. 'When I was a child the people would say, "Look at this one. Who does he belong to? Can he really belong to that man there?"'

'Your father knew well that you were his son,' Shabalala said. 'He had you close in his heart.'

'That's why it pains me that I did nothing to save him.'

'You were not at the river.' Shabalala threw out a lifeline in the hope that it reached the boy's hands. 'The man who shot your father is the one who is at fault in this matter.'

'The wages of sin is death. I knew that and yet I did nothing because what Pa did gave me pleasure also. My mother will hear of this but she will not understand. She will never forgive.'

'Your mother loves you also.'

'She will be in disgrace because of me. Her family will cast her out if I go to jail.'

'You are loved by her.' Shabalala walked slowly towards the boy. 'She will take you back into her arms. It is so.'

The wind rising up from the veldt was cold on Emmanuel's face. Even Shabalala with his breathtaking physical speed would not be able reach the melancholy boy in time to stop him from testing his angel's wings.

'You'll tell her I'm sorry, hey, Shabalala? You'll say to her that I know we will meet one day on the beautiful shore.'

'*Nkosana* . . .' Shabalala sprinted towards the boy he'd seen stumble and fall as a child. His hands were outstretched with the mute promise: 'Hold onto me and I will keep you safe from harm.'

'Stay well,' Louis said and stepped backwards off the cliff and into the Lord's embrace. There the dry snap of branches, then the breath of the wind as it stirred the silence.

Emmanuel stood at the edge of the sheer drop. There was no sign of Louis Pretorius. He wasn't in a crevice with minor injuries or balancing precariously on a tree limb awaiting rescue. The boy had fallen all the way to the veldt floor.

'I must get him,' Shabalala said and headed for the path that led down the mountain. He was breathing hard, his giant chest rising and falling under the starched material of his uniform. 'I must find him and return him to his home.'

'You are not at fault.' Emmanuel felt the black man's pain. It was deep in his flesh like a thorn. 'You did all that could be done for Mathandunina in his last moments.'

Shabalala nodded, but kept his own counsel. It might take years for the thorn to work its way to the surface and fall away.

'We will meet you by the boulder.' Emmanuel let the black constable get on with the job of recovering the boy's body. Nothing he could say would take away the pain that Shabalala felt for failing to save the son of his friend. 'We will wait there until you are ready.'

The Zulu constable started on his journey without looking back at the cave where he had once played. He would not return to this place again without a powerful medicine woman, a *sangoma*, by his side. Ghosts and spirits were so thick in the air a person could not draw breath without choking. Mathandunina's body and spirit must be picked up and together taken back to his home in order to avoid more bloodshed and misfortune.

Shabalala disappeared into the bush and Emmanuel pulled the bottle of white pills from his pocket. A place to stir the heart or crush it, he thought as he chewed the painkillers and looked out over the African plains. The light here was completely different from the cool, white sunshine that lit the sky during the European winter, but with Louis's death he felt the same: old and tired.

'Dear Jesus.' Hansie was on his knees, his hands clasped together in prayer. His words came out between broken sobs. 'Help him. Give him strength to overcome the fall. Raise him up, Lord.'

'He's dead, Hansie.'

'*Ja* . . .' The boy made a mournful sound and rocked back onto his heels. 'I should have helped take him off the mountain when you said.'

Emmanuel didn't have the strength to reprimand Hansie. He waited until the boy's sobs lessened.

'You weren't to know,' he said.

Hansie shook his head as if to clear it. 'I'm sorry, Sarge. I still don't understand what happened.'

'In time. Maybe.'

Emmanuel walked to where Davida sat with the blanket draped over her shoulders. She'd stopped shaking and gazed at the breathtaking vista.

'We have to go.' Where to exactly, Emmanuel didn't know.

Returning Davida to Jacob's Rest was out of the question. As soon as the news of Louis's death spread, she would become kindling for the fire that would engulf the small town. She was safer with her mother out here on King's farm.

Davida stood up and let the blanket drop to the dirt. She walked to the ledge and stared into the void.

'I hope the lions eat him,' she said.

The lights of Elliott King's homestead clustered on the horizon and glowed bright against the night sky. Emmanuel breathed deeply. He felt sick. In the back of the van, Shabalala cradled Louis Pretorius's body: an empty cocoon of flesh and bone now broken beyond repair. The Zulu constable was convinced that Louis's spirit was conjuring a violent revenge against them. The only way to avoid trouble, Shabalala said, was to take the boy's body back to his mother, but Emmanuel couldn't let that happen.

'Park close to the stairs,' he said, once they'd crossed the cattle grid at the entrance to the drive. They had to deliver Davida to her mother, then drive Louis to the nearest morgue. A police inquiry into the death was certain and a public inquest couldn't be ruled out. The spotlight would illuminate all the secrets of Jacob's Rest.

Hansie pulled in behind the red Jaguar in the driveway and cut the engine.

Elliott King and his picture-perfect nephew Winston stood at the top stair to the porch. The world was going to hell while they sipped sundowners and admired their own little piece of paradise.

A black ranger in a Bayete Lodge uniform appeared from nowhere and stood guard at the front of the police van with a nightstick in his hands. Like all chiefs, the rich Englishman had his own private army.

King dismissed the ranger with a wave of his gin and tonic and Emmanuel reached for the door handle. Davida grabbed hold of his arm. She trembled.

'I don't want to go out there,' she said.

'Hepple,' he instructed the constable, 'go into the house and fetch the housekeeper, Mrs Ellis. Tell her to come straightaway.'

Hansie slid out of the driver's side door and took the stairs two at a time. He crossed paths with the King men on their way down to the van.

'Your mother's coming,' Emmanuel told Davida and she pressed closer to his side. 'I have to talk to King.'

'Don't let them near me,' she said.

'I won't,' Emmanuel promised and swung the door open and stepped out. King and Winston peered through the front window at Davida's huddled shape.

'Has she been hurt?' King demanded.

'Where's my Davida?' Mrs Ellis stumbled down the stairs towards the triangle of white men standing between her and her daughter.

Emmanuel waved King and Winston aside so the housekeeper could coax Davida out of the vehicle and into the house.

'Take her inside. I'll get her statement in a little while. Stay with her until I get there.'

'Statement?' The housekeeper was dazed and afraid. 'Why does my baby need to give a statement?'

'Take her inside,' Emmanuel repeated, 'and get her a blanket and a cup of tea. Keep her warm.'

'Davida? Baby girl?' Mrs Ellis leaned into the van and put her arms around the balled-up shape hiding there. 'It's mummy. Come on, darling . . .'

Davida reached up and the two women clung tightly to each other. Emmanuel stepped further away and tried to block out the sobbing.

'Come on, baby . . .' Mrs Ellis said and led Davida towards the stairs.

Emmanuel watched the women disappear into the house. Soon he would talk to Davida about the man at the river.

'Did you do that?' Winston said. 'Did you put those bruises and scratches on her, Detective Sergeant?'

'No.'

'That was Louis,' Hansie cut in. 'He's the one who did it.'

'Louis Pretorius?' Winston asked.

'*Ja*. He took her up to the mountain and washed her with stones under the water. He was trying to save her. That's what he said.'

'He raped her?' King asked.

'I don't believe so.' Emmanuel was sure that something else, possibly just as unpleasant and intrusive, had happened under the waterfall.

Winston seemed stunned and angry.

'I'll know more once I've spoken to her.' Emmanuel kept King and Winston back from the van. He didn't like the look in Winston's eye.

'Well,' Winston said. 'Where is Louis? Is he in custody?'

'He's in the van with Shabalala,' Hansie said. 'Shabalala wants to take him back home to his ma, but we can't. Not yet.'

'What?' Winston moved fast towards the back of the van and grappled with the door handle. Emmanuel grabbed him, spun him around by the shoulders, and pushed him hard towards the house. Winston turned to face him and Emmanuel stopped him cold with two hands on his chest.

'Move away from the van.'

'He has to pay for what he did,' Winston said.

'He will,' Emmanuel said. 'Now move away from the van.'

Winston stared him down for a moment and Emmanuel recognised something in his look. Where had he seen that look before? Winston broke eye contact and strode in the direction of the house. King reached out a sympathetic hand, but Winston pushed him away and climbed the stairs.

Something is going on, Emmanuel thought. Why is Winston this angry about the assault of a housekeeper's daughter?

'You need to move away,' Emmanuel told King. 'I don't want to see you or Winston within ten feet of this police van. Understood?'

King nodded. 'What happens now?'

'I'll take Davida's statement and then we'll transport Louis to Mooihoek.'

'You won't take him home?'

'No,' Emmanuel said. 'Go inside and finish your drink. Constable Hepple will escort you.'

Hansie followed the Englishmen up the stairs and took up position between the *stoep* and the vehicle. Emmanuel unlocked the back doors of the police van and motioned Shabalala out.

The tension in the Zulu constable's face and body was obvious. 'Are you all right?' Emmanuel asked.

'This one –' Shabalala pressed a hand against the doors. 'He will cause trouble wherever he goes. He will try to take one of us with him to the other side. I feel it is so.'

'If we bring him to his house, that will cause trouble also. He won't be easy to handle wherever we go.'

'I know this.' The Zulu policeman made eye contact with Emmanuel. 'You must be careful, *nkosana*. Mathandunina knows it was you who found out about the mountain and it was you who took the little wife from him. You have touched her and he does not like this.'

'I did no such thing.'

'You put his blanket around her, that is what I mean, *nkosana.*'

'So –' Emmanuel said after the surge of embarrassment at his denial ebbed. How could a corpse know about the conversation in Davida's room or the quickening of his senses at the sight of her so close to the wrought-iron bed? 'What must we do, Shabalala? I can't see any way to avoid trouble over Louis.'

'We must tell his mother where he is. Maybe if we do this, things will not go so badly for us.'

'When we get to the place where his body will be examined,' Emmanuel said, 'I'll call Mrs Pretorius and let her know where her son is.'

'That is good.' Shabalala still looked worried. 'I will tell him and if he hears it correctly, he will not want more blood to be spilled.'

'I'd like that,' Emmanuel said. Less blood to be spilled. He'd spent three years hoping for that very thing and yet he'd come home and stepped right back into the company of the dead.

Emmanuel read the handwritten statement a second time and looked across the table at Davida. She was flushed and uncomfortable as if the heat from the kitchen stove had suddenly gotten to her. Mrs Ellis hovered close to her daughter's shoulder like a guardian angel afraid of failing a major assignment.

'The man at the river. You sure you didn't see who it was?'

'Yes.'

'Did you know the man who shot Captain Pretorius, Davida?'

'No.' She was adamant. 'I didn't see who it was. I don't know who it was.'

'He sounded like the molester, is that right? Like someone putting on a voice?'

'Yes.'

'Louis admitted to being the molester,' Emmanuel said. 'But he denied killing his father.'

'You believe that mad Dutchman but you don't believe me?' Her grey eyes sparked with anger. 'White men always tell the truth, that's what you policemen believe. It makes catching criminals easy. Just look for the dark skin, don't bother with evidence.'

Her accent caught his attention. It was not quite to the manor born, but desperate to get there by any road possible.

'Where did you go to school, Davida?'

'What?'

'Tell me where you went to school.'

'Stonebrook Academy.' She paused. 'Why?'

'Your accent . . .' he said, 'it's . . . elegant.'

'So?'

'What are you doing in Jacob's Rest, working for the old Jew and his wife in their little rag factory?'

'My granny and my mother live here,' she said. 'I came to be with them.'

'Surely you were meant for more? An accent like that doesn't come cheap.'

'I like cutting patterns.'

'Did you fail your matric, Davida?'

She flashed an angry stare at him, then thought better of defending herself against the insult to her intelligence. The dangers hidden in the answers she gave were suddenly clear to her. She shut her mouth tight.

'Tell him, Davida.' Mrs Ellis took up the fight on her daughter's behalf. 'She passed with flying colours and got accepted at the University of the Western Cape. Top of her class in four subjects.'

'What happened?'

'She came to visit Granny and me for the Christmas holidays and decided to stay on for a year. She'll be going to university next year, hey, Davida?'

Emmanuel sat forward, pulled towards Davida by a thread of understanding. All those days spent in the company of the old Jew and his wife, reading, dreaming of the world out there. He'd done the same thing at boarding school – gazed out over the dusty fields to the world beyond.

'Look at me, Davida,' he said and waited until she did. 'You weren't going anywhere, were you?'

'No,' she whispered.

'That's why the captain built the hut. A little place out of town for the two of you. A home.'

'That's right.'

'No . . .' Mrs Ellis muttered. 'This doesn't make sense.'

Emmanuel maintained eye contact and the thread with Davida strengthened. Her breath became shorter.

'Pretorius made the arrangement for you to be his little wife . . . that's right, isn't it, Davida?'

'What?!' Mrs Ellis broke from the perfect servant mould and hit the tabletop with the flat of her hand. 'You can't come into my house and talk to my daughter like this. My baby's got nothing to do with Captain Pretorius. She delivered some papers to him for Mr King a couple of times, but that was it.'

Davida looked older and wiser than her mother by a hundred years when she leaned back against the tiles depicting pretty rural scenes and wrapped her arms around her waist.

'Ma . . .'

Silence filled the room for a moment.

'No. No.' Mrs Ellis stepped close to her daughter. 'That life isn't for you, my baby. You're going to go to university so that you don't have to be that kind of woman. You're going to stand on your own two feet and have a profession.'

'What country do you think we live in, Ma?' The question was full of sadness. 'A coloured woman doesn't get to choose the life she wants. Not even after she's been to university. This, here, is how things are.'

Emmanuel wanted to look away from Mrs Ellis's face, the death of her dream for her daughter written clear upon it. He watched the tragedy unfold across the kitchen table.

The housekeeper cupped her daughter's cheek with her palm and brushed away a tear that lay there. 'It's okay, my baby,' she said, spinning a new vision for the future. 'We'll forget this business and go on like before. You're young enough to start again without anyone knowing . . . That's right, hey?'

'Detective Sergeant!' Hansie called from outside. 'Sergeant! Hurry.'

Footsteps and the sound of glass smashing came from the front of the house. Emmanuel rushed out of the stifling kitchen and through the hushed luxury of the primitive-themed sitting room to the *stoep*. Elliott King stumbled against the drinks cabinet, his nose dribbling blood onto the front of his linen suit. Winston stood over him with his fist clenched.

'Fuck.' The Englishman found an embroidered serviette and held it to his nostrils to stem the blood. 'Christ, that stings.'

Emmanuel looked past King and saw the rear lights of the police van fading into the night. He jumped off the steps onto the gravel drive and started to run.

'Shabalala's gone . . .' Hansie called out.

Emmanuel sprinted across the cattle grid and onto the dark ribbon of dirt road that split the King property in two. He ran for five minutes. The sound of the engine faded and then disappeared ahead of him. He stopped and gasped for breath. He rested his hands on his knees and tried to figure out what had happened.

After a minute he straightened and glanced at the stars puncturing the night sky. The one person he trusted to stay by him had driven off with Louis's body because of a native superstition. Black policemen weren't even allowed to drive official vehicles. Emmanuel turned and walked slowly back towards King's house. Is this how it ends? he wondered. Abandoned and empty-handed on a deserted country road?

The silent landscape absorbed the crunch of his footsteps and the hiss of his ragged breath. He'd had worse days struggling across winter-hardened fields but today was the peacetime equivalent. The moment Shabalala delivered Louis's body to his mother, the Pretorius family would explode. King's farm and Davida were going to be the targets of extreme vengeance.

He broke into a steady run, then heard a faint sound behind him. He checked over his shoulder. Red tail-lights blinked in the darkness as the police van reversed down the dirt road towards him. He met the van halfway and pulled the driver's door open once the vehicle had stopped.

'What happened?'

'The young man.' Shabalala's top lip was swollen from a recent hit. 'He fought with *Nkosi* King and then he came to the van and he fought with me. He said he wanted Louis but I would not let him in, so he said he was going to get a gun and "bang" shoot me and shoot the van also. He ran to the house and *Nkosi* King said to drive because the young man, he was serious.'

'Did Winston give you that fat lip?'

'*Yebo*,' the constable said. 'I let him hit me many times, but I do not wish to be hit with a bullet many times.'

'You did well.' Emmanuel checked the lights of the homestead. Something had come loose in Winston. 'Stay here. I'll send Hansie for you when things have settled.'

'I will return when you say so.'

'Thank you,' Emmanuel said. Shabalala had gone against his instincts and given up the opportunity to take Louis back to his mother. Winston's violent threats were reason enough not to return to the homestead, but the Zulu constable held the course.

Emmanuel raced back to the house and found Hansie waiting for him at the cattle grid. The teenager's uniform was streaked with dust and embedded with pieces of loose gravel.

'That Winston pushed me down the stairs,' Hansie said. 'Then he went after Shabalala.'

Emmanuel tried to make sense of Winston's actions. What fool goes after the police? For what reason? He leapt up the stairs, thinking of Shabalala's swollen lip and Hansie's dishevelled appearance.

'Stay out here and make sure no-one comes in or out of the house, Hepple.'

'Yes, sir.'

The *stoep* was empty and Emmanuel went inside. The sound of voices drew him across the sitting room to the kitchen, where he paused at the open door. Mrs Ellis leaned over King and wiped his bloody nose with a wet face towel, while Winston stood in a corner looking at the floor. Davida sat at the table and twisted a spoon in her hands.

'Careful,' King groaned. 'You have to be more careful with me, Lolly.'

'Shhh . . .' The housekeeper whispered close to King's ear, 'It's not so bad, you silly man.'

Emmanuel entered the room.

'You're a family,' he said, stunned by the revelation. 'Mother, father, sister and brother.'

'Don't be ridiculous.' King gave each member of his illegitimate family a warning glance. 'You have no proof of your allegations and if you repeat that slander again my lawyers will deal with you, Detective Sergeant.'

'Shabalala was right.' Emmanuel ignored King and spoke directly to Davida. The undervalued sale of the Pretorius farm suddenly made sense. 'The captain did pay a bride price, but it wasn't in cattle or money, it was in land. The land we're standing on.'

Davida glanced at her father, waiting for a cue.

'King was the one who cleaned the hut up after the captain died,' Emmanuel went on. 'He sent you to get any evidence he'd missed when he wiped the place down. That's right, isn't it?'

'Davida.' King used her name like a blunt instrument. 'The detective sergeant is wearing a suit but he's a police officer and his job is to enforce the law. Do you understand what I'm telling you?'

'Yes, Mr King.'

'You don't have to protect him anymore, Davida. Tell me what happened.'

She shut herself up behind her shy brown mouse mask and Emmanuel wondered how he would break through.

'Bride price?' Mrs Ellis placed the wet face towel down on the table. 'What does that mean?'

'The detective is playing games, Lolly,' King said.

Winston snorted in disbelief and the housekeeper took a half-step back. She glared at the injured Englishman.

'You knew what was going on,' she said.

'No.' King sounded calm but his thumb drummed against his thigh. 'Pretorius was someone I did business with, that's all.'

'You say you don't like the Afrikaner, yet you talked with that one for hours about how you both loved Africa. Why did you spend so much time with him?'

'Business,' King said. 'It pays to have interests in common with whoever you're dealing with. If something happened between Davida and that Dutchman it was her choice, nothing to do with me.'

The slap came from nowhere. An arc of crimson blood sprayed from King's wounded nose and landed on Mrs Ellis's starched uniform and the handpainted tiles. Emmanuel caught the housekeeper's hand before she went in for a second hit.

'Liar!' Mrs Ellis was in a cold rage. 'You said this one belonged to me but you broke your promise. You stole her and you sold her.'

'Lolly –' Red bubbles flew from King's nostrils while he tried to stem the bleeding and talk at the same time. 'Don't. Not in front of the police, for God's sake.'

Years of hard work had made her strong and Emmanuel struggled to keep her away from King. If he let her go, she'd scratch his eyes out.

'How could you do this to her? She was going to study to become a teacher, or even a doctor –'

'Christ above, Lolly. How long do you think it would take a dark-skinned girl like her to earn even close to what we made on the land deal? Fifteen, twenty years if she was lucky? Pretorius was willing to give me far more than she was worth –'

Emmanuel loosened his grip and let Mrs Ellis fly. Elliott King didn't know when to shut up.

'Lolly –' King tried to fend off the blows but the house-keeper slapped him down and tore into the suntanned skin of his neck and chin with her nails. His chair tipped over and King went with it, landing on the floor with a thud.

Mrs Ellis followed him down and her hands began to rip his hair. Emmanuel gave her another moment and when she showed no signs of slowing he pulled her away; he already had one dead body to deal with.

'Okay –' He lifted the vengeful woman up and held her arms loosely by her side until her muscles relaxed and she fell against him fighting for breath. 'It's okay now,' he said.

Winston stepped towards his mother and she surged violently towards him. Emmanuel held her back.

'You knew,' she cried. 'The two of you knew about it.'

'No,' Winston said. 'I was supervising the lodge on Saint Lucia for the last six months. I didn't know anything about the land deal until it was done. I would never have let that Dutchman touch her.'

'You're lying –'

'I will not take the blame for setting up that deal,' Winston said.

'Stop.' Davida pushed her chair back and sprang to her feet. 'Stop it!'

King struggled to stand, holding onto the back of a chair for support. His hair resembled an abandoned bird's nest. Mrs Ellis began to weep quietly and Emmanuel released her into Davida's arms.

The name Saint Lucia rang a bell. Emmanuel dug around in his memory and came up with the sign at the jetty in Lourenço Marques and the beautiful wooden sailboat moored in the berth behind it. 'What's Saint Lucia?' he asked.

'An island.' King was happy to shift the focus away from

the land deal. 'We opened a lodge there at the beginning of this year.'

'What do you do on the island, Winston?'

'I run it,' Winston said.

Emmanuel took that information on board. The captain's killer had slipped into Mozambique. What if the killer had simply gone home?

'What did you think of Captain Pretorius?' he asked Winston.

'*Die Afrikaner Polisie Kaptein –*' Winston mimicked the rough-edged Afrikaans tongue perfectly '– meant nothing to me.'

Davida gasped and Emmanuel turned to her. The blood had drained from her face.

'If I closed my eyes,' Emmanuel said, 'I'd think you were a proper Afrikaner. An Afrikaner used to giving orders.'

Winston went very still. 'Plenty of people can put on that accent.'

'Did Davida ever tell you about the man who molested the coloured women last year?'

Winston shrugged. 'We all heard about it.'

'He put on an accent,' Emmanuel said, 'to cover up his own voice.'

'And?'

'Did Davida ever tell you that man had an accent?'

'I don't remember,' Winston said.

'Did you tell him, Davida?'

'No . . .' Her fingers twisted together. 'I don't remember.'

Emmanuel stared at her. 'Was it Winston's voice you heard at the river?'

'It wasn't him.' She spoke in a rush. 'It was someone else. I swear it.'

'Where were you last Wednesday night, Winston?'

Mrs Ellis stopped crying and the room went quiet again. Davida's face was pinched tight with shock. A horrified realisation had just begun to register on King's bloodied face.

'Were you on the South African side of Watchman's Ford last Wednesday night, Winston?' Emmanuel asked and a phone began to ring in another part of the house.

'He was in Lourenço Marques collecting supplies for the island.' King wedged himself into the conversation. 'I can have a dozen signed witness statements attesting to that fact on your desk by tomorrow afternoon.'

'I'm sure you can,' Emmanuel said. The telephone continued its insistent ring. He walked to the door and called out, 'Constable Hepple! Come in, please.'

Hansie poked his head around the doorjamb.

'Could you please answer the phone and tell the caller that Mr King and Winston are busy.'

'Yes, sir.'

'Now, where were you last Wednesday night, Winston?' Emmanuel asked the question again as the ringing fell silent. 'Take your time and try to remember.'

'I told you. He was buying supplies —'

'Everyone out of the room,' Emmanuel said. 'Winston. You stay.'

'Sergeant —' Hansie stood fidgeting in the doorway. 'It's for you. The telephone.'

'Who is it?'

'It's the old Jew. He says it's urgent and I must get you *now*. Straightaway.'

Davida hurried to him and whispered 'Granny Mariah' so that her mother didn't hear it.

'I'll check,' Emmanuel said, then spoke to Hansie. 'Stand

guard and don't let anyone leave until I get back. You understand? No-one.'

'No-one.' Hansie repeated and took up position in the middle of the doorway, hands on his hips in a direct imitation of a police recruitment poster printed in the English and Afrikaans newspapers. 'Why stay on the farm or serve in a shop?' the advertisment seemed to say. Why indeed when a few months training translated into instant authority over ninety per cent of the population?

Emmanuel walked into the office where King had shown him the native spells kept by Pretorius senior and picked up the telephone on the desk.

'Detective Cooper?' Zweigman sounded like he'd run a mile in wooden shoes.

'Is it Granny Mariah?'

'No, she is recovering. Davida?'

'Recovering also.'

'And the boy?'

'In custody,' Emmanuel said. 'We'll be transporting him to Mooihoek in a few hours.'

'Good.' Zweigman dropped his voice to a whisper. 'Do not come near the town and be careful on the roads also.'

'What's happened?'

'The brothers searched my house and Anton's. Nothing serious. Torn books, overturned furniture. Amateur theatrics . . .' The old Jew was unfazed by the thuggish actions of the Pretorius boys. No doubt he'd seen several libraries' worth of books burned on Nazi bonfires and watched a continent bombed to rubble. He didn't scare easily. 'They are still searching for you,' Zweigman added.

Emmanuel listened carefully. There was no possibility of returning to town, not after what had happened to Louis on the mountain. 'What did you mean about the roads?' he asked. If he couldn't get to Mooihoek this evening he needed to make alternate plans. On the King farm he was a sitting duck for the Pretorius brothers and the Security Branch.

'The Security Branch has sent four teams of men out to set up roadblocks leading to and from town.'

'Why?'

'This I do not know. Tiny was ordered to take his finest liquor to the police station and it was he who passed this news to me.'

'Any idea where the roadblocks are? Or what they're looking for?'

'No idea.'

Emmanuel paused to consider his position. If the road-blocks were set up between King's farm and Mooihoek, then he was trapped until daybreak.

'Doc,' he said after a pause. 'What's the best way to store a dead body overnight?'

Emmanuel sat down opposite Winston at the kitchen table and studied him for a moment. The rest of the family were in the sitting room under Hansie's guard. Winston appeared composed. Zweigman's phone call had given him time to collect his thoughts.

'Let's talk about Captain Pretorius,' Emmanuel began. He kept his tone friendly and relaxed.

'I only met him a few times,' Winston said.

'Funny, the way history repeats itself. Your mother must have been about Davida's age when she took up with your father. Maybe a little younger.'

'I've never done the maths,' Winston said.

'I think you have. You know better than most people the kind of life Davida was headed for.'

'My mother's been very comfortable.'

'One child taken away and dressed up to pass as white, the other traded for a piece of land. That's comfortable?'

Winston got up abruptly and walked to the stove, where he warmed his hands despite the heat in the kitchen. 'I made a mistake,' he said. 'I realise that now.'

'Explain that to me, Winston.'

'I should have gone after my father instead.'

Emmanuel asked slowly and deliberately: 'Did you kill Captain Pretorius at Watchman's Ford last Wednesday night?'

Winston looked him in the eye. 'He took Davida's chances away when she had so few to begin with. That was unforgivable.'

'Did you kill him, Winston?'

'I was in Lourenço Marques on Wednesday night. I bought supplies for the Saint Lucia Lodge. I have five witnesses who will testify to that in court.'

'Only five? Surely your father can afford more.'

'He can. But five will do.'

'I'm curious. Captain Pretorius was pulled into the water,' Emmanuel said. 'Why?'

'Maybe the killer didn't want to leave him on the sand with his fly open and reeking of sex. Maybe the killer felt sorry for him in the end.'

'You have some regrets, then, about shooting Captain Pretorius last Wednesday night?'

A hardness showed itself beneath the surface of Winston's face. Surviving as a fake in the white man's world had taught him how to protect himself and his family at all costs. He smiled but said nothing.

Emmanuel wondered what kind of world Winston King lived in. His whole life was a lie. Even his fair skin and blue eyes were a lie. It didn't help that he lived in a time when the term 'immorality' was applied to interracial sex and not to the raft of laws that took away the freedom of so many people.

'What about Davida?' Emmanuel asked. 'Do you have any idea what will happen to her?'

'She didn't kill Pretorius. She has no case to answer.'

Emmanuel wanted to slap Winston across the face. He showed no remorse for Captain Pretorius's murder and no understanding of how his actions would affect his darker-skinned sister.

'Davida gets to walk into the sunset? Is that what you think?' Emmanuel said. 'All thanks to you?'

'She'll go to Western Cape University and she'll get to live her own life. Surely that's worth something?'

'Davida's a key witness in the murder of a white police-man. She'll be put through the wringer. In court. In the newspapers. The dirt will stick to her for the rest of her life. Do you really think she'll go to university?'

'I didn't think that far ahead,' Winston muttered. 'I didn't think about it.'

'You didn't have to,' Emmanuel said. 'You're a white man. Remember?'

Emmanuel sat down next to Shabalala and considered the health of the case. Sick but not fatal. He had a written state-ment from Davida for the docket and a five-sentence lie from Winston claiming to be in Lourenço Marques buying supplies on the night Captain Pretorius was murdered. No confession, but enough to haul Winston in for formal ques-tioning in the near future. That was the end of the good news.

'A couple of miles along the main road?' Emmanuel repeated the information the Zulu constable had given him, hoping he'd got some part of it wrong. The men from the Security Branch were smack between them and Mooihoek.

'*Yebo*. A car and two men are at the roadblock, waiting.'

'Any chance of getting by them?'

'Across many farms and through many fences, but not at night. Not in the dark.'

The police van was now parked in the circular driveway in front of King's homestead. Van Niekerk didn't have the power to call off a Security Branch roadblock and Emmanuel wasn't inclined to let the major know about the mess he was in.

'They won't let us through without searching the vehicle,' Emmanuel said. 'We'll have to spend the night here and check the roads at dawn.'

'What shall we do with him? The young one?'

'King's icehouse out beyond the back *stoep*. Zweigman said that's the best place for him.'

'Home,' Shabalala said. 'That is the only place for him.'

'Not much of a home after the lies his father told.'

'To live in this country a man, he must be a liar. You tell the truth –' Shabalala clapped his hands together to make a hard sound. 'They break you.'

He fell through the sky, and his body twisted and arched in the air like a leaf on the wind. He smelled wild sage grass and heard the sweet, high voice of Louis Pretorius singing an Afrikaans hymn. A tree branch snapped and he continued to fall at speed towards the hard crust of the Earth. He called out for help and felt a gust of cold wind across his face as he plummeted without stopping.

Emmanuel sat up gasping for breath in the darkness. He felt around him; his fingers brushed a blanket and the hard edges of a wrought-iron bedstead. He had no idea where he was. No memory of lying down in a wide bed with soft sheets in a room that smelled of fresh thatch and mud.

To the right of the bed he found a box of matches and in the weak light cast by the flame found an unused candle with a fresh wick. He lit the candle and tried slowing his breath to normal. The naive tribal designs painted onto the bare concrete floor helped place him. He knew where he was. A just-completed guest bedroom attached to the back of Elliott King's homestead.

The quiet rustle of the reed mat at the foot of the bed alerted him to her presence and he held up the candle to cast light further into the room. She sat on the floor with her chin on her drawn-up knees like a pensive child.

'Did your father send you?' he asked. 'Or your brother?'

'Were you dreaming about the mountain?' She shuffled forwards and placed her elbows on the mattress. He was sweat-stained and shaky, but she showed no fear of him.

'Yes.' Emmanuel saw no point in lying and it was a relief to tell the truth to someone who had been there. 'I was.'

'Was he in the dream?'

'Just his voice. Singing,' Emmanuel said. 'I fell off the side of the mountain and went down like a stone. You?'

'He was washing me under the waterfall and when I looked down, the skin on my arms was torn to ribbons. I saw the white of my bones through the flesh.'

'He's gone. The dreams will stop but it might take a while,' Emmanuel said. After the ordeal on the mountain, he knew he represented a safe haven from all the terrible things Louis had done to her in the name of purity. All victims of war and violence felt a bond with those who saved them. The bond was fragile, however, and should not be encouraged. Now was the time to tell her to disconnect. Life would resume and they would be strangers to each other again. That was as it should be.

She moved closer and Emmanuel didn't stop her.

'Do you think I'm a bad person?' she asked.

'Why would I think that?'

'Because of the captain and what I did with him.'

'You had good reasons for everything you did,' he said and realised, with a sense of discomfort, that this was the first personal conversation he'd held with a non-white person since his return from Europe. Interviews, witness statements, formal and informal questioning: he came into contact with every race group in the course of his work, but this was different. She was talking with him. One human being to another. Her skin shone velvet brown in the candlelight.

'Do you think God knows everything?'

'If there is a God, He'll understand the position you were put in. That's as close to philosophy as I come in the middle of the night.'

'Hmm.'

The sound was low and thoughtful. She tasted the idea of an understanding God. She reached out and touched the scar on his shoulder. He glimpsed sanctuary in her eyes and felt the warmth of her skin and her breath. Easy now, Emmanuel told himself. This is a police operation: a murder investigation in which she figures centrally. This was no time to give in like a vice cop at the end of the shift.

'You're hurt,' she said.

The sleeve of her nightdress fell back to her elbow and he touched the long red scars along her arm.

'So are you.'

She leaned forwards and kissed him. Her mouth felt lush and warm and yielded to his. Her tongue tasted him. She climbed onto the bed and slid herself between his legs, then rested her hands on his knees as the kiss continued, an endless dance.

He pulled back. Not far enough to convince himself or her of his intention to disengage. 'Why are you doing this?' he asked.

'I want to be in charge this time.' Her hands slid over his thighs to his wrists, which she held in place with a firm grip. 'Will you let me be in charge, Detective Sergeant Emmanuel Cooper?'

She gave him power and asked for it back in the same breath. It was exciting and shaming: that raw appeal to his rank.

'Yes,' he said.

Sleep pulled him under, past riptides and eddies to a place of safety. He slept like the dead but the dead did not bother him. He was in the burned-out cellar of his dreams with the woman curled against his back for warmth.

'*Get up!*' The command was barked loud and clear into his ear. '*That is an order, soldier!*'

Emmanuel pushed his face deep into the pillow. He wasn't ready to leave the cocoon. The war could go on without him.

'*Up. Now!*' the sergeant major said. '*Put your shorts on. You don't want them to find you bare-arsed, laddie.*'

The bottle of white pills, still almost half-full, stood next to the spent candle stub. Emmanuel reached for it and saw, through half-opened eyes, the pale pre-dawn light that crept through the curtains.

'*Forget the pills,*' the sergeant major said. '*Shorts first and then wash your face, for God's sake. You smell like a Frenchman.*'

Emmanuel sat up, alert to the rumble of voices on the other side of the bedroom door. He reached for his shorts and pulled them on, then touched Davida on the shoulder. 'Get up,' he whispered. 'Put your nightgown on.'

'Why?' She was sleepy and warm, the crumpled sheets wrapped around her body.

'Company,' he said and lifted her up by her shoulders so he could drop her cotton shift over her head. 'Whatever happens, stay low and don't say anything.'

She was now wide awake and alert to the footsteps outside the door. She slid off the bed and sprang into the corner like a cat.

Outside, King's voice was raised in protest. 'There's no need for this —'

Emmanuel stood up and the door smashed inward. Silver hinges flew into the air and Dickie and Piet appeared as solid black silhouettes against the grey dawn light in the open doorway.

'Down! Down!' Piet's handgun was drawn, hammer cocked, finger on the trigger. 'Get down.'

Emmanuel sat on the edge of the bed, conscious of Davida hidden in the dark corner behind him. She was low to the ground and silent, but it was inevitable that Piet and his partner would find her.

'Get the curtains, Dickie.'

Two more Security Branch men pushed King back towards the main rooms of the house.

'That's my property!' King fumed. The Security Branch officers pressed him into the kitchen. One of the men remained on guard in the corridor while the other returned to the destroyed doorway. Piet and Dickie had come with backup. Thank God the mad Scottish sergeant had woken him up. He had his shorts on and Davida had her nightdress on. That was something.

'You're in a world of trouble,' Piet said. 'The Pretorius brothers are opening the icehouse now. What are they going to find, Cooper?'

Emmanuel tried to get a handle on that information. Did Shabalala leave his lonely vigil outside the icehouse and walk to Jacob's Rest with the news? No. Shabalala would never leave Louis alone, not for a second.

The sound, half scream, half howl, was terrible to hear. The Pretorius boys had found their baby brother lying cold and blue amongst the bottles of fizzy soft drinks and ice cube trays. Emmanuel got to his feet, thinking of Shabalala facing the rage of the grieving Pretorius family alone.

'Sit down.' Piet clipped his gun back into the holster and began to walk a slow circuit of the room. He kicked a pile of discarded clothing with his foot and randomly lifted artifacts and books. He stopped at the foot of the bed and peered into the corner.

'Well, well, Cooper,' he said, 'this explains why this room smells like a whorehouse.'

A cold finger of fear touched Emmanuel's spine. He had to get Piet away from Davida, even if it spared her only a few minutes of his special attentions.

'Is that the only place you get to be with a woman?' Emmanuel said. 'In a whorehouse? Makes sense with a face like yours. I hope you leave a decent tip.'

'Secure this package, Dickie.' Piet indicated Davida's hiding place and lurched towards the bed where Emmanuel remained standing.

'You are in my world now, Detective Sergeant Cooper.' Piet was unnaturally calm. 'You should show some respect.'

In Piet's world, fear and respect were the same and Emmanuel wasn't going to show either without a fight. Davida cowered in Dickie's shadow and he went on the offensive.

'What are you doing here?' he asked. There were rules about how white policemen dealt with each other and Piet was walking a thin line.

'I was invited.' Piet fumbled in his grubby jacket and pulled out a fresh pack of cigarettes. The stench of stale beer, sweat, and blood wafted from him. 'King sent one of his kaffirs to the police station to ask for our help. A hell of a thing, the old kaffir making it there on a bicycle in the dark.'

'Why would King need you?' He already knew the answer. Why wait for a team of Hebrew lawyers to get to work when it was possible to play one branch of the police force against the other and muddy the waters even further? King had smelled his separation from the main task force and used it against him: basic warfare tactics. There was only one flaw in the plan. The rich Englishman hadn't planned on the Security Branch finding Davida in the room with him and against all reason Emmanuel found he was glad of the knowledge. Davida had come to him of her own accord.

Piet lit a cigarette and inhaled. 'We got a confession last night,' he said. 'The colonel is on his way from Pretoria to pose for photos. It's going to be a big case. Everyone wants a piece of the action.'

'He signed?' Emmanuel asked. Nobody, but nobody in government, was going to look too closely at the confession of a known communist, least of all van Niekerk, whose ambition was to rise on the political tide. Piet and Dickie were bulletproof and Emmanuel himself was half naked.

'Of course,' Piet said. 'So you can imagine my surprise when I heard you had someone else in line for the murder. A murder that I have a written and signed confession for.'

If he dropped it now and said he made a mistake about Winston King's involvement, then apologised for the inconvenience he'd caused, maybe he'd get to fight another day. The Security Branch had outmanoeuvred him and now a black man from Fort Bennington College was going to hang for crossing the river on a Wednesday instead of a Saturday.

Piet smoked the rest of his cigarette in silence and blew smoke rings into the air schoolboy style. A bad sign. He walked over to the pile of clothes, picked up Emmanuel's discarded jacket, and rifled through the pockets until he found what he was looking for.

He held up Davida's statement between thumb and forefinger. 'Your evidence?' he said.

'A statement.' Emmanuel didn't give him any more.

Nothing was going to stop Lieutenant Lapping from reading over the long list of damning allegations levelled at Captain Pretorius: adultery, manufacture of pornography, physical assault, and criminal misconduct as defined under the Immorality Act.

Piet unfolded the paper and read the handwritten statement. He finished and looked to the corner where Davida huddled at Dickie's feet. 'You write this?' he asked.

Davida pressed deeper into the corner, afraid to look up, afraid to answer. Dickie reached down and slapped her across the face with an open hand, drawing blood from the corner of her mouth. Fear kept her silent.

'Answer,' Dickie said.

'Yes.' She pressed her hand against her throbbing cheek.

'Look –' Emmanuel got Piet's attention. 'You have your confession. This is nothing compared to what's going on at the station.'

Piet smiled. 'I'll leave after you have been punished for disobeying orders and for getting on my fucking nerves and not a moment before, Cooper.'

The pockmarked lieutenant stepped away to reveal Henrick and Paul Pretorius standing side by side in the smashed doorway. He held the piece of paper up for them to see.

'Know what this is?' Piet asked. 'It's a statement claiming that your father was a deviant and a liar who defiled himself by blood mixing. What do you have to say to that?'

The Pretorius brothers moved towards Emmanuel in a rage. He blocked a punch from Paul and ducked under Henrick's sledgehammer blow before a jab to the stomach sent him reeling back onto the bed. The wooden beams of the ceiling tilted at a crazy angle above him. Paul breathed down on him.

'You're going to pay,' he said. 'For Louis and for the lies you're telling about my pa.'

'Every word, true,' Emmanuel said and tried not to tense when the punches hit him from every direction. He tasted bile and blood and heard the wet smack of his flesh yielding to fists. So, this is what Donny Rooke felt like out on the kaffir path: a punching bag in the Pretorius family's private gymnasium.

'Stop, stop, stop,' Piet ordered. 'You can't take it out of him all at once like that. It's dangerous. You have to slow down. Consider where you're delivering the message and how.'

Emmanuel struggled to sit up. If Piet was calling the shots he was in deep, deep trouble. The Security Branch officer could keep him alive and in pain for days. Piet took off his jacket and rolled his sleeves up to the bicep.

'Henrick. Hold him down and keep him down,' Piet instructed.

'I'm a police officer,' Emmanuel groaned. 'What you're doing is against the law.'

'I'm not doing anything,' Piet said. 'This is a private beating carried out by two men whose brother you killed and hid in an icehouse.'

That did sound bad. Inaccurate, but a jury would think twice about punishing the Pretorius boys for taking out their anger on the man who Louis had said tried to molest him.

'Now,' Piet continued. 'Start with a slap. Open-handed. Not soft and not hard. Just enough to get his attention.'

'You have my attention,' Emmanuel said and Paul delivered a stinging hit across his cheek. Not too hard and not soft either. The tin soldier was a natural.

'Good.' Piet was impressed. 'Now pose a question and wait for the answer.'

'Why did you tell those lies about my pa?'

'No lies,' Emmanuel said. 'Your pa liked to fuck dark girls. Outdoors and from behind.'

Paul hit him hard across the face and sent the blood and spit flying from his mouth. The skin above his left eye burned and he focused on the enraged Paul Pretorius, who was struggling against Piet Lapping's hold.

'Calm down,' Piet said. 'That was too hard too early.'

'He said —'

'The detective sergeant is testing you,' Piet pointed out with a scholarly fussiness. 'The stronger prisoners will do that. Your job is to remain calm.'

'I almost forgot —' Emmanuel blinked away the blood that ran from a cut in his eyebrow. 'Louis was the one molesting those coloured women last year. Your pa sent him off to a crazy farm. Check if you don't believe me.'

'*For Christ's sake, shut up,*' the sergeant major whispered as Henrick rose off the bed and hammered his fists indiscriminately into whatever patch of flesh he could find. Piet's little talk on remaining calm clearly had no impact on Henrick.

'Get him off,' Piet instucted Paul. 'We don't want a dead policeman on our hands.'

Henrick's weight lifted off him, but the pain remained and surged in waves from his toes to his cranium. His mouth was puffed and cut, which made taunting the Pretorius boys a linguistic challenge. He heard his own breath, ragged and defeated. An hour more and he'd be sausage meat.

'You understand now, don't you?' Piet said. 'You are in shit up to your elbows.'

Emmanuel shrugged. He knew he was in trouble: he could feel it in his face, his chest, and his stomach.

'Bring the girl,' Piet told his partner and Emmanuel sat up straight. He was scared: for himself and for Davida, who appeared slight and nymphlike in her white cotton nightdress. This morning was going to be bad for everyone. What was Mrs Ellis going through, knowing her girl was locked away with armed and violent men? Even King must know that he'd opened his door to a force he could not control.

'Don't be frightened,' Piet said to Emmanuel when Davida was pushed roughly around the foot of the bed. 'The physical work is done and now we move to a longer-term punishment. One that you have kindly handed to me in the form of this girl.'

Emmanuel tried to stand but Henrick slammed him down. Davida's face was streaked with tears, but she didn't make a sound.

'Was she worth it?' Piet asked. 'I hope so, because you're going to spend the next couple of years in jail wondering why you flushed your life and your career down the toilet for one night between the sheets.'

Emmanuel worked his swollen tongue against the roof of his mouth until a semblance of feeling returned. He wanted Davida out of the room and out of harm's way even if it meant going against van Niekerk's orders about keeping the past hidden.

'No law broken.' Emmanuel managed to get the three words out, slurred but recognisable.

Dickie sniggered. 'Have you forgotten what country you're in? You've been caught with a non-white. You're going to jail.'

'Not white,' Emmanuel said, even as he thought about van Niekerk's response to what he was doing.

'I know she's not white,' Piet said. 'That's why you're going *down*.'

'Not white,' Emmanuel repeated.

Piet stared at him dumbfounded. 'Fuck off.' He grabbed his hand and checked the skin underneath Emmanuel's fingernails for dark pigment. It was an old wives' skin colour test passing as science. He dropped the hand with a grunt. 'You're as white as me and Dickie here.'

Emmanuel reached down and lifted one of his leather shoes onto his knee. He slid a finger under the inner sole and pulled out a single piece of paper.

'The missing intelligence report . . .' Piet smiled. Most interrogations were intensely boring: the repetitive questions, the strangled denials, the hour-long beatings. There were no real surprises left on the job anymore.

Piet opened the page and whistled low in response to the information.

'Little Emmanuel Kuyper,' he muttered. 'I remember the photographs of you in the newspaper. You and your little sister. You had the whole country crying.'

'What are you talking about?' Dickie tried to keep up with the conversation. He didn't read much, not even the lowbrow daily papers that carried more pictures than print.

'Emmanuel Kuyper. That was his name before he changed it; probably to avoid the connection with his famous parents,' Piet explained. 'Cooper here is the boy whose father was acquitted of manslaughter after the jury found he had good reason to believe a half-caste shopkeeper had fathered his children. A part-Malay, if I remember.'

'Bullshit,' Dickie said. 'There's not a drop of Malay blood in him. Look at him. He's white, white.'

'That's what caused the scandal.' Piet lit up again, lost in memory. 'Half the country thought the father's story was a pack of lies while the other half thought the mother was a whore. During the trial, the father's side of the family put the children up for adoption. An Afrikaner couple who didn't want them turned over to a coloured orphanage took in Cooper and his sister. You were brought up in a proper Afrikaner home till you left school, hey, Cooper? Probably threw a torch onto the bonfire with all the other Voortrekker Scouts at the Great Trek celebration.'

The feeling in Emmanuel's mouth returned. He was going to burn a couple of bridges in the next few moments, but he didn't care about the consequences. So long as Davida walked out unharmed and he could follow her.

Piet squinted hard and flicked the intelligence report to the floor. 'Your mother may have been fucking the Malay,' he said, 'but there's not a drop of brown blood in you.'

'Prove it,' Emmanuel said.

There was a pause while Lapping examined the problem from every angle.

'Interesting,' he said. 'We can't charge you under the Immorality Act if you're mixed race but that doesn't mean your life isn't about to go down the drain if I pursue this claim and get you reclassified.'

'Go ahead,' Emmanuel said.

'You'll lose your job,' Paul Pretorius joined in. 'You'll lose your home and your friends. Everything.'

'He's going to lose all that anyway once he's charged under the act.' Lieutenant Lapping circled Davida, thinking aloud all the while. 'This way he saves himself and the girl from a public court appearance and makes them both innocent parties as they've committed no offence. Clever.'

'He's trying to weasel out of it.' Dickie was furious. 'He's changing the rules on us. Look at him. He's white.'

'I think he is,' Piet said mildly. 'But there's no way to prove it, which is why the detective sergeant has chosen to give us this report. Claiming to be non-white is his easiest way out. No prison term and as much black snatch as he can poke. Right, Cooper?'

Emmanuel shrugged. His life was spinning down the drain while Piet imagined him living it up in a shebeen full of black women. It didn't surprise him. Blacks and coloureds laughed louder and longer . . . or so it seemed to whites. He was going to miss the job, his sister, and his life.

'He gets to walk away.' Paul Pretorius couldn't believe it. 'Reclassification isn't enough to pay him back for Louis.'

Piet ground his cigarette butt under his heel and immediately lit another, as if it were oxygen and not nicotine that was poisoning his bloodstream. He sucked deep until the tip of the cigarette glowed hot and red.

'Cooper is forgetting that a non-white man has little protection from the law.' The lieutenant handed the cigarette to Paul. 'We will now be forced to make the punishment for what happened to Louis immediate and physical in the extreme.'

Shit, Emmanuel thought. Was there no way out of Piet Lapping's carnival of perpetual pain? The Security Branch officer in the doorway swung around and faced into the house, hand on his gun holster.

'Speak —' The officer barked the command down the corridor.

'Lieutenant Lapping?' Mrs Ellis's voice, sharp with fear, called out from the sitting room. 'Lieutenant Lapping?'

'Mummy —' Davida whispered before Dickie cupped his hand over her mouth.

'*Ja*?' Piet pursed his bulbous lips. The sound of a female voice put a damper on the high he experienced during physical questioning: like having your mother walk in on you just before the climax.

'Phone call,' the housekeeper said quickly, aware on a base, instinctual level that the men in the room were unused to a woman interrupting their dark business.

'What?' Piet moved to the destroyed doorway and listened. He was ready to leap and strangle the housekeeper if she made a wrong move.

'There's a man on the phone. He asked to talk to a Lieutenant Lapping right away.'

'The colonel?' Dickie asked.

'No,' Piet said and unrolled his sleeves and buttoned them, careful of appearances outside the room. 'He doesn't know we're here.'

So – Emmanuel's brain formed the thought with sluggish determination – Piet was keeping this excursion secret. He was determined to clear any obstacles that could throw doubts over the confession he'd extracted from the communist last night.

'Put the cigarette out and don't do anything until I get back,' Piet said and left the room to answer the phone.

'Take a break.' Dickie stepped into the boss's shoes and found them quite comfortable. 'Cooper and his friend aren't going anywhere.'

The Pretorius brothers retreated to the window and fell into a whispered conversation while Dickie pushed Davida into a chair and stood over her. Emmanuel sank his throbbing head into his hands. It was his fault that Davida was here, in this room with men who stank of violence and hate. Their pleasure had come at a high price.

'Look up.' Piet Lapping was back in the bedroom and he was not calm. 'Look at me, Cooper.'

Piet paced back and forth in front of the bed, his fingers flicking the flame of his cigarette lighter off and on like a lighthouse beacon. Something had set him off and destroyed the mystic calm he insisted was a mainstay of the 'work'.

'You're really something,' Piet said through tight lips. 'You and your sissy friend van Niekerk.'

Emmanuel had no idea what he was talking about. Van Niekerk was in Jo'burg and unaware of the disaster with Louis or that the Security Branch interrogation was taking place at Elliott King's game ranch. How the hell had van Niekerk tracked him down?

'What happened?' Dickie asked.

Piet ignored him and bent down in front of Emmanuel, his pebble eyes wet with rage. 'Mozambique. That's where you got them. Am I right?'

Emmanuel lifted an eyebrow in response. Piet could go fish.

'What?' Dickie walked to his partner's side but kept plenty of space between them in case he needed to duck out of the way in a hurry. Lieutenant Lapping was unpredictable when he was angry and he was rarely this angry.

'I should have known,' Piet mused aloud. 'That day you left for Lourenço Marques to question the underwear salesman. I smelled something was wrong . . .'

'What underwear salesman?' Dickie was trying his best to get involved and be a genuine partner, not just a muscleman.

'Shut up, Dickie,' Piet said. 'I need to get this straight so we don't do anything foolish. I need to think.'

Piet flicked the lighter on and off, the sound of it like gunfire in the tense atmosphere. A muscle jumped in the cratered skin of his cheek and Emmanuel held his breath.

'He's going to release the photos if we touch another hair on your pretty head,' Piet said after a long while. 'He wants you to call him in ten minutes to verify that you're safe, like a fucking virgin at her first dance.'

Emmanuel stood up, his body stiff from the beating he'd taken. He didn't care what the Security Branch threw at him. Van Niekerk had the photos and their power couldn't be pissed away by slinging childish insults. He glanced over at Davida and saw that she understood. They were going to walk out of the room and then they were going to run.

'You're going to let him go?' Paul Pretorius pointed an

accusing finger at the pockmarked lieutenant. 'You promised us he'd get what was coming to him.'

Piet caught Paul's finger and twisted hard until the finger snapped out of its socket.

'Agghh –' Paul Pretorius groaned and sweat broke out on his forehead.

'We are letting him go because your pa couldn't keep his pants buttoned up and that slippery fuck van Niekerk has proof of it.'

'That's a lie.' Paul was red-faced with pain. 'He's lying.'

Piet let go of Paul's finger. 'I did consider the possibility that he was lying, but he has something, this van Niekerk. It was in his voice. I could hear it: the pleasure he takes in having power over us. Over me.'

Dickie marshalled a decent thought and threw it into the ring. 'Maybe he's just a good liar.'

'Consider the facts,' Piet said patiently. 'Van Niekerk knows my fucking name, he knows where I am when even the colonel has no idea. This is not someone to be taken lightly and that is why I cannot take the risk that he is just playing with us.'

Emmanuel limped past the bickering Security Branch men and held out his hand to Davida, who was perched at the edge of her chair, ready to make a run for it. 'Let's go,' he said.

She stood up and took his hand. Her fingers curled around his and squeezed tight. Emmanuel turned to the door and noticed pockmarked Piet staring at them with evil intent. Not good. Emmanuel started walking. Please, God. The shattered doorway was so close now. Just four more steps.

'So sweet,' Piet muttered. 'The way you looked at her just then. It's as if you actually like her.'

Davida's fingers slipped from his and Piet pulled her back

into the room with a yank. He held her in the tight band of his arms. Davida twisted and kicked but remained imprisoned against the foul-smelling white man with the cratered face.

'Don't do this.' Emmanuel heard the pleading tone in his voice and tried again, stronger this time. 'Let her go, Lieutenant.'

'The deal,' Piet said, 'was for your release. We keep her.'

'No!' Davida arched her back and tried to wriggle free but she was no match for Piet's bullish strength coupled with his experience in subduing troublesome prisoners. 'Let me go!'

Piet lifted her in the air, as easily as he'd lift an empty laundry basket, and threw her back on the bed. The springs groaned. He straddled her in one quick move and pinned her arms above her head.

Emmanuel was close behind. His battered body found a sputter of speed from a reserve located behind his damaged kidneys. He smacked Piet hard in the side of the head and got no reaction. He went in for a second hit and connected with air. Dickie and Paul pulled him back and threw him into the chair. The dark fear from the dream consumed him and grew stronger.

'Good,' Piet said as Davida's body strained and pressed against his inner thighs. 'I like spirit in a woman: a bit of fight.'

'You have everything you want,' Emmanuel said. 'She's of no use to you.'

'I want the photos. The photos for the girl, that's the trade.'

'If van Niekerk won't give them up?' Emmanuel asked. That was a real possibility. 'What then?'

'Well . . .' Piet pressed a thumb against Davida's mouth and forced her lips apart. 'You can fuck off out of here or you can stay and watch me work on her. Your choice, Cooper.'

'No.' Emmanuel struggled against the mother lode of Boer muscle holding him in the chair but couldn't break free. 'Don't do this.'

'You cannot imagine –' Piet's breath was coming hard as the body underneath him continued to buck and grind '– how beautiful my work can be. I will get to know this woman in ways that are beyond you. I will break her open and touch her soul.'

'Please –' Davida recoiled from the evil man leaning close to her. 'Emmanuel, help me –'

'Wait,' Emmanuel said. He needed Piet to stop and listen. 'Wait. I'll talk to van Niekerk and try to make a deal.'

'The girl for the photos. That's the only deal I'm interested in. I'm not going to let your major hang onto evidence that might spoil my case further down the track.'

'Okay,' Emmanuel said. 'Let her off the bed and sit her in the chair. I'll make the call.'

Piet shifted his weight and considered the request. He was reluctant to break away from the bruising and intimate tango that prisoner and interrogator danced together in the dark of the holding cells. He lifted his body and let the girl wriggle from under him. If he didn't get the photos, he had this to look forward to. The task of breaking the woman to his will.

Emmanuel sat Davida down in the chair and let her feel his touch, gentle and unforced. It hurt to look in her eyes and see the stark terror flickering in the dark circle of her pupils.

'Don't leave me,' she whispered. 'Please don't go.'

'I have to,' he said. 'I'll come back in a few minutes. I promise.'

'You promise?'

'Yes.' He didn't know if he was coming back with the keys to her release or with nothing at all. He had to roll the dice.

'Go with him,' Piet said to Dickie. 'Make sure he doesn't start trouble.'

'I'm going alone,' Emmanuel said. 'Van Niekerk won't talk if someone else is listening in. Or is that what you're hoping for, Lieutenant? A no from van Niekerk so you can get back to work on the girl?'

'Piss off,' Piet said and fumbled for his cigarettes. 'You have ten minutes.'

'Fifteen,' Emmanuel said and shuffled out of the room past the guard in the hallway.

He made slow progress towards the office, his bruised muscles twitching with five different kinds of pain. The cut on his eyebrow had opened again and he stopped to wipe away the trickle of blood obscuring his vision. Through the red haze he saw Mrs Ellis standing in the doorway to the kitchen, neat and trim.

'My God . . . my God . . .' she whispered. 'Did they do this to you?'

Emmanuel nodded. He was still in his undershorts: a sorry, beaten man with skin pulsing red, yellow and bright purple.

'My baby –' Mrs Ellis gave voice to her worst fears. 'My baby is alone with those men?'

'Yes,' Emmanuel said and limped to the office. He had fifteen, twenty minutes tops to turn things around. 'I'm trying to get her out.'

'Trying?' Elliott King appeared in front of him, his face pinched tight with impotent rage. 'You lured her into that room. It's your fault she's in this position.'

Emmanuel slammed Elliott King hard in the chest and sent him flying back into a wall. He leaned to within an inch of King's suntanned face. 'Your daughter came of her own accord and she would have left of her own accord but for you and your half-baked attempt to manipulate events. This has been your doing right from the start.'

'I sent for the police, not a gang of Afrikaner thugs. I should have known not to trust the Dutch.'

'You entrusted Davida, body and soul, to a Dutchman in exchange for a piece of land,' Emmanuel said. 'Now you're not even in charge of your own house. How does it feel, Mr King?' Emmanuel turned his back on him and limped to the office.

Winston King was inside with the phone to his ear and a crossed-out list of names balanced on his knees. He hung up and rubbed the flat of his palms over his eyes.

'No takers,' Winston said. 'Botha will try to contact the commissioner of police in an hour or so to see what can be done. No promises, though. Nobody wants to mess with these Security Branch fuckers. For once, the size of your donations isn't big enough.'

'The commissioner won't take the call,' Emmanuel said. 'A member of the Communist Party confessed to Captain Pretorius's murder last night. The Security Branch has a signed confession. Nobody is going to go up against them.'

'Shit.' Winston looked sick. 'Fucking hell.'

'I'll take that as an expression of genuine regret for your actions,' Emmanuel said and signalled him out of the office. 'It comes a little too late for the poor bastard who was beaten into a confession and it comes too late for Davida. Two other people are going to pay the price for you, but you're used to that, aren't you, Winston? Someone else picking up the bill.'

'Davida doesn't mean anything to those men,' Winston protested. 'Why hold her?'

'She's currency,' Emmanuel said. 'They want to exchange

her for a piece of evidence that could derail their case in the future.'

'I'll tell them —' Winston's face was ashen. 'I'll confess to everything if they let Davida go. I'll put it in writing.'

'Wait —' King said from the doorway. 'I'll give them a good price to walk away. How much do you think they'll take?'

'This might be hard for you to understand,' Emmanuel said and sank into the office chair. 'But this situation is above money. Those men believe they are guarding the future of South Africa. Your cash means nothing to them. Not with a communist ready for trial.'

'No-one is above money,' King stated with certainty.

'Fine.' Emmanuel lifted the phone. 'You and Winston go in and offer them a bribe, see what happens.'

The King men eyed the blood dripping off his chin onto the beaten flesh of his torso.

'You'll make the deal for her?' Winston blushed at his own cowardice.

'I'll try,' Emmanuel said and placed the phone to his ear. 'Now get out. Both of you.'

Emmanuel pushed the casement window up und leaned out to take a deep breath of fresh air. The sun was over the horizon and a golden light shone onto the meandering river and squat hills. It was going to be another fine day, full of wildflowers and newborn springbok. The office door opened behind him but he didn't turn around. He didn't have the heart or the stomach to face anyone right now.

'He won't exchange the evidence for my girl, will he?' Mrs Ellis said.

'No,' Emmanuel replied. 'He won't.'

Van Niekerk had been blunt to the point of insult. There was nothing in the proposal for him. No reason to exchange the ultimate blackmail tool for a frightened girl. He already had a maid and a cook. He had no use for another non-white female.

'They're not going to kill her.' The major had been brutal in his summation. 'I've seen the photographs and there's nothing those men can do to her that hasn't already been done. Disengage and walk away, for Christ's sake.'

He could imagine van Niekerk doing just that. Walking away from a helpless human being without a second thought. That was his strength, and it would take him to the very top.

'What can I do?' The housekeeper was humble in her powerlessness. 'What must I do to help my baby?'

Emmanuel heard the clink of cutlery and smelled the freshly brewed coffee. He checked his watch: 6:50 am. He had three minutes left to make a decision. Go with van Niekerk and rise to the top of the pyramid of evil. Or stay here and go down fighting in defence of what was right.

He turned to Mrs Ellis. She'd brought him a mug of coffee and a buttered ham sandwich cut on the diagonal. It was enough to light a spark.

'What's in the pantry?' he asked.

'Everything,' she said. 'We're very well stocked. Mr King insists on it.'

God bless the greedy rich, Emmanuel thought as the spark struggled to become a workable idea.

'Meat?' he asked.

'Bacon. *Boerewors* sausages and wild game steaks.'

'Sweet things?'

'I have some jam biscuits made up and a sponge cake for afternoon tea. Also some dried fruit and store-bought sweets.'

'Is Constable Hepple still here?'

'He's out on the veranda waiting for you. He told Johannes and Shabalala that he couldn't go back to town with them. He couldn't desert his post.'

'Bring Hansie, Elliott King and Winston in here,' he said. 'We have to move fast.'

Emmanuel limped back to the spare bedroom with the mug of coffee in one hand and a half-eaten sandwich in the other. He stood in the doorway and sipped at the drink. The hot liquid singed the cut inside his mouth, slid over the lump in his throat, and continued down to the aching knot of fear in his stomach.

Sunlight filtered into the room but the Security Branch officers and the Pretorius brothers retained a greyish cast, the result of too little sleep, too little food, and too much beer.

'Well?' Piet was lounging on the bed, no doubt keeping the space warm in preparation for the woman's return. Cigarette butts littered the floor around him.

Emmanuel forced more coffee into his bruised mouth and went to check on Davida: scared stiff, but holding up. He handed her the coffee which she drank down in a few thirsty gulps. She reached for the sandwich but he kept that firmly in his hand. It was a long shot. Relying on a plain ham sandwich to save Davida's skin. He saw Dickie out of the corner of his eye. The big man was looking at the sandwich and at nothing else.

'Major van Niekerk wants more time to think about it. He's going to call back in half an hour with an answer.' Emmanuel took a bite of the homemade bread and chewed it before continuing. 'Can you wait that long?'

Piet stood up and flicked ash from his pants. 'The answer is yes or no.'

'What do you want most, Lieutenant? The photographs or the chance to drop your pants for your country?'

Piet flushed. 'And what the fuck are we supposed to do while your major prances around?'

Emmanuel shrugged and checked his watch. Any minute now Mrs Ellis was going to fire the opening salvo of the battle. He took a bite of the sandwich and felt the hungry gazes of Dickie and the Pretorius brothers follow the movement of his hands. He licked butter from his fingers.

'Where did you get that food?' Dickie blurted. 'And the coffee?'

'This?' Emmanuel held the sandwich up. 'Housekeeper gave it to me from the *braai* plate.'

'What *braai*?' Dickie said and sniffed the air like a hound dog. The smell of woodsmoke began to rise and mix with the aroma of bacon, onions and fried sausage.

'That bastard, King.' Emmanuel shook his head. 'He's got enough food in the kitchen to feed an army. Although I never had anything like that when I was marching through France. No *boerewors* or sponge cake in my ration pack.'

Dickie's stomach gurgled and the Pretorius brothers stepped towards the smashed doorway. The sizzle of oil and meat called all men.

'Wait,' Piet ordered. 'This is a set-up. Why would anyone light a *braai* at this time of morning?'

The lieutenant was a pure freak of nature, always on the lookout for danger. He didn't need food or sleep so long as the 'work' remained unfinished.

'Practice . . .' Davida leaned forwards in the chair with the empty coffee mug held close to her chest. 'Mr King is going to have a breakfast *braai* for the guests when the lodge opens. He likes to test the food and pick what he wants.'

'What happens to the food he doesn't eat?' Dickie asked.

'He gives it to the workers,' Davida said. 'The ones building the huts.'

Dickie groaned at the thought of all that white man's food going into the mouths of black workmen who were happy with a cob of roast corn and a piece of dried bread twice a day. He sniffed and thought he smelled brewed coffee amid the aroma of roast meat. 'Lieutenant . . .' he begged. He was a big man. He liked six-egg breakfasts wiped up with a loaf of bread and washed down with a pot of black coffee. His stomach started to eat itself from inside. 'Please . . .'

Piet eyed his men and saw the beginning of mutiny stirring. He'd been negligent; they hadn't had a real meal in forty-eight hours. He pulled the woman over to the bed and secured her to the frame with his handcuffs.

'Half an hour,' Piet said.

Emmanuel handed Hansie a plate piled high with three kinds of meat and a fat slice of bread on top. The Security Branch crew hoed into the feast served up by Mrs Ellis and King himself, who'd donned a servant's apron for the occasion. Winston served coffee and tea with the oily charm that melted the knickers off English girls and made men dig deeper into their pockets for a tip.

'Take this to the man guarding the bedroom,' Emmanuel told Hansie. 'Tell him the lieutenant said to eat it in the kitchen while you stand guard.'

Hansie went off and Emmanuel waited. Everything was going according to plan, but for Piet's restlessness. He ate and drank with his men but stopped every few minutes to check his watch and scan the area.

Emmanuel waited until Piet did his security check, then slipped into the house and bolted for the bedroom. He estimated he had two minutes. He pulled a set of keys out of his wrinkled pants and handed them to Hansie, who now stood guard outside the bedroom.

'You know what to do?'

'Of course,' Hansie said and grabbed the keys.

'Good . . .' Emmanuel checked the corridor. Empty. 'Remember, don't stop until you get to Mozambique.'

'Yes, Sarge.' Hansie took off; the car keys jangling happily in his hands.

Emmanuel unlocked Davida's cuffs and set her free. Her wrists were marked with blood, but that was child's play compared to what Piet Lapping would take out of her if she was still here when he got back.

'We have to be quick. Go out the window and run straight to the night watchman's hut. Fast as you can.'

She had to be out of the room and sprinting before Hansie fired up the sports car and drew the men to the front of the house. The window creaked open and Emmanuel lifted her in his arms.

'You?' she said.

'I'll be fine.' He slid her out of the window. 'Run,' he said.

She bolted across a patch of bush in her white cotton shift. She ran hard and did not look back. A memory surfaced as her form flew away from the house . . .

Emmanuel's little sister ran fast down the alley, barefoot in her nightgown with the blue forget-me-nots embroidered on the collar. Emmanuel ran alongside her. He smelled wood fires in the air as they raced towards the light of the hotel on the corner. Fear blocked out the cold of the winter night. Anger burned in him at not being strong enough to stop the blade. When he was older, bigger, he'd stand

and fight. Behind them, the screams of their dying mother chased them farther and farther into the darkness . . .

The sports car started with a roar and a spray of loose gravel as Hansie sped out onto the road. Emmanuel imagined the grin on the boy's face as he revved the sleek Jag across the veldt. He heard the blast of a horn, then footsteps and voices raised in surprise. The Security Branch was taking the bait. Car engines turned over and wheels spun. The pursuit had begun.

He listened for Davida, but with luck she'd made it to the night watchman's hut and escape. The plan was to transport her to a safe place known only to King and his faithful servants.

Emmanuel turned to leave. By all conventional standards, this case was a failure. The wrong man beaten into a confession, the Security Branch triumphant, and van Niekerk set to blackmail his way up the ladder. Rescuing Davida would have to be the saving grace. It would have to be enough for him.

'You think you know pain?' Piet stood in the doorway, calm as a cobra eyeing a field mouse. 'A bullet wound and a few bruises? They are nothing. The scribbling of a child on your body.'

Emmanuel swivelled and jumped for the open window. He was getting out with his liver, lungs and spleen intact. Iron hands pulled him back into the room and Lieutenant Piet Lapping began the lesson in earnest.

Emmanuel tasted blood. It was dark. It was painful to breathe. He drifted in and out of consciousness on a tide controlled by pockmarked Piet. His blurred outline hovered over him and he thought: the Pretorius boys know nothing about administering a proper beating. Piet is right to give lessons.

There was a dark smudge of movement behind Piet's head

and the smash of glass. The lieutenant went down and a splash of whisky landed on Emmanuel's cut lip.

He struggled to sit up and concentrate. 'You?' he wheezed.

Johannes, the foot soldier in the Pretorius army, pulled him up and dragged him to the open window. Emmanuel's muscles quivered and he tried to stand. No dice. He had the strength of a bowl of jelly.

'Why?' Emmanuel grunted as the hulking Boer lifted him up and stuffed him through the window like a sack of smuggled animal hides.

'Found the photos under Louis's bed when we took him home,' Johannes said. 'Burnt them. Everything you said about Louis and my pa is true. Got to make things right.'

'Oh . . .' Emmanuel slid over the sill and onto the strong width of a shoulder. A solid khaki uniform blocked his vision for a moment, then he caught flashes of bright yellow wildflowers, red dirt, and green tufts of veldt grass. He heard the singing of the trees and smelled the promise of spring rise up from the wet ground. He was moving across country on the shoulders of a giant. His eyes closed.

Constable Samuel Shabalala and Daniel Zweigman sat side by side and watched the first light of day appear on the horizon. Shabalala pointed a finger at the sliver of pale pink that pushed through the curtain of night. 'God's light,' he said.

'Yes,' Zweigman agreed. 'I'd forgotten what it looked like.'

Emmanuel forced his eyelids apart. The muddy outline of the two men filled the space at either side of him. He focused all of his energy on keeping his eyes open for one second longer.

'Ahh . . . you are back with us, Detective.'

Blurred faces, one white and the other black, leaned in close to examine him. He tasted a bitter liquid in his mouth and struggled to swallow it. Everything hurt.

'A half dose of crushed pills mixed with wild herbs gathered by Constable Shabalala from the veldt,' the white face explained. 'You are my first patient to be treated with this miraculous combination of German and Zulu medicine. You are a lucky man.'

Zweigman. The name stuck with Emmanuel. Zweigman the shopkeeper and Shabalala the policeman. The two men who'd tipped van Niekerk off to his location and saved his skin.

'How long?' Patches of sky winked through the branches of a thick-limbed tree. He was on the veldt somewhere, wrapped in blankets and lying on a thin bedroll.

'Three days,' Constable Shabalala replied. 'You went a long way away, but now you are back.'

'Davida?'

'Gone.' Zweigman pressed his fingers against the bruised muscles of Emmanuel's torso. 'Soon you will be well enough to travel. You have a fierce will to live.'

'The lieutenant and his men are gone also,' Shabalala said. 'They left in many cars with the communist man in wrist irons. Many newspaper cameras followed after them. They are the *indunas* now.'

Emmanuel felt himself gently lifted into a sitting position and tasted cool water in his mouth. He looked out from swollen lids. Veldt surrounded him on all sides in wide ribbons of green and brown. A dove cooed and the grass swayed in the early morning light. The landscape was golden and it hurt to look at, so he closed his eyes.

'I came back . . .' Emmanuel mumbled. He could have stayed in England with his new wife and learned to tolerate the rain and the cold. But he'd come back, knowing how cruel the country was and how hard the God that ruled over it.

'*You love this fucking place, laddie.*' The sergeant major put forward his opinion. '*This is the country where you chose to stand and fight. Simple as that.*'

'Got my backside kicked. Lost the match,' Emmanuel said, thinking of the innocent man about to stand trial for Pretorius's murder.

'Delirium,' Zweigman said and laid him down again on the thin mattress.

'What about you?' Emmanuel continued his conversation with the Scotsman. 'What are you doing here?'

'*You invited me,*' the sergeant major said. '*But I don't think you need me anymore. You've got the German and the African, so rest easy, laddie. Rest a while.*'

Zweigman took the detective's pulse, then wrapped the blankets tightly around his bruised body. How he had survived the beating was a mystery, but he would carry the scars, some visible and others hidden, to his grave.

'One day,' the German shopkeeper said, 'I will tell you how I came to be hiding in Jacob's Rest. For now I will tell you this: my wife and I are leaving and that is a very good thing. I will open a practice and start again. I have decided to stand up and see if I am knocked down.'

'Why?'

'Feel the sorrow, yet let good prevail. What else can men like us do, Detective?'

Emmanuel felt the rough ground underneath him and heard Shabalala's deep baritone voice singing a Zulu song. His life was saved by a black man and a Jew, his physical being reawakened by a mixed-race woman, and his crushed body lifted to safety by a proper Afrikaner. It was a jigsaw of people that fitted together despite the new National Party laws.

He closed his eyes and drifted off to sleep. Shabalala's voice carried him out of the dark cellar of his dreams and into the sunlight. He saw himself lying on the open veldt, beaten but not defeated. Zweigman was right. What else was there to do but get up again and take another swing at the world?

Acknowledgements

If it takes a village to raise a child, it takes two villages to raise a family and write a novel. These are the people of my village to whom I owe thanks.

Imkulunkulu the great, great one. The ancestors. My parents Patricia and Courtney Nunn for love, hope and faith. Penny, Jan and Byron, my siblings and fellow travellers on the dusty road from rural Swaziland to Australia.

My children Sisana and Elijah, lovely beyond compare. My husband, Mark Lazarus, who gave me time, space and the use of his impeccable eye for story. You are the roof and the walls of my little hut. Many thanks also to Dr Audrey Jakubowski-Lazarus and Dr Gerald Lazarus for their generosity and support.

Literary agents Siobhan Hannan of the Cameron Creswell Agency and Catherine Drayton of InkWell Management who bridge the gap between my writing desk and the world with focus and enthusiasm. I could not be in better hands.

For historical and cultural help I send special thanks to: Terence King, author, police and military researcher and historian; Gordon Bickley, military historian; Audrey

Portman of Rhino Research, South Africa; Susie Lorentz for Afrikaans help and her honesty. Aunty Lizzie Thomas for Zulu help. Any errors or omissions are entirely my own.

Thanks also to members of the Nunn and Whitfield clans for stories and memories, both light and dark, of life in southern Africa.

To the Randwick 'Gals' (Cass, Tash, Julia, Julie W, Una, Ilsa, Mary and Julie N) and the Kingsgrove 'Gals' (Angie, Julie I and Jodie) for being a great posse of women with whom to ride out the transition into motherhood. Kerrie McGovan for introducing me to the mysteries of the intrawebs and delicious restaurant-quality meals. Loretta Walder, Maryla Rose and Brian Hunt who lit the path on the darkest nights.

Members of the 'Blind Faith Club', an invaluable group of friends who, in the absence of proof, believed I would finish the book and that it would be published. They are Penny Nunn, the terrific Turks Yusuf and Burcak Muraben, Tony McNamara, Steve Worland, Georgie Parker and Paula McNamara.

Double thanks to Pan Macmillan for giving my book an international home. Maria Rejt in London. Rod Morrison and James Fraser in Sydney. You have re-invigorated my belief in lucky stars. Editors Kylie Mason and Anna Valdinger who simply made the book better. To all the Pan Macmillan staff for their warm welcome and hard work.

Ngiyabonga. Thank you all.

picador.com

blog
videos
interviews
extracts